# Cape Cod Pilot

# Cape Cod Pilot

*by*
Josef Berger
(Jeremiah Digges)

*With a Foreword by*
Edward Gorey

NORTHEASTERN UNIVERSITY PRESS
*Boston*

First Northeastern University Press edition 1985

First published in 1937 by Modern Pilgrim Press and
The Viking Press in the American Guide Series, with
the editorial and research assistance of the Federal
Writers' Project, Works Progress Administration for
the State of Massachusetts

Library of Congress Cataloging in Publication Data

Berger, Josef, 1903–
Cape Cod pilot.
Reprint. Originally published: Provincetown,
Mass.: Modern Pilgrim Press, © 1937.
Bibliography: p.
Includes index.
1. Cape Cod (Mass.)—Description and travel—
Guidebooks.    I.   Title.
F72.C3B39  1985    917.44'920442    85–4884
ISBN 0–930350–72–3 (pbk. alk. paper)

MANUFACTURED IN THE UNITED STATES OF AMERICA
90  89  88            5   4   3   2

# PREFACE

This book deviates from the form used in others in the American Guide Series, for it attempts to present guide material as a personal experience. Though it is a collective task, the editors felt that the folklore and yarns that constitute the major part of the book would be enriched in presentation by the use of the personal pronoun. Jeremiah Digges is one of the Federal Writers' Project workers, and he is rightly credited with the major writing, rewriting and editing of this book.

Credit for invaluable assistance, generously offered, is due Mr. Nathan Halper, Mr. Gilbert Rich, of the Provincetown Public Library; to Mrs. Mayme Claxton, Mr. Jazzaniah Snow and a host of other men and women on Cape Cod who gave the authors first-hand information and reminiscences of early days on the Cape. Special thanks are due to the skippers and crews of many vessels, trap-fishermen, surfmen, draggers and seiners of Cape Cod and, particularly, the crew of the schooner *Mary P. Goulart.*

Indebtedness is due to many publications and historical works often mentioned and sometimes quoted in this book. A brief bibliography of these publications and works is given preceding the Index.

THE EDITORS

# CONTENTS

# ILLUSTRATIONS

ix

*Lighthouse on Buzzard's Bay, Mattapoisett, September 1940.*
Photograph by Walter Payton, U.S. Dept. of Agriculture,
Farm Security Administration, courtesy of the Library of
Congress.

# FOREWORD

*Cape Cod Pilot* was first published in 1937 as part of the American Guide Series produced by the Federal Writers' Project of the Works Progress Administration. Jeremiah Digges was the pen name taken by Josef Berger, a reporter and writer who had come to Provincetown with his wife and small daughter, and who in the winter of 1936 was hired by the FWP to work on the Massachusetts State Guide. He put in the requisite four days a week on material for this; the other three he spent writing a personal book about the Cape based on scrapbooks of local newspaper clippings and his own interviews with people who could remember something of the Cape in its heyday before it declined into what is primarily a summer resort.

As he escorts us along the Cape, Berger regales us with "whacking good yarns" about everything from religious practices in Harwich "before the cranberry" to the brawls in Eugene O'Neill's house in Provincetown that "rattled [it] like a loose stove." Berger brings to life the very soul of Cape Cod with an insouciant charm that seems to defy the Depression years. What is surprising and paradoxical, however, is that the book was a sensitive and reliable guide to the Cape of its time, and remains so today.

The Cape now is indeed a very different place from what it was then; what you notice and how you feel about it depend on who you are and how long you have known the Cape. For the first-time visitor, *Cape Cod Pilot* remains an excellent, in fact one of the best, guides of all. It should perhaps be added here that the Cape has passed from being rural to suburban, and that a current guide of some sort should be consulted for actual directions.

It seems worthwhile to mention various aspects of the Cape that have come into being since the book was written. The two most important are the Mid-Cape Highway and the National Seashore.

The construction of the Mid-Cape Highway (whether it will ever be completed as projected seems to remain a moot point) was long-over-due. As its several sections were opened, they absorbed all through traffic and allowed once more for leisurely driving down the main streets of the original villages and along the more picturesque roads between them, always one of the most popular ways to enjoy the Cape. For the tourist who chooses the highway, it offers, in addition to its negative virtues of speed and convenience, various rest and picnic areas, and several panoramic views of the Cape, most notably the one near Exit 6, just west of Hyannis.

Almost certainly the single most consequential event for the Cape as a whole in this century was the establishment of the National Seashore as part of the national park system. Taking over as it did all the land of the Lower Cape not occupied by the villages themselves from Provincetown through Eastham, it has permanently determined the face of that area and, indirectly, had great influence on that of the Upper Cape.

Probably its most important efforts have been directed at protecting the always fragile and imperiled seashore itself, but its other projects have been many and varied. It has set up a number of nature trails of different lengths and kinds, and has provided access to historical sites such as the first landing of the Pilgrims and the Marconi Station. Extensive bicycle paths now run among the dunes outside Provincetown, thanks to the National Seashore, and its headquarters and other buildings have provided the Cape with its only distinguished contemporary architecture. And of course by its mere existence the National Seashore has prevented all that might have happened in the way of unbridled commercialization of the area.

In the same spirit, similar efforts at preservation on a smaller scale, both natural and cultural, have taken place and continue to do so all over the Cape. More and more conservation areas and nature trails are in evidence wherever you go; more and more historical houses and small museums are preserved and open to the public. Historical districting extends from Sandwich to Orleans on the north side of the Cape wherever there is a concentration of old houses; thus whole neighborhoods will continue to retain the charm of the Cape's most attractive architectural period.

And so, though the Cape changes, and does so at an ever increasing pace, the older Cape Cod continues to exist as tenaciously as ever, possibly more so because of an increasing consciousness of what can be lost. In a way then, there is more to be seen and appreciated by the first-time visitor than ever before.

The Cape goes on being a special place, not quite like any other. I know that I for one would not want to live anywhere else.

EDWARD GOREY

# Cape Cod Pilot

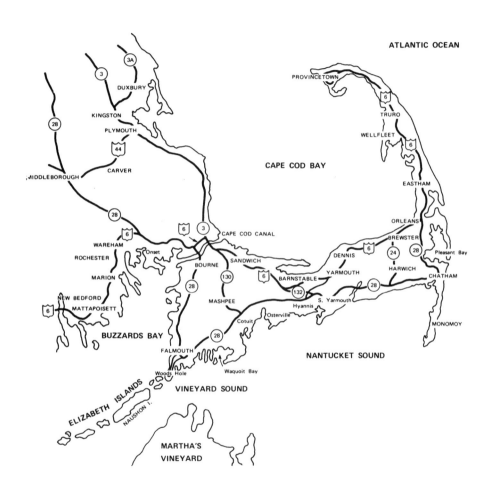

# CHAPTER I

## INTRODUCTION

In the museum of the Old Dartmouth Historical Society in New Bedford there is a gilded mirror, and under it a card informing the open-mouthed visitor that here is a:

MIRROR IN WHICH GENERAL GRANT
AND ABRAHAM LINCOLN BOTH LOOKED

Invariably, the attendant at the museum says, the tourist looks up quickly into the glass—and is a little disappointed at seeing only himself there.

A guidebook should have better manners, I suppose, than to point back to the tourist as one of the "principal features of interest." But manners or no manners, a Cape Cod guidebook must single him out for this distinction; for within the past two decades, the tourist has stepped into the leading role; "summer business" has overshadowed all others; for most of the towns, it is now the mainstay.

There has been other commerce for the people of this sandy sliver of New England, industrial booms on which enduring fortunes were built. But the whaling, the foreign trade, the ship-building, the salt-making, all have passed; and the same evolution that wrote finis to each of these has brought the motor car and the hard-surfaced highway.

The Cape had no choice. It put its house in order for a new day, said farewell to the deep water and hung out a shingle, "Tourists Accommodated." Financially, it proved to be a happy way out of a lean era. As a magnet for tourists, Cape Cod was charged with so many historical currents, on the one side, and so many physical attractions on the other, that success was pretty well assured from the start.

A strange community evolved—"home" to a small, anciently settled population which carefully drew the line between "native Cape Codder" and "off-Cape furriner," took pride in its history and grimly tried to safeguard its traditions; and "resort" to an annual influx of four or five times as many people, some merely vacationing for a week or two, others buying homes and coming back each summer. In the 1936 season, the Cape Cod Chamber of Commerce estimated, 175,000 people visited the peninsula, a record to that time.

For the Yankees, these proud "natives," adjustment to the new order was neither simple nor wholly pleasant. It meant dropping the seclusion which their rugged little villages had cherished through ten generations. Time was when these towns could "warn out" residents of doubtful status; and even when the townsmen themselves began voyaging over the seven seas for their living, they were still most particular in having it understood that their homes were strictly their own.

When the Old Colony Railroad, now the down-Cape spur of the New Haven, was put through as far as Plymouth, and the company wanted to carry the line on to Provincetown, Cape Cod refused to accept the charter agreement. The old stagecoach scudded along fast enough—when the wind was fair—and the Lord only knew how many furriners would be stowing down in "the cars."

Editor Phinney of the Barnstable *Patriot* went through the towns, speechifying valiantly in favor of the railroad. Why, folks in other places, when they saw a chance like this, would sign on the dotted line and then run out to touch off fireworks!

But the folks of this place were "deef as a haddock." Then, one day, the resourceful editor warned them that if the British should ever again attack the United States, the first place they would strike was Provincetown, and without a railroad, Provincetown and her neighbor villages would be cut off without escape. Editor Phinney knew his people. "The cars" came down-Cape.

While this controversy was raging, the Cape had no inkling, of course, of the use which furriners of a still later day were to make of this same old stagecoach route—which has been followed in the Cape Cod extension of U. S. Highway No. 6. A police check on a Sunday in the summer of 1936 showed that 55,000 motor cars passed over one of the canal bridges in twenty-four hours.

First an Indian trail, and then a wagon track, the route of U. S. Highway No. 6 had been known from Old Colony days as the "King's Road." By an act of the General Court in 1920, it was officially designated "The King's Highway," and markers were placed all down the line.

But the natives of Cape Cod didn't like that name. They never had liked it—at least not since the signing of the Declaration of Independence. The town of Orleans, especially, was in a stew over it, and after eight years of agitation, Orleans adopted a resolution in town meeting, "viewing with an interest that approaches grave concern this attempt, neither historically nor geographically correct, to rewrite American history."

Headlines began to appear in the Boston newspapers:

KING'S HIGHWAY GALLS CAPE COD

Other towns began passing resolutions. They not only viewed it "with an interest that approaches grave concern;" they "considered it a deplorable situation," they even "contemplated it with growing alarm." And then, mysteriously, the "King's Highway" signposts began to disappear, one by one, first from the Orleans roadside, then through other towns. More years passed, more signposts vanished, and the name of the down-Cape road remained a highly debatable matter, until in February, 1937, the Governor of the Commonwealth signed a new law, which designated it "Grand Army of the Republic Highway."

It was a master stroke. Nobody bothered to pronounce the road's new name. Everybody was satisfied.

Because I have been stopped on the street in Provincetown—the "jumping-off place" at the tip-end—by motorists who, having come that far, wanted to know "which is the way to Cape Cod?" I feel that a word on the geography of the Cape should be included here. Better than any words is a map, and the Cape Cod Chamber of Commerce will provide you with a big detailed one, at no charge (address "Hyannis, Mass.")

On the way from the Canal to Provincetown, your sense of direction may have a hard time keeping up with you, and a glance at the map will show you why. Your course is a spiral, "boxing the compass," as the mariners say. As you set out from the Canal, you are headed eastward, but when you enter Provincetown, you are going west. And if that does not confuse you enough, someone along the road probably will. One local historian, writing in the nineties, has left to posterity his grave discovery that Provincetown is "the only city in the United States where the sun rises in the west and sets in the east."

From the Canal, the Cape widens at the base to about twenty miles—the section embracing Sandwich, Falmouth and Mashpee—but beyond that point the sixty-five-mile peninsula keeps within a width of six miles, and in places narrows to little more than half a mile.

The inner shore is known as the "Bay Side;" the outer as the "Back Side" on the east, where it faces on the Atlantic Ocean, and as the "South Shore" where it faces on Nantucket Sound. Inlanders who have known the Cape only as a curlicue on the map, a tiny pothook sticking out over the continental shelf, will find the circuit of these shores crammed with surprises. The night-like pine woods of Sandwich and Mashpee, the salt marshes of Barnstable, the bleak hills of Truro, the costume-jewelry harbor of Provincetown—all are like odds and ends tossed together in Mother Earth's catchall without the slightest regard for sorting and matching.

The "Bay Side" skirts Cape Cod Bay with a

border of broad flats and wide beaches, little used inlets, salt marshes, shallow harbors, wooded knolls and a string of villages vaguely hyphenated by scattered houses and a network of old wagon roads. Along the "Back Side" lies the great unbroken beach, part of which Henry Thoreau tramped for the material in his book, *Cape Cod*. As contrasting with the "Bay Side," here are surf, lonely bluffs, the eerie dune country of Eastham and the Lower Cape, and all alongshore that strange, wild dominance of the sea which holds the beachland in its spell and works its witchery on all who come to look. It is a hard-shelled traveler indeed who departs this part of Cape Cod untouched, who carries off with him no memory, no feeling that for a moment in his life he has been at one with the sea.

"Back Side" and "Bay Side," then, are terms to remember when you visit Cape Cod. A prim Wellfleet housewife who rents rooms to summer people once confessed to me that she had somehow shocked her guests by a "perfectly civil answer" she had given them. They wanted to know the best place to take a sun-bath. And, of course, she told them the best place was on the Back Side.

From Chatham, at the "elbow" of the Cape, westward to the corner at Woods Hole, the continuation of the Back Side faces on Nantucket Sound and Vineyard Sound, and in making the turn, it undergoes a marked change. Here it is called the "South Shore," facing the "South Sea," and people living here refer to the Bay Side, across-Cape, as the "North Shore," and to Cape Cod Bay as the "North Sea."

In a circuit of the towns, our general course follows Route 6 all the way down-Cape, taking in

Sandwich, Barnstable, Yarmouth, Dennis, Brewster, Orleans, Eastham, Wellfleet, Truro and Provincetown. These are the "Bay Side" towns. On our return, we retrace on Route 6 to Orleans, and there swing south into Chatham, on Route 28, the "South Shore Road." Thence we continue westward through Harwich and a string of South Shore villages in the towns of Dennis, Yarmouth and Barnstable, then through Mashpee to Falmouth, and finally up the shore of Buzzards Bay to Bourne and the Canal.

As the visitor from broad, inland America drives down the length of this sandy curlicue, and observes that it is taking him well out to sea, and that in spots it seems to be hanging as if by a thread, he may wonder at the durability of this land, its permanence as the living-place of people, the site of solid villages linked by old roads. On the map it looks as if it might carry away with the first good breeze, or go under before any big sea that should catch it broadside. There are points along the way whence both shores can be seen, and there is more than one spot where Father Neptune, congratulating himself on a particularly lively spree, has joined his hands, making a temporary channel.

But the inquiring visitor finds Cape people curiously indifferent to any prospect that the ocean might some day swallow their little peninsula in one gulp. "Narrow in the beam" though it is, the body of the Cape has proved seaworthy, its underpinnings have withstood all attacks within a period estimated by geologists at thirty thousand years. Battering surf and besieging tides are forever remodeling its coastlines; islands are on record which no longer exist; sand is washed from one corner to be deposited in another; windblown dunes bury whole forests. But all this mobility, plus earthquakes of which there were two in 1935, has failed to make Cape Cod "drag anchor."

Geologically, the Cape has been a grand hook for scientists to hang theories on. That it is a work of glaciers—a terminal moraine—all are agreed; but from here on, the scientists do not hold together even as well as the glaciers did.

A moraine is an accumulation of earthy rubbish pushed together by the glacier—like the ridges of egg left on my small daughter's breakfast plate when she gets through pushing around with a piece of toast. The lines of egg left by the sides of the toast are lateral moraines; but if she should suddenly get tired of eating egg, as she very often does, and should stop pushing and throw the piece of toast across the room in disgust, the line left on the plate by the front edge of the toast is a terminal moraine. And in explaining Cape Cod, that seems to be about as far as the geologists can agree.

Another glacial riddle, variously solved, is the Cape's long string of fresh-water ponds. Cape folks used to say there was a pond to drown every town gossip in. At any rate, there are nearly 300 such lakelets, with an aggregate area of about 40,000 acres—one-fifth of the fresh-water acreage of the State of Massachusetts. Almost down to the very tip-end of the Cape one passes them, and the narrowness of the land and their proximity to the salt sea on both sides appear to be no hindrance.

These ponds are invariably beautiful, where they have been let alone. There is something sad and wasteful, I think, about a natural pond that has been "landscaped" and fitted out with a set of swans and a marble statue; but only a few in the South Shore towns have been thus abused.

Cape Cod owes its name to the good judgment of the English navigator, Captain Bartholomew Gosnold. Crossing the ocean in the *Concord,* he sighted land on May 15, 1602. At first he called it "Shoal Hope," but apparently realized that he could do better than that. "Near this cape," says his log, "we came to anchor in fifteen fathoms, where we took great store of codfish, for which we altered the name to Cape Cod."

In a racier version of the incident, as given in an old poem by Benjamin Drew, the explorer is pictured as sitting on the deck of the *Concord,* contemplating the Cape and scratching his head for a name—finally deciding to call for a line and hook and name it for the first fish he caught.

> *Old Neptune heard the promise made,*
> *Down dove the water-god—*
> *He drove the meaner fish away*
> *And hooked the mammoth cod.*
>
> *Quick Gosnold hauled. "Cape . . . Cape . . .*
> *Cape Cod!"*
> *"Cape Cod!" the crew cried louder;*
> *"Here, steward! take the fish along*
> *"And give the boys a chowder!"*

An introduction to Cape Cod cannot properly close without a word about the weather. No greeting, no conversation is valid here until some reference has been made to it. Governor Bradford himself sets the fashion in his *History of Plimouth*

*Plantation.* On August 15, 1635, he is revisiting the Cape when there arises:

> . . . *such a mighty storme of wind & raine as none living in these parts, either English or Indeans, ever saw. . . . It caused ye sea to swell up above 20 foote, right up & downe, and made many of the Indeans to clime into trees for their saftie.*

And three hundred years later, to the day, Al Higgins, of Cape Cod, grants an interview to a reporter for the New Bedford *Standard-Times*:

> *I got up early to see how the hens were making it. I no sooner got the henhouse door open when my best rooster hopped out into a gust of wind that stripped him to the pin-feathers and tossed him against the chopping-block with such a thump that the axe fell and cut off his head, slick as a whistle. There he was—killed, picked, and ready to clean. I don't believe there ever was such a gale.*

They tell weather yarns and they use weather talk under oath in the courts. A Provincetown woman, testifying in a divorce suit against her husband, told the judge:

"I came home one night, your honor, and Henry was snoring so hard you'd think the fog was coming in." And His Honor, having heard the Provincetown foghorns all his life, knew exactly what sort of noises Henry had made.

Their knowledge of the weather comes of lifelong study. There is the story, for instance, of old Cap'n Phineas Eldridge, retired skipper who took to growing turnips on a farm in Eastham, but who had grown weatherwise through many years in command of a coasting schooner. One evening the Cap'n was late for supper, and his wife, glancing out the window, saw a light flitting about the turnip field. Then the Cap'n dashed in, spun the telephone crank and shouted, "Give me Chatham, quick! Hello, Chatham? I want Sam Paine, the postmaster. Hey, Sam! My hat's just blowed off and got clear of me, but she's scudding due south in this breeze, and allowing for the reef in the brim, I calculate she'll just about make in to your place in fourteen minutes more. Mail her back to me, will you, Sam?"

The hat, of course, fetched up on the specified doorstep in Chatham, in exactly fourteen minutes after the Cap'n hung up the receiver, and was sent back to him next morning by parcel post.

# CHAPTER II

## SANDWICH

*Cross Canal over Sagamore Bridge (U. S. 6); turning right at information booth, one mile.*

The golden wedding days that crowd Cape Cod's calendar had a romantic precedent long ago in the town of Sandwich.

By a two-minute departure from the highway, you can start your tour with a visit to two ancient graves which the townsfolk still call the "Saddle and Pillion"—reminders of one of the first golden weddings in the New World. Historically they are unique among the markers of New England.

To reach them, turn left when you come to the information booth on the highway, about a mile beyond the Sagamore Bridge. One-tenth of a mile further, at your right, you will see two crude steps, making a break in a low stone wall at the roadside. The path from these steps leads to the graves of Edmund and Elizabeth Freeman.

Edmund Freeman of Saugus (Lynn) who had come over on the ship *Abigail* in 1635, was among those adventurous souls who "looked for greater matters than they found or could attain unto, aboute building great houses, and such pleasant situations for them, as them selves had fancied; as if they would be great men & rich, all of a sudaine; but they proved castles in ye aire." He and nine other men decided to take the ancient Indian trail to "Cap-Codd."

In April, 1637, the little band started off, and with Edmund went his wife, Elizabeth, and their two small sons. They had broken all ties with the mainland; they would build in the wilds, live there, and there "sleep till the trompe of Judgement Day."

"I fancy they came here," writes a local historian, "to worship God and make money, thinking a frontier town, as this was, a singularly convenient and likely place to be let alone."

But Edmund, a genial soul who had in him the gift of peace-maker, was not let alone. Others soon joined the settlement, and a scramble for land followed. Disputes arose. Quarrelsome neighbors needed a man of his talents. "Everybody, parson as well as people, bought and sold land, which ranged from a shilling an acre, both up and down." Time after time Freeman was called in as moderator, and finally he rose to a position as assistant to Governor Bradford.

Meanwhile Elizabeth, braving the terrors of the "salvage forreste," with its packs of "ye hongrie ravening wolvs," set about getting a house in order. Unlike the "castles in ye aire" of which her husband had dreamed, unlike even the "latched, thatched and daubed" dwellings of later years, these first homes of Sandwich were put together with "creek stuff" and anything else that came to hand.

But for Edmund and Elizabeth, it was home enough, and as he achieved leadership, he provided more handsomely for an ever expanding family. He and Elizabeth grew old together, and in 1676, Elizabeth died. They had been married 59 years, and now Edmund was 86. Grimly he called his sons and his many grandsons to him, and led them to the top of the knoll near his house; and there he buried Elizabeth, putting down "a large flat rock resembling a pillion." * Beside it he placed another stone, oddly shaped like a saddle. Then he turned to his sons.

"When I die," he told them, "place my body under that stone. For your mother and I have travelled many long years together in this world."

The old man's wish was fulfilled. Then, for two centuries he and his beloved lay peacefully under the pines that lined Tupper Road, forgotten by the town of Sandwich, unknown to the rest of the world. Research workers later established the identity of the two strange graves, and bronze tablets were set down in the stones—one for Edmund on the saddle, one for Elizabeth on the pillion.

The town of Sandwich has done little to call attention to the graves, and up to now the great influx of people who come each summer to "see Cape Cod" has sped by on the highway, hardly more than a stone's throw away, because they had never been led to the spot. Recently a research worker for the New England Historical Genealogical Society has reported that Edmund and Elizabeth are among the ancestors of President Franklin D. Roosevelt.

Ever since Edmund Freeman's time, Cape Codders have been "traveling many long years to-

---

*Cushion attached to a saddle, on which women rode while accompanying their husbands.

gether in this world." They begin looking forward
to their old age when they reach 90. Living long is
so much the practice here that people say "it must
be something in the climate"—though one spry
octogenarian has confided to me that "it's only because it takes such an etarnal long time to convince
a Cape Cod Yankee of anything."

William Nye, the Sandwich historian, died in
1936 at the age of 96; but Grandma Holway was
well and hearty at 95, and she had a host of friends
near her own age; and young Charlie Pope, only
74, was in the same year giving his exhibition per-
formances—on roller skates—and had arranged
with Henry Ford to go to Dearborn the next year
and there challenge any man of 70 or over to a contest in "plain and fancy figgers."

All down the Cape you will meet them—an alert
legion marching towards 100, most of them not
even "chairbound." Falmouth has a "town cane"
which its oldest resident is allowed to keep. It
hasn't been very useful, however—most of those
who have held it didn't know what it was for. In
Dennisport, Captain John Wixon and his wife,
Sarah Jane, celebrated their seventieth wedding
anniversary in the spring of 1937, and Captain
Elijah Eldridge of that village was still carrying
on at 91 the trade he took up when he quit the sea
—repairing towerclocks.

In Brewster, Dorcas Howland is 96, and Deziah
Hutchins of High Brewster is 95; and Eastham
has its Frank Ellison, past 90 and working his
thirty-acre farm. An off-Cape doctor once tried to
perform a "mercy killing" on Frank, with lethal
pills, when he had been so badly battered that it
seemed worse than useless to try to save him. The

"killing" didn't take, as Frank relates it. The doctor has been dead thirty years.

The Sandwich which is your first taste of Cape Cod is not slapped on a plate and pushed under your nose; to get to it, you must go around the counter. And so, when you have returned from the Freeman graves to the intersection, instead of turning onto the highway again, continue straight across, passing the information booth on the detour leading to the beautiful old village.

On your way you pass Bay View Cemetery, where Joseph Jefferson is buried. Jefferson, greatest comedian of his time, won renown as Rip Van Winkle, as Bob Acres, and in a score of other leading roles. On that corner of the Cape where the Canal now opens into Buzzards Bay, he and Grover Cleveland were neighbor summer residents, both attracted by the hunting and fishing in Sandwich woods. Jefferson wanted to buy a house in Sandwich, but Sandwich didn't want Jefferson. To the townsfolk, "the stage" was a remote, godless world, whence no good neighbor could have come. Jefferson went south, but before he left, he bought a lot in Bay View Cemetery, and told his friends, "They won't let me live in Sandwich, but I'll stay there yet!" And he is staying—yet.

Of Cleveland, too, there is a story worth retelling. The then President was lost in the Sandwich woods. Drenched by a heavy rain and tired from his day's fishing, he knocked at a lonely house in a clearing. A voice from aloft asked what he wanted. "This is the President," Cleveland said. "I'm lost, and I'd like to stay here tonight."

"Well," came the answer, "stay there." And down went the window.

When I saw this story in the old "Cape Cod Magazine," I was not inclined to take it seriously. But not long afterwards I saw a sign on a fence farther down-Cape, in Brewster:

NO HUNTIN
NO FISHIN
NO NOTHIN

If the average American can tell you nothing of Sandwich as one of his country's first settlements, at least he has heard of it as the place Sandwich glass comes from. A kind of second-hand halo has been hung over the town by collectors of this commodity.

In 1825 Deming Jarves came down from Boston to propose a glass industry to the town. He saw, in the great pine forests, the chief requisite—fuel to keep the furnaces hot. Pittsburgh glass works could afford to pay their men as high as $2 a day, he said, and the labor was neither dangerous nor too arduous. In that same year a factory went up, skilled workmen were brought in, and glass-blowing was begun.

On outlay, Jarves found that he had overshot his mark, and two years later formed a stock company, the Boston & Sandwich Glass Company. The business itself, however, was profitable from the start.

This company, nearly a century before the United States Steel Corporation began owning its own railroads and ships and cement plants and what-not, had to buy up 2,000 acres of forest land, to operate what amounted to a large lumbering industry, to build homes for the workmen it had imported, to set up company stores, to install a horse railroad to the waterfront and operate its own scows, and even to own its own steamboat, for the transportation of sand, pearl ash, salt-petre, nitrate of soda and other necessary commodities. The steamer kept a regular schedule, Sandwich to Boston, for ten years, carrying passengers as well as freight.

The "gaffers" as the expert glassmakers were called, were a lordly crew, able and proud, and about them and their skill arose a tradition in Sandwich. Elizabeth Reynard, in her colorful book of Cape lore, *The Narrow Land,* mentions the cloudy rose that, "held in a woman's hand, unclouded to reveal virginity." Also among the tales to which the "rosin monkeys" listened as they sat around the glory-hole, was that of Gaffer Bonique, the mysterious Frenchman, who knew many things besides glass-making, and who—for all anyone knew—might even have been the Lost Dauphin of France.

As interesting as the spectacular ascent of this industry was its decline. The shutdown in 1888 has been ascribed to "labor trouble," which is a distortion of the picture. While a strike was the immediate cause, what really ended the Sandwich industry's career was its inability to compete with the mechanized glass factories that had sprung up in Pittsburgh and Chicago. The very thing that now endears its product to collectors—the touch of the hand-craftsman—stamped it as obsolete, doomed it when its time was outlived.

The men joined a union, and in 1887 they threatened to strike for better wages. The company is
said to have warned them that if the fires in its
furnaces were once allowed to go out, they would
never be relighted. Then, according to W. E.
Kern, one of the workers, an immediate issue arose
over the company's refusal to make good a short-
age of 87 cents in the week's pay of Nicholas
Black, glassmaker. The men recalled that it had
paid Gaffer Rice Harris of England $5,000 and
expenses for six months' work. There was on hand
a large order for lamps when the dispute over
Black's pay arose. The men went on strike, and on
New Year's Day the plant closed—for all time.

There were a few later attempts to revive the
glass trade in Sandwich, but none succeeded. Early
in this century the molds and other equipment were
sold for junk, the iron ones melted down, the
wooden ones burned. Many tourists have come to
Sandwich with shovels, to unearth small fragments
of the glass, spoiled pieces that were once tossed
into the "cullet-box," and now even these are gone.
If you feel like prospecting when you come here,
you can still find the bricks, covered with molten
glass, that were once in factory floors, but that is
about all that remains. Children of Sandwich play
where once the great gaffers of France, England
and Belgium made magic and "did fey things"
with blowpipe and punty-rod. One of the last of
the Sandwich gaffers, George Thatcher, died in
Falmouth in 1936, at the age of 82.

There was a time, in the infancy of that great
American manufacturing industry which turns
out "genuine antiques" in mass production, when

Sandwich glass was a hard nut to crack. It was difficult to reproduce the "quare silver tint" of old Sandwich. Machinery had not been devised for putting in the irregularities of hand-made or blown ware, chemists had not yet found a substitute for the Sandwich formula, long kept secret, for fine ruby and other tinted glass.

With the further advance of machine methods, however, processes have been perfected which will produce glassware quite as imperfect as the most cross-eyed, near-sighted, palsy-fingered workman could have made it by hand in the old days. The way was made easier by the fact that no trade mark appeared on the Sandwich product. Now "Sandwich glass," made forty years after the Sandwich factory closed down in 1888, looks the same, rings the same to a thump of the thumbnail, even breaks the same.

What many enthusiasts do not seem to realize is that the Boston & Sandwich Glass Company was itself a mass production industry—one of our earliest of its kind—and it was interested in making quantities of anything that would sell, among which were many cheap and practical items, like ten-cent lamp chimneys. At its peak of production, in the 1850's, it was employing 500 men and boys, and turning out annually goods with a value of $600,000. And much of this output was pretty atrocious stuff, designed to bedazzle at the lowest possible figure.

Some day, experts point out, the market for Sandwich glass, based on scarcity value, will level down to a recognition of only those articles which, made in Sandwich, could not be duplicated elsewhere; and these were not, strictly speaking, a product of the factory, but rather of the individual workers. They are the "off-hand" pieces, which were fashioned by the gaffers, the blowers and gatherers and made in their off-hours.

These pieces are rare and generally beautiful, for many of the men were artists. They spent their evenings at the glass-house, making trinkets and ornaments for their homes, for their wives and their sweethearts. As works of the artist, such glass is rightly cherished, and is readily recognizable by experts. The antique shops selling "genuine Sandwich glass" generally don't handle it.

The site of the old glass factory is down by the railroad station, where there were once several large buildings belonging to the plant. Only one structure remains.

There are several collections of Sandwich glass on the Cape. The museum of the Sandwich Historical Society has one, the museum in Provincetown another. In Sandwich, you will find the museum in the white building on the town green. If it is closed—and the chances are six to one that it will be—you can still gain admittance by telephoning the curator.

Other items are worth seeing there, including a glass-blower's kit, a collection of arrowheads, and an old flint-lock musket credited with ending the ravages of a persistent wolf at Sandwich's door in 1675.

Wolves terrorized the town for two hundred years. Bounties were offered, and a wolf's head once occupied the most prominent place on the front of the meeting-house. At one time the town weighed a scheme of building a wall all the way across the Cape to shut these brutes out, but one canny townsman objected that such a wall would keep the wolves in instead of out. Poor as the people were, they offered from £2 to £4 for a dead wolf. The last big wolf was killed about a century ago.

This same gun likely was used by many a Sandwich youth on the pestilent "blackbirds," in compliance with the law in this and other Cape towns that forbade a man to marry until he had killed his quota. "Old men over 70 were excused from the blackbirds," a local historian says—though he does not add, as would seem only fair to me, that blackbirds above a certain comparable age should not count either. But he does point out that it was a hard law, and he pities the young man "going out afield with his gun. Birds and a wife or no birds and no wife; so the law said. How could he shoot straight, so perturbed?"

The town of Sandwich had many other strange and wonderful laws. One of these required that a pig's snout must be ringed, and Richard Bourne was among those fined, "not because the swine had done mischief, but that the law might suffer no damage."

Sabbath-breaking was a more serious offense than "drinking overmuch," fines being respectively thirty shillings and ten shillings, with an hour in the stocks thrown in for each. For working on Sunday, which was breaking the Sabbath in the worst way but one, a severe thrashing at the whipping-post was prescribed. There was also a law providing that "if any man make motion of marriage to any man's daughter or maid, without first obtaining leave of her parents, guardian or master, he shall be punished by fine not exceeding £5, the price of a cow." Cows were rare in the Old Colony, and the intent of the law was not often violated.

The museum has a case of trinkets brought home by Hannah Burgess from the voyages she made with her husband, Captain William Burgess of the clipper *Challenger*.

Will was only 22, and Hannah was very proud of him, as, certainly, she had a right to be; for to a Cape sailor of any age, the command of a clipper ship was the top of the ladder.

Hannah found only one fault with him. When first she went to sea, she observed that his crew often took the name of the Lord in vain! And not long afterward, in a spell of thick weather, she also observed that Will did the same thing! Yet, "in his letters written to me at sea," Hannah wrote in her diary, "William appeared to enjoy sweet communion with his God!"

Hannah tried to cure him of the astonishing habit. She was not very successful, but through the diary runs the assuring line, "I am happy in the love of my husband."

Their roving romance, however, was to endure only two years. While the *Challenger* was loading at Chincha, an island group off Peru, Will fell sick. He was too sick to navigate his ship, and the nearest doctor was in Valparaiso. The mate knew nothing about reckoning position at sea, but Hannah did, for she had made Will explain what those endless figures were in the tables of his *Navigator,* and in her spare time had studied them. So

Hannah navigated to Valparaiso; but two weeks before they made the port, Will died.

Hannah had him brought back to Sandwich for burial. She lived out her life in the village, and when she died, left the case of her souvenirs to the museum. She left pictures, too, of Will and herself.

To Cape Codders, there was nothing startling in Hannah's willingness to go to sea with her husband, nor, in fact, in her ability to reckon from the tables of the *Navigator;* rather it was regular practice among many sea captains to take their wives aboard ship—whether they liked it or not—and the ladies, having time on their hands, studied navigation. What some of these young New England shipwives had to endure from husbands who were alive and healthy was as bad as Hannah Burgess's plight with a dying one, and sometimes rather worse. There was the gentle lady of Provincetown, for instance, who came back from years in the Arctic a chattering lunatic—but I shall leave her story until we can pick it up on the scene.

The largest "memorial boulder," the most elaborate bronze tablet, will never bring back the past as an old house does. Unfortunately, the "town fathers" of many of our ancient villages have allowed the houses—most intimate reminders of those who lived in ages past—to go to ruin, but have spent money dotting the country with "historical markers" commemorating the acts of these same dead. I suppose the preference for the markers arises from the fact that they are the creation of those who honor the dead, whereas the houses were the creation of the dead themselves.

But of dwelling places, there are still many staid ancients in Sandwich, and there are few pleasanter ways of studying history than by looking at old houses. The village claims the "oldest house on Cape Cod," in that gray-shingled "salt-box" (long slant of roof in rear, short slant in front) which nestles beside the glassy-green waters of the mill pond, and which is called the Hoxie House. To reach it, pass the Old Mill Shop and turn right, along the pondshore. You will find it at your right, about fifty yards from the road.

Whether these jasmine-bedecked walls are the very oldest on the Cape or not, I do not pretend to know. Certainly they are old enough, and beautiful enough, to be in no need of trivial superlatives. There is evidence that in the year this book goes to press, 1937, the house is dozing through its three-hundredth birthday.

Lodowick Hoxie, whose descendants still own the house, came to Sandwich in 1658, and among other achievements, gave his children the names of Solomon, Gideon, Hezekiah, Jubal, Bathsheba and Content. One of these Hoxie totsies sold, gave or lost the house, which is next recorded as in possession of the Reverend John Smith, who in turn moved away in 1688 with his thirteen children— possibly, though not stated, because a fourteenth could not be crammed in. This was the same Reverend Smith "whose tolerant principles had rendered him obnoxious to the majority," in the words of the historian, so that he moved to New York.

Another Hoxie, Cap'n Abraham, bought the old house back into the family nearly two hundred years later. Just as men out west looked a horse in the mouth to determine its age, on the Cape they

looked in the fireplace of a house. And Cap'n
Abraham, exploring into the past of this home of
his ancestors, took a brick out of the hearthplace
on which the date was marked—1637.

On the west side of School Street, you will find
a white house with a long piazza, the birthplace of
an author whose books are among the best-sellers
of all time. His public falls asleep over the adventures of his heroes, yet his works have sold nearly
five million copies. For the books are "Bedtime
Stories," the author Thornton W. Burgess, the
heroes Peter Rabbit and his companions.

Burgess spent his boyhood in the village of
Sandwich, and on the beaches and flats, in the
woods and along the brooks. When he began making up stories about little animals for his own small
son, he drew upon the scenes he had known himself. The original Briar Patch of Peter Rabbit, the
Green Forest, the Wide Marsh, and many more,
are here in Sandwich. And for other parts of his
stories, too, Burgess has drawn upon his Cape Cod
memories.

> . . . It was a mass meeting of angry citizens. . . .
> Of course Jerry Muskrat was there, and his uncles
> and aunts and all his cousins. Billy Mink was there,
> and all his relations, even old Grandfather Mink,
> who had lost most of his teeth and was a little hard
> of hearing. . . . And everybody was looking very
> solemn, very solemn indeed. When the last one had
> arrived, Mother Muskrat climbed up on the Big
> Rock and made a speech. . . .
> "It is no longer safe for our little folks to play
> around the Smiling Pool or along the Laughing
> Brook. What are we going to do about it?"
> Everybody looked at everybody else in dismay.
> Then everybody began to talk at once. . . . Such

*excitement! Everybody had a different idea, and nobody would listen to anybody else. Old Mr. Mink lost his temper and called Grandpa Otter a meddlesome know-nothing. . . .*

And if Mother Muskrat was not presiding over a regular New England town meeting, such as Thornton Burgess must have attended many times in Sandwich, I shall humbly take my place beside Grandpa Otter as a meddlesome know-nothing.

The Old Mill Shop near the Town Hall straddles a brook that once turned Sandwich's grist mill. A part of the old machinery has been preserved there. Miller William Nye shut up shop about forty years ago because, as he once explained to me, "nobody brought any more corn to grind."

The church in the Center, like many others built a century ago on the Cape, is spired in a design of Christopher Wren, and this one stands not far from the site of the first meeting-house. No trace remains of that structure, which was called "old" in 1644, and which "looked like a thatched barn," nor is there anything of the building which replaced it in 1756, where Mordecai Ellis and Joshua Fish were appointed "to take care of the young people who are very often rude on the Lord's Day, and when any do offend, to return them to the law." Men and women were properly separated, each sex on its side of the center aisle, but Mordecai and Joshua had to keep a bright lookout. They returned to the law, among others, "two young females for laughing."

Cape Cod's first settlers lie in the little cemetery beside the mill pond in Sandwich. Here, where

willows overhang the soft, green banks, "mossy
marbles" are already surrendering to eternity; the
dead sleep on, while the stones crumble and are no
more.

The oldest marker standing now is dated 1680,
but Sandwich has buried its dead here since 1663,
and in a record book in the possession of the Pope
family, all the graves are listed, and the epitaphs
given.

Many an ancient romance could be retold if the
stones of this burying ground were given tongues,
if the ripples of Shawme Lake could whisper
words. Here lie the two wives of Richard Bourne,
famed minister of the Mashpee Indians.

Richard's first wife, Bathsheba, fell ill of a fever
which neither the minister's "dosage and pills" nor
the Indian herbs could cure. His second wife was
Ruth Winslow, a widow of Marshfield—"a little,
lively, smart Gentlewoman of very good sense and
knowledge, of ye strictest Piety, an excellent Spirit
of Family Govt, very good skill in ye Diseases of
Women and Children, very helpful to her neighbors."

In 1676, shortly after Bathsheba's death, Richard wrote to the widow:

"I have had divers motions since I received
yours, but none suits me but yourself, if God soe
incline your mynde to marry me . . . I doe not
find in myselfe any flexableness to any other but an
utter loatheness."

The following year he met her in Barnstable,
where she was visiting relatives, and there he married her. Elder John Chipman of that town had
tried to dissuade him. The widow, he said, was a
worldly creature—yes, much too worldly for Rich-

ard Bourne. And when his arguments had failed, the Elder attended the ceremony, but stood shaking his head throughout, and whispering to his wife that the widow was too worldly for Richard.

Five years later Richard Bourne died. Then Hope Chipman, wife of the Elder, "changed this life for a better ye 8th of January, 1683." And the year following, Elder John Chipman came to Sandwich and married the "worldly" widow himself!

Your respect for Cape Cod as a good solid bit of the earth, for all its frailty on the map, will be enhanced by a trip across-Cape from Sandwich village on Route 130. The way to Peters Pond passes through the Shawme State Forest, a tract of 8,500 acres in the townships of Sandwich and Bourne, in which a large conservation project has been undertaken. Two CCC camps were put at work here in 1933 to build thirty miles of dirt roads, clear the swamps, place fire-fighting equipment and lanes, and plant new trees—white pine, Scotch pine, American red pine and white spruce.

Some of the titles to these acres went back to the time of the earliest settlers, and the State ran into many a problem in tracking down ownership when it set out to acquire the land. In 1936 a fire got beyond control and spread over hundreds of acres, and the smoke could be seen in a great cloud from across Cape Cod Bay, in Provincetown.

Back in Sandwich, as you pass the Daniel Webster Inn, forget Daniel for the moment—they have merely borrowed the glory of his name because he stayed there at times—and let this house tell you

its own story, which certainly needs no trumping-
up with a statesman's renown.

Henry Thoreau has mentioned the Eastham
minister of old, who sat upon a cliff and watched
for drift whales because the town fathers had voted
to appropriate for his support a part of the value
of every whale that came ashore. But originally
these proceeds all belonged to the crown; and it
was one Reverend Rowland Cotton, of Sandwich,
who conceived the ingenious scheme of taking over
the whales to pay the pastor, "putting himself in
the place of the King in the matter of drift whales,
which then abounded in yonder bay."

The result is the house you see before you. It
was built as the parsonage in 1694, and how many
drift whales went into it only the good parson
and a generous Providence knew. Dame Cotton's
dowry was said to have been of considerable assistance—she was one of the Saltonstalls of Boston
—but then, she had to have her silk and brocade
dress and her mourning ring, and the other features of "a select toilet."

Samuel Sewall, in his diary, writes a synopsis of
one of Reverend Cotton's sermons—"a long one, a
Gospel sermon, full of meat." And a later Sandwich minister pays tribute to him as a "clever and
painstaking preacher." Whatever the pains or
other matters he took, he passed on to his reward
in 1722, and the Reverend Benjamin Fessenden
took over at the meeting-house.

Now skip a century, and look once more at the
big house on the main street. No more does the
ink congeal with cold, while a man of God writes
frugally on little sheets his two-hour sermon for
the coming Sabbath; no more does the communion

bread freeze and rattle in the plate as the deacon prepares it in the pantry. Now, as the Fessenden Inn, the old house is kept warm and bright, and while a long line of ministers turn over in their graves, it is known far and wide as the one "wet" spot in this part of the Cape. Sandwich was then the only wet town, and the Fessenden Inn, turned into a stagecoach stop, was the only house licensed to sell jug liquor tapped from barrels and measured out with a wooden ladle. Thither the farmer, who was not to be without his ration of grog, brought his earthen jug over many rough miles; thither, too, came the weary traveler who knew of it as the "ordinary" on the stage line between Boston and the down-Cape towns, and often he took along a supply promised to his friends and neighbors down the Cape.

Webster was among those who put up at the Fessenden, in the years before 1825, when he came to hunt and fish in the Sandwich woods. When the glass workers began hunting and fishing too, Webster found it hard to see the woods for the hunters, and went to Marshfield. He liked the glass, however, and bought much of it, and in 1850 a bowl, "the largest piece of flint glass made by machinery in any part of the world up to that time," was presented to him. Two mechanics worked six months making the mold alone for Webster's "Union Bowl."

Across the road from the East Sandwich depot is the house that Barnabas Holway, expert boatbuilder, put up in 1720, with its great kitchen, wide-planked and brick-ovened; its fine old furniture, including a handsome tip-top table of more than a hundred winters; and its long low shed in the yard where Barnabas and his family built whaleboats for many a blubber-boiler when these vessels started going afar for oil. The shed, walled with planks more than two feet wide, now bears a sign above the door, "Old Boat Shop." It is said that Barnabas, as a young man, toiled and tinkered, building his beautiful shop. With a workman's love of his tools, he safeguarded them by putting a strong lock on the narrow door at one end of the building. Then he proceeded to build a beautiful boat, and when it was all finished, stood there wondering how to get the boat out of the building.

If you wish to carry further your quest for homes that have lived long, Old Sandwich will reward you on Valley Road, where are more good examples dating back beyond the turn of 1700. Also, there is the 1699 Seth Pope homestead, the story of which is told in a booklet, *Cape Cod Legends,* which the Cape Chamber of Commerce has published.

"Seth the Peddler," according to his story, in 1669 was ordered to depart from the town of Sandwich lest he become a public charge. He went, but as he trudged off toward the King's Road, he flung back the boast that he would return and "buy up the town."

Seth went to New Bedford, worked and saved, and built himself a wharf and warehouse. He became selectman and representative to the General Court. And, good as his word, "in 1699 he came back and purchased nearly all the land in the village," and built a house for each of his sons. Then he turned upon the community that had "warned him out," and announced that although his children could stay there if they chose, as for himself, he "would not live in the damned town." And off he went again; but the house known as the "Seth Pope House" has remained in the family to this day. This house is on Grove Street, across from the cemetery. The fifth house, after you turn off the highway, is Seth's; and over the door is the date, 1699.

In an antiquated secretary in the Seth Pope House are many letters and documents, and scrawled upon one of them is this:

> "*May 9, 1777, received of Paul Wing five pounds lawful money, being his fine for refusing to serve as one of the constables for the town of Sandwich 1777.*
>
> *Joseph Nye*
> *one of the Selectmen.*"

Paul Wing was a Quaker, and Quakers could not, in conscience, bear arms. Hence Paul's refusal to serve as constable. But the story of the Quakers in Sandwich goes back, more than a hundred years before Paul Wing's time—and forward also, for nearly two hundred years, to the present. If you turn left on the dirt road a little beyond the village, marked "Friends Meeting House," you come to a large, bare clapboarded structure which is the oldest Quaker meeting house in America. Quaker services are still held there each Sabbath evening.

Then take the macadam road at the left of the meeting house, and you will find a tablet to Paul Wing's ancestor, Stephen, who was Sandwich's first Quaker. The second white house on your right is Stephen's. For a time in the early days the structure was used as a blockhouse. Its walls are eighteen inches thick.

The Reverend John Wing came to Boston in 1632, bringing his mother and his wife, Deborah, and his brothers, Daniel, Stephen and Matthew. In 1637 they all came to Sandwich to settle. The Reverend John moved down-Cape, settling in Brewster.

In 1641 Stephen built the house you see here, and here he stayed through the four bitter years, 1657-1661, of "lamentable controversy," while the "renegade Episcopal minister," George Barlow, carried out with such eagerness the statutes enacted against the heretics.

Stephen Wing was one of the growing faction of Sandwich settlers who were "unsettled in their church relations, who were doubtful of the propriety of stated preaching," and who, to put it bluntly, considered Sandwich's long-winded Reverend Leverick an ass. So, when Christopher Holder and John Copeland came to town from Rhode Island in 1657, Stephen Wing hearkened to them. When they called upon him to "quake at the word of the Lord," he quaked. And within the year, seventeen other families of Sandwich joined him in his new faith.

Intolerant Plymouth devised even harsher laws against this pernicious sect which "sowed their corrupt and damnable doctrines in almost every town;" Boston cut off the outer rims of their ears, and when that did not stop them, banished them on pain of death. Sandwich, for which claims of a greater mildness are made, merely thrashed them thoroughly and plundered all that they owned. In three years, 129 cattle, three horses and nine sheep, "in value about £700," were filched by the town, mainly through the offices of Marshal Barlow, from twenty-one of his victims.

Among these was William Allen, once a man of good estate, who was forced to pay it all out in fines, and who ultimately was thrown into prison in Boston. His wife, Priscilla, kept the children as best she could on stale bread and water; for Marshal Barlow had taken away almost everything the family possessed, even to the last cow and a bag of meal. Barlow, drunk partly with power and partly with grog, came to make a last raid on the helpless Priscilla, and seizing a copper kettle, snorted:

"Now, Priscilla, how will thee cook for thy family and friends, thee has no kettle?"

And Priscilla answered:

"George, that God who hears the ravens when they cry, will provide for them. I trust in that God, and I verily believe the time will come when thy necessity will be greater than mine."

George Barlow's necessity, after he had grown rich on "the spoils of the innocent" and then poor on the books of the Tavern, was verily greater than Priscilla Allen's. In his old age, so Sandwich loves to relate, back he tottered, craving charity that "never was refused; yet he was to the last ungrateful, and lived despised and died unregretted."

How any Quaker managed to come out of this pious thievery with a shilling to his name, or a foot of land, is a question that stumps the local chroniclers, who can only point out that they had "tough hearts of English Oak," and they "held their meetings in Christopher's Hollow, with the advantage that Plymouth Court could not fine the green woods of Almighty God 40 shillings for entertaining a harmless people."

There were more Quaker troubles in Sandwich than in any other town in the Colony—"not because Sandwich was more cruel," say its apologists, "but because there were more Quakers here." Yes, the forgiving little town of Sandwich even gave these troublesome folk a burying-ground of their own. In 1695, thirty years after Charles II had ordered all persecution to cease, it set aside half an acre, and there it allowed the weary dead to lie unmolested—until its enterprising minister, the Reverend Cotton, was voted the privilege in town meeting of 1715, of "pasturing his horse therein."

Leaving Reverend Cotton's horse to fatten on the grasses that have grown out of this "most monstrous deluded set of people," you may take the by-road, from the highway, which leads to the fish hatchery. The exhibit of darting young trout and salmon—thousands of them kept in shallow pools according to size—is worth the short jog it takes to reach it.

The object is to put fish in the ponds of Massachusetts faster than the fishermen can take them out, and at a clip of 130,000 baby fish annually, the hatchery has been holding its own. For biological details of this achievement, see the director of the hatchery. He lives in the old Nye House, hard by. The house has its own story, which goes back centuries before the fish hatchery. It was built by Goodman Benjamin Nye in 1685. Helen Nye ("Grandma Holway") was the ninth generation to live in it. The Nye family gave it to the State in 1914.

Three miles further along the highway, another by-road turns off to the State Game Preserve, a 200-acre tract given over to the breeding of pheasants and quail. The birds do their part ably, but the world seems equally prolific in turning out hunters.

# CHAPTER III

## BARNSTABLE

*On U. S. 6, between Sandwich and Yarmouth. Eight miles between Barnstable town lines.*

An ancient ghost town, long overgrown by the lush salt meadows, lies half a mile shoreward from the highway at the Sandwich-Barnstable town line. Here were once a swampland and a freshwater pond, and upon its shores, "Iyannough's Town." Sachem Iyannough of Cummaquid was, by all accounts, the sort of Indian who deserved that favorite adjective of the historians, "noble." Edward Winslow, of the *Mayflower,* described him as "a man not exceeding twenty-six years of age, personable, gentle, courteous and fair-conditioned; indeed, not like a salvage except in his attire."

Iyannough and his people spent the winters across-Cape at the "South Sea," and the summers in his "Town" at this spot. The long finger of duneland across the harbor, now called Sandy Neck, was Cummaquid—"long point"—and the whole region embraced by the Sachem's domain also was known by this name. On the point, the tribe held its lobster, oyster and clam feasts, the shells of which are still uncovered when a violent storm digs out new contours in the beach.

Winslow was with a party of ten men of the *Mayflower* company when he met Sachem Iyannough in July of 1621. The Pilgrims were searching for young John Billington, a lad of "one of ye

38

profanest families amongst them," who had run
off and gone astray in the woods. After they had
made in at Barnstable Harbor, low tide left their
shallop grounded. Some of Iyannough's subjects
were fishing for lobsters, and on meeting the English, invited them ashore.

Iyannough himself was in town at the time, and
he happened to know that the Billington boy was
with the Indians at Nauset. After providing Winslow's party with "cheare plentiful and various,"
the Sachem accompanied them in their shallop to
Nauset, where they picked up the youth. On the
return trip, they stopped again in Iyannough's
town, where they were given presents, and dances
were performed for them.

If Iyannough had any thought of reward for
such hospitality, certainly it was not the reward
that came to him less than two years later, when
he and his subjects were driven by the guns of the
English into the swamps, there to die of pestilence.
Rumors were heard of an "Indian conspiracy,"
and the swashbuckling bantam hero, Miles Standish, leading at that time an extermination cam-
paign, drove the Sachem of Cummaquid and several other chieftains into hiding, and to their
deaths. Yellow journalism was not yet born, but
Standish needed no jingoistic editorials to fortify
him for war—especially at a time when the Indians had not yet learned how to use firearms. History, it seems to me, owes something to the rakish
Morton, who in his chronicles of the day first
bestowed on our valiant Standish the nickname,
"Captaine Shrimpe."

The Billingtons—the family of the runaway
lad—had been a trial to their fellow Pilgrims, and

nine years later John Billington, Sr., was "found
guilty of willfull murder," in waylaying a young
man, whom he "shote with a gune, wherof he
dyed." Billington was executed for this crime.
"Thus, as it was ye first execution amongst them, so
was it a mater of great sadnes unto them."

Cummaquid, long after Iyannough's tribe vanished from the scene, became a try-yard for the
town of Barnstable. Here the versatile Reverend
Cotton of Sandwich boiled down his drift-whales
between prayers for a stray school, and here his
successors in the oil business carried on until the
drift-whales grew scarce and small coasting craft
could not find enough of the creatures in nearby
waters to keep the works busy.

The whale is a simple, trusting fellow. He swallowed Jonah without even taking a trial nibble,
and for a hundred years after the Pilgrims came
to Cape Cod, he continued to swim close inshore.
Being unable to consult the tide table, he frequently was beached, and promptly boiled.

Occasionally whales and blackfish, a smaller
species, still become stranded in the waters about
Cape Cod. Scarcely a year passes that some town
along the line does not report a school of blackfish
gone aground—"puffin' pigs," they call them—or
that news of them fails to get literally in the wind.
These animals are from ten to twenty feet long,
weighing up to two tons, and any town that re-
ceives one of their group calling-cards in its sea
breezes must send men to the beach at once to tow
them to sea or bury them.

The great leviathan—the species that came in
answer to the Reverend Cotton's prayers—is now

an infrequent caller at the Cape. Spouts are sighted in Provincetown waters, usually in April or early May, but a full-sized whale high and dry on the beach is now an arrival to make the front page of Cape newspapers.

In the winter of 1936-37, a sixty-foot sulphur-bottom whale rolled in on the tideflats of West Dennis, on the Back Shore. He was dead, and there he lay, in three feet at low water. The town of Dennis achieved publicity all the way up and down the coast, but paid for it through the nose for four days, when a fishing vessel was finally commissioned to tow old Sulphurbottom out to sea—at the end of a long line. He drifted back to Popponesset Beach in Mashpee, and this time the Coast Guards towed him out and blew him up with a bomb. The few old Cape Codders who could remember back to the days when they risked life and limb to make fast to such a creature shook their heads and muttered that "times had certainly changed."

But never start a Cape Codder on the subject of whales. I have had one old skipper glibly tell me that he once milked a cow-whale, that he had tried the milk, that it was very tasty. Said he christened her Magnesia.

The Cape Cod Indians, having no training in white man's real estate, called a swamp a swamp. For the four thousand acres of salt-hayland which the highway passes through now, their name was Moskeehtuckqut—Great Marshes. For some reason that escapes the record, the white settlers did not alter this to read "Shady Acres" or "Mountain View," and Great Marshes it remains.

Over these stubbly fields, where now a few unused supports are all that remain of old Barnstable's hay industry, our forefathers wrangled endlessly among themselves. Every other stalk of stubble here represents, at some time in the past, a law-suit. They measured and cut and sliced and whittled and chiseled away at this meadowland, and at each other, until in the end it was doubtful whether more effort had gone into the cultivation of the land than into the litigation over it. For ten years, from 1694 to 1703, they did more suing than sowing, and so many committees were appointed to settle disputes that everyone eventually became a committee member; and then, of course, the deadlocks began all over.

The salt hay grows wild now. Each Maytime the green of the Great Marshes freshens and spreads, each summer the patches turn tawny. But before the November frosts, no one comes to harvest. Salt hay, it was found in later years, had undesirable effects on the cattle. In some seasons it would come up saltier than in others, and Cape farmers would find their critters "well nigh cured on the hoof."

One farmer there was who owned broad tracts here, and no story of the Great Marshes of Barnstable would be complete without an account of him.

"Oh, for a cot in the wilderness! If the damned pox be not upon me now, 'tis only by the grace of God and a taut baize shirt! Giddap, Mehitable!"

Dr. Abner Hersey raced his erratic mare over the piny South Sea road and muttered maledictions upon the head of Seth Hyllier, whose home

he had just visited while on his "rounds" and whose
person he had found livid with the symptoms of
the dreaded smallpox. The year, 1786, was marked
by the plague.

To the mare Mehitable he communicated his
agitation, just as he communicated everything else
to her while the sulky rocked and rolled like an
apparition sweeping through the frosty night. She
sweated and flew. The doctor sweated and swore.
Nobody on the Cape lived in greater fear of catch-
ing the pox than Abner Hersey himself. It was
more than a disease; an affliction that consumed
you with ague when you had it and consumed you
with fear when you didn't.

He was eccentric—"a compound of caprice and
whim"—but he "could read the character of a visi-
tation" and that was the secret of his success. His
whims did not intrude upon his work; they were
domestic, not professional. He touched no "ardent
spirits."

On his bed were twelve all-wool blankets. In the
summer he rolled back ten, sleeping under two;
as the season progressed, he added blanket after
blanket, until in January it was "eleven blankets
cold," and in February "twelve blankets cold."

Once his sister-in-law called on him, bringing
along a friend. "Madame," he told her, "I cannot have you here. I am sick. My wife is sick. I
have no hay for your horses. I have no servants in
my family. And I had rather be chained to a galley
oar than wait on you myself!"

Nothing daunted him—except the damned pox!
Now, as he dashed through the woods, the feeling
of dread came over him again and again.

"Yes, a cot in the wilderness!" he repeated. "A cave on the mountain-side! Some island of refuge! Half an hour, good Lord, of peace!" Shuddering in the completely enclosed sulky—an outlandish contrivance of his own design—he made up his mind that when he got home he would shut himself up in the house for a whole week—provided he lived that long, and in case he did not, he swore he would haunt Seth Hyllier's scabrous soul and titillate the plague-spots on his body until the man should writhe and squirm and make moan as none other in Barnstable County ever had!

Suddenly he started, and began scratching under the ponderous great-coat which was made of seven calf-skins. The sweat trickled into his collar.

"By the great everlasting, what can this itching be in my left leg? Ah, thunder of Jehovah!—the pox! The end has come at last! Come, come, Mehitable, stir your stumps!"

Quite probably, it was during the week that he made himself a prisoner in his house, following this visit to Seth Hyllier, that the eccentric angel of Cape Cod composed his will. The involved document must have taken at least a week to draw up, and certainly he was in the mood for it then. Besides, never since he had begun his practice at the age of 19 could the doctor possibly have found the time for it while making his "rounds." These covered the entire Cape, sixty-five miles each way.

The history of medicine in modern times can offer no parallel to the practice of Abner Hersey— in point of distance certainly, and probably in point of variety as well. No other doctor served the Cape in his day, and probably none other would have been acceptable. Everybody knew him. Anybody who had seen him, dressed in his personally designed overcoat, could never forget him.

The proceeds of his practice, which were big in spite of modest fees, Doctor Hersey invested in farm lands, among them several large tracts in the Great Marshes. He was a shrewd buyer and an exceedingly able farmer. No land that he bought had ever failed to pay for the fencing, and most of it did much better than that. When he died in 1787, his broad planting lands were under high cultivation.

His will, besides giving £500 to Harvard to support " a professor of Physic and Surgery," left the use of the farm land to the thirteen Congregational Churches of the Cape, upon the death of his wife. He had carefully apportioned to each church according to the amount of practice the parish held for him!

"And it is my will . . . that the deacons of the churches do from time to time let out or rent such real estate for as much as it will fetch." There followed orders for keeping the land in fertility and the equipment in repair, and the doctor went on to specify how the proceeds should be spent. Part of it must buy books, books of sermons on the "Christian temper" and on the rise and progress of religion—"eighteen sixty-thirds on Dr. Doddridge's *Salvation by Faith,* etc.

For one hundred years, these thirteen parishes were to enjoy the benefits of Abner Hersey's labor. Then, the doctor added, he intended to come back and see how things were going, to reassure himself of "the immortality of his fields."

Thirty-nine deacons, three from each parish, came together once each year at Lydia Sturgis's

tavern in Barnstable to "manage the estate." The
tavern was a diverting place. The small beer was
good, the ardent liquors better. And there was card
playing through most of the night in that part of
the building nicknamed "Hagar's Bedroom."
Most of the "managing" the deacons did was on
the expense accounts they handed in after the meeting. At the end of ten years the proceeds from
neglected and deteriorating acres had shrunk, and
the padded expense accounts of the managing deacons had swelled, until the two figures met.
"However pious they [the deacons] may have
been, they certainly were not good farmers. They
reinaugurated the old system of cropping without
manure." So well had the doctor planned and prepared, however, that it took 29 years of the deacons' management to bring the fields and forest
lands to utter waste. When there was no more
money for liquor at the tavern, the deacons petitioned the Legislature to sell the estate, pointing
out that " the management of said real estate in
common is attended with great inconvenience."
In 1816, Abner Hersey's "immortal fields" were
sold at auction. To posterity is left only the brief
note that the money which the churches received
"they have devoted to other purposes than those
for which it was given."
Whether the good doctor came back when the
hundred years had expired, to see how well his
acres were being put to the uses of the house of
God, no one in Barnstable knows. But he had
scheduled his return inspection for the year 1887,
and in that year, on the night of January 9, a
townsman passing the old graveyard in West Barnstable, stopped when he heard a clatter of hoofs

down the King's Highway. A creak of old wheels faded off across the bare brown flats that once were green with hay, and into the stubble-lands where Abner Hersey's forests had stood thick with pine and oak. And faintly across the marshes a voice called, a voice weary with disillusion:

"Thunder of Jehovah, what have they done! Ah, I had as lief be chained to a galley-oar as go through it all again! Giddap, giddap Mehitable! Oh, for a cot in the wilderness!"

The burying ground you pass in these marshlands goes back to Old Colony days, and is noteworthy mainly for the presence of Governor Thomas Hinckley's bones. Thomas's father, Samuel, died about 1640, and left a large estate for that day. Among the more important items were two cows, Prosper and Thrivewell.

Thomas, fiery tempered public servant for fifty years, served as governor from 1680 to 1692, and is cited by local historians as a model, for those times, of liberal politics and religious tolerance. Instead of ordering that the ears of the Quakers be cut off, as was being done in Boston, Thomas merely had the heretics horsewhipped.

Most of the Governor's sixteen children were girls. He gave them names that were in vogue then —Bathshua, Mehetable, Admire, Experience, Thankful, Reliance and the like. When his wife, Mary, died, the gruff old statesman shed a tear and penned some very bad verses. That the poetry achieved publication is standing evidence of his power among men. There was once, in this cemetery, a monument to Mrs. Hinckley, which has long since crumbled to pieces, and upon which was inscribed, "Here Lyeth Ye Body Of Ye Truly Virtuous And Praiseworthy Mrs. Mary Hinchley, Wife to Mr. Thomas Hinckley, Died July Ye 29, 1703, In Ye 73d Year Of Her Age." As may be observed in most of these inscriptions, spelling was the least of the Old Colony's worries. To the other epitaphs in this cemetery I shall not give space; they are there for you to read, they have been there a long time, and probably they will be there for the writers of guidebooks centuries hence to copy off. But one other of the "eternal tenantry" deserves a word—Captain John Percival, an aide of Admiral Nelson in the Battle of Trafalgar and also commander of the U. S. S. *Constitution* in a round-the-world sail in 1844-46. His eccentricities at sea earned for him the nickname of "Mad Jack" Percival.

You will not find any reference to acts of cruelty at sea on stones that mark the graves of ship commanders, naval or merchant. But the tradition itself was a cruel one—made and kept so largely by owners who had these skippers in their hire and who made ruthless demands upon them. In the merchant marine, ideas of ship's discipline were kept at a curious parallel to those of the Navy itself. Shipping was a speculative business, hazards were large, and humane treatment was a luxury which the business could not or would not support. It was a courageous skipper indeed who would cross the set policies of his employers.

How these owners felt about the dangerous business which other men carried on for them is made clear in many a letter of instruction and other old shipping record. The experience of Captain William Sturgis of the ship *Atahualpa* is a case in point.

Captain Sturgis was a 21-year-old Barnstable skipper. On a voyage to the Far East in 1809, his vessel was attacked by a fleet of sixteen "ladrones," manned by Chinese pirates, while she lay at anchor in Macao Roads.

The cruelty of these raiders was well known to American sailors, and before they would allow themselves to be taken captive, Captain Sturgis and his men were prepared to blow up the vessel and themselves, with a barrel of powder. In the meantime he trained two small cannon on the enemy, and fired away. The shots took effect on the crowded junks, and the *Atahualpa* shot her way out of reach of the raiders.

Upon bringing the vessel safely to Boston a few months later, Captain Sturgis made a report to his owners of the encounter. Their reaction was to "reprove him for taking the cannon with him in the first place," and to make him pay the freight on them!

William Sturgis, despite all such handicaps, became one of the most successful of a long list of Barnstable sea captains. He was among the first to plunge into the hazardous Pacific Northwest fur trade, which required the long voyage around the Horn and up the other side of the Continent, to shores still largely unexplored. Able both as navigator and trader, he made a large fortune.

To many another Barnstable man, the sea was not so kind; and to some it was not kind at all. There were twelve townsmen in the crew of the brig *General Arnold,* which sailed from Nantasket

Roads on the day before Christmas, 1778, with a total of 105 men aboard.

On Christmas morning she ran into a blizzard, accompanied by wild northeast gales over Cape Cod Bay, and in the hope of riding it out, she dropped anchor off the Plymouth shore. The gale continued, and next day rose to hurricane force, whipping a heavy snowfall before it. The ship began to drag anchor. The crew worked desperately to keep her off the shoals, where she might pound herself to pieces, but it became a losing struggle. Closer and closer she edged inshore, and in Plymouth Harbor, in plain sight of the beach, she struck.

The crew, unable to go below now, were suffering terribly from the cold. Some of them filled their boots with rum, in the hope that it would keep their feet from freezing. That night—December 26—thirty men were frozen to death, some lying stiff on the deck, some covered by the snow, others washed overboard.

Next morning the gale abated, but the thermometer kept at zero. Those who were still alive were numbed. There was no movement aboard the vessel.

Rescuers were not able to reach the *General Arnold* until the following day—the 28th. By that time the quarterdeck was completely covered by the dead. Only one of the twelve Barnstable men was still alive.

Barnabas Downs was conscious, but he was unable to move. Desperately he tried to attract the attention of the rescue workers as they searched back and forth among the bodies for signs of life. At last—by frantically winking—he succeeded.

When he was taken ashore and treated, the heels and toes of both feet had been frozen, and the flesh fell away, leaving only raw stumps.

The Congregational Church of Barnstable, which can be reached by turning right at the stoplight just beyond the graveyard, is one of the oldest buildings on the Cape, dating from 1717. The church society traces its existence back to the formation of the Congregational Church of Southwalk, London, in 1616, and asserts that it is therefore the oldest such unit in America.

There was considerable persecution of the founders, and the Reverend John Lothrop, Cambridge graduate who was the society's second pastor, spent two years in a London jail. In 1634 he brought thirty followers with him to Boston, and they went to Scituate to settle; but five years later Pastor Lothrop led his flock, now twenty-five families, down the Cape trail to Barnstable.

To its church the old village confided its life-and-death secrets; and these, ghost-secrets now, peer out from between the sedate lines of the clerical record where they were tucked away.

On June 4, 1649, Mrs. Judith Shelley is excommunicated for calling the pastor dirty names. "Wee had long patience towards her, and used all courteous intreatyes and persuations; but the longer wee waited, the worse she was. She is wondrous perremptorye in all her carriages."

Mrs. Shelley has a daughter, Hannah, 12 years.

March 9, 1652—Hannah Shelley, 15, is married to David Linnel, 25.

May 30, 1652—David Linnel and his young wife Hannah, "children of the Barnstable church,"

are summoned and attend a meeting of the church
and there, before the congregation, confess their
fault ("fornication in unlawful accompanying,"
before their marriage). They are both, by the sentence and joint consent of the church, "pronounced
to be cutt off from that relation which they hadd
formerlye to the church by virtue of their parents
covenaunt."

Plymouth, June 3, 1652—Mr. Thomas Dexter
and John Chipman, grand jurors from Barnstable,
make complaint of the "publique fame" in the
Barnstable church. The Court condemns both
David Linnel and Hannah Linnel "to be publicly
whipt at Barnstable where they live."

June 8, 1652—Sentence is executed upon David
and Hannah Linnel.

On your left, half a mile further along the highway, you pass a memorial boulder marking the
birthplace of James Otis, able lawyer for the colonists in pre-Revolutionary days and an eloquent
moving force for rebellion. Of Otis, John Adams
said: "I have been young and now I am old, and
I solemnly say that I have never known a man
whose love of country was more ardent or sincere—never one who suffered so much, never one
whose services for any ten years of his life were
so important and essential to the cause of his country as those of Mr. Otis from 1760 to 1770."

The first of the Crockers to own a tavern or
"ordinary" on the Cape was John Crocker, who
came over with his brother William in 1634, and
got his license in Barnstable in 1649. That tavern
is gone, but later Crockers, descendants of Wil-

liam, kept other "Crocker Taverns" in Barnstable, and one of these public houses still stands.

Now known as the "Coach House," it was for many years the property of Cornelius Crocker, more than two centuries ago. Cornelius, born club-footed, took up the trade of a tailor, but he could drive a bargain as sharp as his needle, and he rose rapidly to become one of the richest men of the parish. He owned two farms, two houses, a wharf, a fish-house, a grist mill and the tavern. His daughter, Lydia Sturgis, was a widow for 62 years, during which she ran the public house as "Aunt Lydia's Tavern." Ezekiel, another Barnstable Crocker, married a girl named Temperance and then opened a saloon.

It was in Aunt Lydia's Tavern that the Whigs gathered during those exciting days just before the Declaration of Independence. And it was here that a band of the young blades of that party held a long conference one night to decide what should be done about that incorrigible Tory, the Widow Nabby Freeman.

The Widow Nabby owned a little grocery store next the courthouse, and when the "Vigilance Committee" had asked her to surrender her stock of tea, they received a piece of her mind instead. She was uncompromising, and because she had a fine knack for speechifying and exercised it on the least excuse, the Whigs had long had it in mind to "put a bridle on her tongue."

On the Town Green, which is now marked by a small sodded triangle at the left where Rendezvous Lane meets the highway, these men had planted their shiny, gold-tipped "Liberty Pole." The

Widow Nabby would emerge from her little store, pass within earshot as they stood beside it, and addressing no one in particular but making herself heard all too clearly, she would remark that "somebody ought to heave up thet dead tree." Then she would disappear from view in Otis Loring's Tavern, across the road, where the Tories made their headquarters.

One night Aunt Nabby's wish was mysteriously fulfilled. The patriots found their Liberty Pole lying on the Green—"hove up" just as the widow had said it ought to be. They propped it up, then marched to Aunt Nabby's home.

"She had retired for the night," writes Amos Otis. "They obtained an entrance, took her from her bed to the Green, besmeared her with tar and covered her with feathers. A rail was procured from a fence in the vicinity, across which she was set astride, and either end thereof was placed on the shoulder of a stout youth. She was held in her position by a man who walked at her side, holding her by the hand. When they were tired of the sport, and after they had extracted from her a promise that she would no more meddle in politics, they released her."

The "new house" which the Reverend Lothrop, the town's first settled pastor, built for himself in 1644 still stands, as part of the Sturgis Library. When he lived in it, it was 21 feet across the front and 29 feet deep. The chimney was on the west side, with an oven projecting outside the wall.

The minister's first home, erected when he brought his flock from Scituate in 1639, was taken down in 1824. The frame was of great timbers, covered with planks an inch and a quarter thick. But the walls were not plastered, and the roof was only thatch. The pastor complained that the draughts had brought on "a stitch in his side," and the house which is now part of the library was therefore provided. When the "ancient house" was razed, the memorial brick was found, on which was inscribed the date, 1639. A hotel was going up at the time, and the brick, then nearly two centuries old, was unceremoniously carted off, to be plastered, inscription and all, into the hotel chimney.

The wills, deeds and other documents which have "made it legal" when Cape property changed hands, were kept in the County Court House in the village of Barnstable. A fire in 1827 destroyed much of this historically valuable material. Before the carelessness and indifference of "public servants" towards such matters as the safeguarding of ancient records, the student of history stands aghast. Only last year the clerk of one of the old down-Cape towns admitted to me that he had several volumes of town records in his home—a frame building which the winds from the Bay would fan into flames in a twinkling if ever it caught fire. He explained that it made no difference whether he returned the records at once or kept them indefinitely; the town hall was a frame building too. The records were original material, going back years before 1700. There have been half a dozen such fires in which old Cape records were lost forever.

Fortunately, copies had been made of some of the records lost in the Barnstable fire.

The will of John Goodspeed, who died in 1721,

mentions separately a looking-glass among his bequests. He also leaves a set of carpenter's tools, a "whaleboat and tacklin' " and four hives of bees. John Davis, in a will dated May 10, 1701, bequeaths "to my daughter Mercy for her tender care and labor past done for me and her mother, £20 in money and £5 a year so long as she continues to attend me and her mother, or the longest liver—her diet, washing and lodging, in the family with her brother Benjamin, 1 cow and heifer, 2 sheep, 2 swine, and at her mother's decease, ½ the household stuff and bedding forever, and the southward end of the house so long as she shall live a single life."

When John Bacon, Esq., died in 1731, he left his negro slave Dinah to be sold by his executors "and all she is sold for shall be improved by my executors in buying of Bibles, and they shall give them equally alike unto each of my grandchildren."

Upon proving the will of Captain Matthew Fuller, wealthy citizen of Barnstable, in 1678, an item inventoried as "pearls, precious stones, and Diamonds, at a guess £200," was missing. Robert Marshall, Captain Fuller's Scotch servant, was suspected, and the charge so affected the faithful, dog-like Scotsman "that he took no food and finally died of starvation." To this day his grave, on the northeastern declivity of Scorton Hill, is pointed out, and some timorous people dare not pass it after nightfall. Robert Marshall is looking, looking for the jewels.

In the making and observance of Cape Cod wills, precision has ever been an outstanding virtue. In Truro a house was once cut in half to carry out the wishes of the deceased. The house of Captain Josiah Hopkins is still standing in Tonset, a part of Orleans. The Captain, who died in 1854, left his widow two-thirds of the chimney, among other bequests. To a son he left certain other parts of the house, so divided that if the son wished to go from the front to the rear of the section he owned without trespassing, he had to step outside and walk around to a rear door.

The "crime news" of the Old Colony is set down in the Plymouth court records, and there one finds many an item from Cape Cod. For example:

> *November 21, 1681—Indian James, thou art here indited by the name of James, for that thou, haveing not the fear of God before thyne eyes, in the town of Barnstable didst felloniously, willfully, and of mallice aforethought, with intent to murder, kick Samuel Crocker on the bottom of his belly, whereof the said Samuel Crocker three weeks after died; which thou hast don contrary to the law of God, of England, and this collonie, and contrary to the peace of our sou.'r Lord the Kinge, his Crowne and dignity.*

But for all this iniquity, the jury finds Indian James "nott guilty of willfull murder."

There have been four courthouses of Barnstable County since the first was built in 1685, and at least as many jails. Whenever it begins to look as if the jail is in danger of collapsing about the ears of the prisoners, the county puts up a new one. Henry Ford slipped badly when he failed to acquire for his museum-village the fine antique jail that preceded the present structure in Barnstable. One of its difficulties half a century ago was bathing the prisoners. The gaoler left a diary which has been preserved. He tells how a bathtub eventually was built for the jail, and how it was discovered that the completed tub wouldn't fit through the doors. They couldn't get the tub in, and they couldn't let the prisoners out.

The courthouse boasts another aged exhibit, a bronze bell which is sometimes declared to be the oldest in America. I am not at all sure of this, in view of the fact that some of the Californian and Mexican missions are still standing, and I do not care at all. As the bell itself says, in a Latin inscription around the bottom, "If God Be For Us, Who Can Be Against Us?"

The bell is now mounted and on view in a corner of the law library. Its story goes back more than two hundred years, to March 12, 1697, when a foreign vessel was wrecked off the coast of Sandwich, and all hands, including Captain Peter Adolph, were lost. Men of Sandwich found the bodies as, one by one, they were washed up on the beach. They were taken to the First Parish Church, and next day, with fitting ceremony, laid away in the burial ground. Letters in Captain Adolph's pocket identified him, and the pastor wrote to Frau Adolph, informing her of the tragedy.

The widow, grateful for the funeral given her husband, bought the bell from a German craftsman and presented it to the Sandwich parish.

For seven years it called the faithful to worship, and then, in 1703—probably to deprive the faithful of any excuse based on failure to hear the little bell—a town meeting voted "to authorize Benjamin to sell it and purchase another for the church." Benjamin sold it to the Barnstable Court. A Boston connoisseur has estimated that the bell was cast about 1675. The town of Sandwich, I am told, now wants its bell back. And the town of Barnstable has no intention of returning it. Sandwich's only reminder of the incident is a stone beside the mill pond with the inscription:

> *Here lyeth ye body of Capt. Peter Adolph of New Yorke who died by shipwrack in this bay and was washed on shoar 3 miles below this towne.*

The two cannons at the courthouse entrance were sent here during the War of 1812, to protect the salt works from the British. On the "Common Fields" the Crocker brothers owned the most elaborate salt works on the Cape, and they prayed the Government to send the guns. No shots were fired, but the guns had their big moments in years following, when it became the custom for the boys of the neighboring villages to see who could carry them off on each Fourth of July. The feat was said to have been accomplished several times.

Across the street from the courthouse is the Barnstable Inn, which used to be called the Eldredge Hotel, and in the chimney of which—I presume—still is lodged the 1639 memorial brick taken from Reverend John Lothrop's "ancient house." Mention the Eldredge Hotel to almost any old-timer on the Cape and he will start telling you about the County Fair, and declaring that those were the days. And indeed, for Cape folks, they were. They were the days when the Agricultural Society once a year held festivities worth retelling to the grandchildren, including everything from ploughing contests to ladies' exhibition riding.

The Society was organized in 1843, and the County Fair continued as an institution on the Cape until 1931. There were years when the attendance rose above 15,000, and you could ride on the Old Colony Railroad at half-fare rate, with all cows, chickens, pigs, corn, turnips and other exhibits going free. The Governor and other high-ups from Boston would be there, and all the down-Cape towns were "represented by their most beautiful ladies, who, with their escorts, danced for six hours to music by Gilmore's Quadrille Band."

They danced the Polka, the Waltz, the Schottische, the Caprice. And they did the old-time square dances too, the Quadrille, the College Lancers, the Saratoga, the Virginia Reel and the Soldier's Joy. What the people down east were calling "the Portland Fancy" was danced here as "the Sicilian Circle." Many of these dances required a prompter, and prompting was a very specialized business. One of the few professional prompters still living told me, a few years ago, that he had spent most of a lifetime developing "his technique." Naturally he deplored the coming of the tango, followed by the lame duck, Irene Castle's half and half, and the fox trot—"newfangled shuffles that don't call for a single jot of real able gittin'-about." I told him I had heard of a move afoot to revive the old square dances in this country. He said they'd never do it, because the dances can't be done without good prompting, and that "takes years."

In 1860 the County Fair went in for horse-trotting, and a race track was built. Half of the best families of Barnstable entered their horses, while the other half went to church overtime and prayed for their souls.

The farm exhibits, like everything else at the fair, were in all respects the ultimate superlative. The only squash on earth that ever grew bigger than the 55-pound marrow squash that Bill Gray had brought from his Yarmouth acres was the one that Bill Gray had left at home, to keep for himself. That one was so big the oxcart started to give way when he let it down with a tackle. Then Clark Hoxie of Sandwich showed up with a squash that weighed 62 pounds, but explained that the sandy base of his farm had proved too weak to support the weight of his best specimen, which had kept sinking as it grew, until it had gone down, down, "clear to China, by Godfrey!"

There will never be another County Fair in Barnstable, at least none under the auspices of the Society, which wound up its business in 1936, but while a turnip yet grows in Eastham, or a strawberry in Falmouth, or a haddock on Georges Banks, there will always be a tall tale to grow with it. This sandy soil, when it ceases to nourish anything else, will produce yarns while it remains above tidemark. Only the other day the newspapers carried the story of a young man of Chatham, who has discovered a new and easy way to catch fish. He merely dips his hook in molasses—"long-tail sugar," Cape folks call it—and casts it high in the air. The molasses attracts bees. Then, when the hook drops into the water, the bees are stuck and go in with it, and that makes them mad. The fish sees the hook with what look like real flies attached, and when he goes for it, the wet, angry bees sting him to death.

The name of Cummaquid now applies only to the east part of Barnstable. As you pass the Cummaquid postoffice, you traverse what once were the pestilent swamplands where young Sachem Iyannough and his braves were driven to hiding and to death, probably of the smallpox. Just behind the postoffice is the Sachem's grave. If you have come through Plymouth, this may confuse you, for in the museum in that town, you may have seen the bones of—whom but the Sachem Iyannough, so labeled! Upon the stone erected here in Cummaquid is the inscription: "On This Spot Was Buried The Sachem Iyanough, The Friend And Entertainer Of The Pilgrims, July, 1621."

The Cape Cod Historical Society, which put up the stone, might have explained that "On This Spot *Was* Buried The Sachem," etc. For David Davis, one of the innumerable descendants of the early Cape settler, Dolar Davis, turned up a copper kettle with his plow in 1860 at this spot, and then turned up the Sachem with a spade. Thereafter the museum at Plymouth acquired his find, and the Sachem whom the museum has on display is fairly well established as the genuine article—all of which does not greatly matter except to sound a cautionary note concerning the ways of historical societies when local pride gets the upper hand over full-bodied history. The innocent traveler will often find that in the effort to catch his interest, no holds are barred.

Curiously incidental to the discovery of the bones of this Sachem by Farmer Davis is the fact that some two centuries before, in 1666, one of his own ancestors, Nicholas Davis, son of Dolar, had purchased a large tract of Barnstable lands from a "Sachem Yanno." This was a later Sachem of the same name, which is spelled and pronounced a dozen ways. From the name comes "Hyannis," the village on the South Shore, and "Wianno," another South Sea community.

In East Barnstable, on the old Indian trail across-Cape, there is a pond, and in the woods beside it once stood a lonely house where the Devil was said to have had a standing welcome. For there lived Lizzy Tower Hill, the Witch of Half-Way Pond.

Poor Lizzy had been a member of the church, in good standing, before the stories of witchwork got abroad; but once the whispers started, they followed her to her death in 1790.

There was unholy dancing o' nights at Half-Way Pond, so the rumors said, and strange lights shone in the forest. A Mister Wood of West Barnstable went further. He brought charges against Lizzy, declaring that she "put upon him a bridle and saddle and rode him many times to Plum Pudding Pond in Plymouth, where witches held nightly orgies." He had no supporting evidence, and the case was dropped. But Mister Wood went on talking about Lizzy.

Then there was Dr. Richard Bourne, 71-year-old physician of Barnstable, who passed that way on Christmas Night, 1810.

The doctor considered himself indispensable at any party, chiefly because of his singing. He sang only one song—"Old King Cole"—but with each drink it was so vastly improved over the last version that no one recognized it as the same piece.

It was midnight, and the doctor was riding back

on the Indian Trail from a Christmas party in Hyannis. And this night, as he jogged through the woods, he made them ring with "Old King Cole" —less recognizable than it had ever been before.

Snow lay on the ground, hard-crusted and bejewelled by the moonbeams. A northwest wind moaned in the trees and whipped the doctor's shawl out behind him. Suddenly he drew rein, then walked the mare a little way into the woods.

Lizzy Tower Hill had been dead a score of years. Yet there, according to the doctor's story, he had caught sight of a rotten stump which shone with a warm red light. He imagined it was a fire, and as his feet were very cold, he dismounted, pulled off his boots and placed his feet on the stump.

When sufficiently warm, his story continues, he remounted; but "unfortunately omitted to put on his boots."

All night the doctor wandered about in the woods at Half-Way Pond, failing to find his way out until long after sun-up. He reached the road at last, and he had not gone far when he met several townsmen of his acquaintance. Bowing a greeting to them, the doctor inquired:

"Gentlemen, can you tell me whether I am in this town or the next?"

The town of Barnstable, like a mackerel seiner with a full trip of fish, carries the biggest part of her story "below water line." From the wealth that is stowed in her hold I have pitched up only a few items here. But better this than to dismiss the centuries in the manner of old Captain Peleg Hawes on a voyage to China.

"Now then, Arathusy," Captain Peleg told his wife, "it's twenty minutes to sailing-hour. Better start your crying and get it over with, so's I won't be holding up the vessel."

As he pursed his lips and began tidying up his ditty-box, an obedient sob escaped his wife.

"Oh, Peleg, 'twouldn't be so hard, if you'd only write me a letter while you're away on these etarnal long v'yages! Promise me, Peleg, you'll write this time—just one letter!"

The Captain groaned and promised. And eighteen months later, Arathusy, all a-tremble, tore open an envelope and read:

*Hong Kong, China,*
*May 21, 1854.*

*Dear Arathusy:*
*I am here and you are there.*

*P. Hawes.*

# CHAPTER IV

## YARMOUTH

*On U. S. 6, between Barnstable and Dennis. Three and one-half miles between Yarmouth town lines.*

A "good sermonizer" was the Reverend Timothy Alden, of Old Yarmouth, with a nice eye for timeliness in the choice of his texts. For fifty years his little flock had faithfully supplied firewood for the parsonage, in accordance with his salary agreement, and for fifty years the Reverend Alden sermonized in return, ever finding the word of God that best befitted the occasion. But one cold winter in the 1790's, the day set for delivery of his firewood passed, and it appeared that this little item had been let to lapse. The following Sabbath, the pastor announced his text from Proverbs XXVI, 20:

"Where no wood is, there the fire goeth out."

Whether to insure a long line of warm-hearted ministers, or merely for love of a leaf-arched road, a citizen of Yarmouth fifty years later planted elm saplings along the highway, which have grown into the tall green guardians of the town, locking their arms overhead today. The man who planted them was Amos Otis, local historian and genealogist. In addition to these trees, he performed herculean labors to reconstruct the family trees of Cape Codders, digging back through generation after generation in the town of Barnstable, in his struggles with the eternal question of who begat whom. In the case of one family, the Crockers, he gave up in despair, after many pages of Nathaniels and Jobs and Jeremiahs, "not because my subject is exhausted, but because I am."

I have heard recently that these grand old elms are dying fast, and a few that were cut down to make room for highway improvements were found to be rotten inside. Unless another foresighted townsman of Yarmouth arises to save the peculiar beauty of this village, all that will remain of Amos Otis's forestry will be his family trees, those laborious lists of Shubaels, Thankfuls and Ezekiels, which keep on thriving without noticeable need of outside help.

In these volumes of genealogy, Otis has recorded many bits of information and folklore that have placed later writers deeply in his debt, certainly myself included. But concerning his everlasting Cape Cod family trees, I would much prefer to see *them* get the Dutch elm, or whatever it is, and the green boughs that rustle over the King's Road keep alive.

None of the Cape towns can well support a claim to a saltier history than its neighbors. Brewster, which was a sort of snug harbor for deepwater skippers who had traded their way to affluence, cites a record of ninety-nine sea captains who have owned homes, at one time or another, within its bounds. Yarmouth, on the other hand, can point to one time when fifty such skippers were living in homes that lined the highway between its town limits, all contemporaries. And so, as you drive through, you are geographically as close to the old days of sail as you can be anywhere on earth.

In recreating these old seafaring towns for an inland public of today, no honest reporter bears down too heavily on the "romance" of going to sea; which is to say—at the risk of getting an axe in my neck—that the majority of the literature on seafaring of old just hasn't been honest. Men went to sea for two rewards—first, bread and butter; and second, enough laid aside for future bread and butter to enable them to quit going to sea. Certainly the calling was hazardous and exciting, and Cape Cod boys went down to the sea with their eyes shining. There were even a few hardy souls who actually felt enough "lure" and "fascination" to keep at it after their fortunes were made, and there was no further necessity; but to picture the old Cape Cod sea captain as a man drawn offshore by an adolescent craving for excitement or by a song-writer's nostalgia is simply bilge. As one Yarmouth skipper put it, "any man who would go to sea for pleasure would go to hell for pastime."

In his book, *Shipmasters of Cape Cod,* Henry C. Kittredge gives a realistic and fairly unbiased account of the doings of these men of Yarmouth and the other towns. He tells of the coasting schooners (called by the foreign traders the "appletree fleet" because they were never out of sight of the orchards alongshore) which carried everything from sheep's wool from Nantucket to mahogany logs from Santo Domingo; of Ebenezer Sears, first American skipper to take a merchant vessel around the Cape of Good Hope; of Stephen Sears, too, who was seized by the Spanish in the Mediterranean while trying to sell a cargo of salt fish; of Elisha Howes, who, on making Boston with a load

of figs from Smyrna, "improved his shore leave"
by getting engaged to Hannah Crowell of Yarmouth; of the three celebrated Eldredge brothers,
Captains John, Oliver and Asa, who skippered
Liverpool packets and made great names and good
fortunes; and of the races between such clipper
drivers as Captain Frederick Howes of Yarmouth,
in the *Climax,* and Captain Moses Howes, of Dennis, in the *Competitor,* who took exactly 115 days
each, Boston to San Francisco, around the Horn,
while the whole shipping world waited, with
money placed on the one or the other. Before the
race was over, it was said that the disappointed
Boston waterfront was exclaiming, "A plague on
both of your Howeses!"

There is no question but that these men loved
a good ship, a fast ship. Among the thousand Cape
Cod yarns that are variations on this theme is the
one about Captain Eleazer, skipper of one of the
trimmest schooners in the "Injies trade." His vessel, the *Bulldog,* was "built to split a drop of water
into a halfmoon while she heeled," and he had let
the town know he was proud of her. He married
a girl named Abigail Bangs, and townsfolk began
asking him if he planned to change the name of
the vessel to the *Abigail S* as a token of affection
for his bride. His reply was, "No, I don't see fitten
for to change the vessel's name. But if Abigail
keeps on steady being a good girl like she is, I've
been thinking I might have her rechristened Bulldog."

So go the yarns. There was actually precious
little of the hearts-and-flowers kind of sentiment
in the love of these men for their ships. It was an

affection based upon speed and seaworthiness, and upon nothing else. If a ship had these qualities, she was beautiful, she was loved. And they meant, in the order of their importance: first, money, for upon speed were based rates and other rewards, as well as the volume of business a ship-owner could attract to his vessels; second, safety of cargo, both from deterioration through a slow voyage and loss through a "broken" one; and third—and last— safety of life and limb.

To go back to the Yarmouth of Old Colony days is difficult, because in 1674 the town clerk, like my friend in the down-Cape town, kept the records in his home. And his home burned. The historians do know that Anthony Thacher, John Crow (Crowell) and Thomas Howes obtained grants and settled here in 1639.

The place called by the Indians Mattakeese, or Mattachee, or Mattakesset, extended across the boundary from Barnstable into Yarmouth. Where Sachem Yanno's domain ended, eastward through Yarmouth and Dennis lay the realm of Massamtampaine. You may pick out any way that suits your fancy to spell these names. As Eva March Tappan wrote:

> *We drove the Indians out of the land*
> *But a dire revenge the Red Men planned;*
> *For they fastened a name to every nook*
> *And every boy with a spelling book*
> *Will live to toil till his hair turns gray*
> *Before he can spell them the proper way.*

The apologists for the land-lust of our pioneer settlers never fail to make the point that all land taken from the Indians here was duly paid for.

A Yarmouth document dated May, 1658, is a good example of this policy of paying off the Indians, and especially of the considerations that were given in payment. For relinquishing his tribal claim to certain large "tracts of land to the town of Yarmouth forever, and defend and save harmless from time to time the said townsmen of Yarmouth," Sachem Yanno was to have the handsome compensation of six coats, six pairs of small breeches, ten hoes, ten hatchets and two brass kettles. Let us hope that at least the small breeches were not too small!

I cannot say how smooth your road would be through Yarmouth if it were not a U. S. highway, for at the August term of court, 1643, the town was "given until the next court to mend their highways or be fined."

It was in that same term that Mr. Anthony Thacher was licensed to "draw wine" in Yarmouth. The house of his son, Colonel John, built in 1680, you will find on the highway, at left just beyond the red-front Economy store.

Anthony Thacher sailed from Ipswich in 1635 in a bark bound for Marblehead. A fierce storm, heightened by a twenty-foot tide, drove the vessel onto the rocky shoals of Cape Ann and ground her to pieces. Thacher and his wife were the only ones to survive, of a ship's company of twenty-three, which had included their own four children.

"Now look with me upon distress," he writes, "and consider of my misery, who beheld the ship broken, the water in her, and violently overwhelming us, my goods and provisions swimming in the seas, my friends almost drowned, and mine own poor children so untimely (if I may so term it without offense) before mine eyes drowned, and ready to be swallowed and dashed to pieces against the rocks by the merciless waves, and myself ready to accompany them!"

The tall twin lights on the Cape Ann rocks near the spot where the vessel piled up are named the Thacher Island Lights.

Anthony Thatcher, like Amos Otis, had an active fondness for trees. He and Thomas Howes planted pear trees whenever they got the chance, and although Anthony's grave is unmarked, the tradition is that he was buried where his beloved blossoms of the pear could shower upon his resting place every spring.

John Thacher was born in Marblehead, where Anthony and his wife stayed four years. When John was one year old, they came to Yarmouth. Among the things Anthony brought with him was a scarlet coverlet, which has come down from one generation of Thachers to the next, and is still in their hands.

John Thacher grew up to be an army officer, a colonel, very handsome, very dashing, and a terror to the hostile Indians. Colonel John divided his time between the virgin forests abroad and the virgins at home. But in 1664 he married Rebecca Winslow, and though he was always a bit playful, to Rebecca he was wholeheartedly devoted. If he teased her now and then, Rebecca knew it was innocent; and certainly, when it came to choosing a husband, she might have done worse than that.

One day, not long after their marriage, John and Rebecca called on the John Gorhams at their home in Barnstable. The Gorhams had a baby daughter, Lydia, and the Colonel was fascinated by the child. Suddenly he picked her up and held her in his arms.

"Allow me," he said to Rebecca, "to introduce to you my second wife."

Nineteen years later, in 1683, Rebecca Thacher died. The Colonel spent several weeks writing sad verses about her. But one day he went calling in Barnstable, and at the Gorham house he saw Lydia again. She was twenty now, and very lovely. The poetry of Colonel John changed its cadences. And on New Year's Day, 1684, Colonel John Thacher married Lydia Gorham.

The Thachers have also preserved a cradle made of rifted oak, with a little arched hood over one end—one of the most heart-warming relics of Old Colony days that I have ever seen. As Colonel John had 21 children and they in turn were each blessedly eventful, the little cradle was "in great request" at all times. Colonel John was the first in Yarmouth to enjoy such satisfaction as may come of having a gravestone with an inscription on it. When he died in 1713, the family imported a stone for him from England.

One of the Thachers became a judge and later a Congressman. In an argument on the floor with a fiery southerner, Judge Thacher's dry Yankee wit became so maddening that the southern gentleman wildly challenged him to a pistol duel.

"I cannot deny the gentleman from Kentucky

his right to challenge me to a duel," the Judge said gravely. "But as I could not hit him anyway, there is no use in my being on hand. I would suggest that he draw my outline on a wall with a piece of chalk. I'll be glad to pose for it. Then, if the gentleman from Kentucky scores a hit with his pistol, I will concede that he has won the duel."

A fine, intimate and endearing glimpse into the lives of these men of Old Yarmouth—the best that I have read—is offered in the sketch by Elizabeth Reynard in her book, *The Narrow Land,* under the head, "Andrew Hallett." Miss Reynard bases her reconstruction mainly upon material in the genealogical notes of Amos Otis, but she touches it with the magic of immediacy, and as you go through the town of Yarmouth today, you may look upon its three-hundred-year-old scene as ground not wholly unfamiliar, your eyes will not have been wholly alienated by the passing of the centuries.

When General Washington was seeking an expression of confidence from the Massachusetts government, this spunky little town voted, a fortnight before the signing of the Declaration of Independence, that "the inhabitants of the town of Yarmouth do declare a state of independence of the King of Great Britain." They made it subject to the action of Congress, but they voted for it to a man.

Thus, while many towns in the state were hesitant, and some, like Sandwich (by a vote of 42 to 33) actually opposed any move towards independence, Yarmouth set down her own declaration. The women folks stayed up all night in an ancient house that stood on the corner of Hallett and Wharf Streets, and while their men made ready to leave for Dorchester at dawn, melted their household treasures into bullets. One "liberty pole" was not enough for Yarmouth, and so there were two, one in front of the West Parish meeting-house and the other on the Hyannis road.

But in the War of 1812, which paralyzed her maritime activities, Yarmouth was just as decisive on the other side of the fence. Town meeting, the nineteenth of September, 1814, "voted unanimously that as this town have ever expressed their decided disapprobation of the present ruinous and unhappy war, and have hitherto refrained from engaging in same; we are still determined not to engage in, encourage or support it any further than we are compelled to do, under the laws of the country of which we are citizens."

In 1817 Yarmouth went dry—in its own peculiar way. It voted to allow one taverner, "for the accommodation of travelers," but the taverner had to give bond of $100 not to sell to inhabitants!

The Universalist Church, the little white clapboarded building with the tower clock, observed its 100th anniversary in 1936. Except for a modern parish house, the church building has never been altered or remodeled.

Another Yarmouth institution celebrated its 100th birthday in 1936—for on December 15, 1836, the first edition of the Yarmouth *Register* was jerked out of the press, and through good years and bad, the little newspaper has carried on without a break since. From its office, on a side road leading off the right of the highway in Yarmouth-port, have come local histories and a long shelf of genealogical pamphlets for the benefit of those Cape Codders who can readily trace their lineage to the *Mayflower* and beyond, and sometimes for those who cannot do it so readily, but manage it somehow.

The *Register* has a background rich in historical color, and has itself played exciting parts in times of stress. In the turbulent administrations of Jackson and Van Buren, its editor made the tempests to rage and the air to crackle in his bitter personal battles with the staff of the Barnstable *Patriot,* publishing since 1830 and still going strong. The parallels were deadly, sarcasm magnificent, inferences poisonous. And the customers bought both papers and were doubly thrilled. The only place where the *Register* fell down was in its poetry, but this appears to be the case in most Cape publications. "There are many unpublished manuscripts in the possession of old Cape Cod families," the Cape Cod Magazine said in 1921, "showing poetical talent on the part of their ancestors." I think this must be true, for the published manuscripts have been so bad for the most part, that I cannot believe there is not some variety, somewhere. For its size, the Cape has produced more bad poetry, I am convinced, than any other section of the United States. The inhabitants have ever been a daring lot.

In Yarmouth the unsuspecting visitor runs into the first of the Cape's tall tales of the Vikings— stories which every good New England tourist should know, because he will run into them so many times in the course of his travels.

There is some interesting circumstantial evidence in Provincetown that the Norse voyagers of the eleventh century *may* have touched there. For the rest of the theorizing on the visits of the Norsemen to this country, there is no tangible proof of the locations. Those named as such are entirely conjecture, some of them pretty farfetched. They have been based on descriptions given in three Copenhagen manuscripts which students of the Norse sagas designate as the "Flatey Book," "Hauk's Book" and "A. M. 557." The manuscripts themselves conflict, the interpretations conflict and the present-day local civic organizations of the various claimant towns conflict.

It is said for Yarmouth that young Thorwald, after repairing the keel of his vessel in Provincetown and calling that place "Keelness," sailed across the Bay to this town and came ashore, was shot with an arrow, and as he lay dying, called the spot "Crossness." Upon the date, 1007, and the narrative details, there is some agreement. The young Viking, mortally wounded, is said to have told his men, "Bury me here; place a cross at my head, another at my feet, call it 'Crossness' forevermore."

But at least half a dozen places on the Atlantic Coast contend that Thorwald said "Bury me here." The bewildered tourist, hearing these statements, which are blithely offered as fact, gets an impression similar to that in Florida, where one finds in a single town three "Fountains of Youth," all discovered by Ponce de Leon; or in England, where the "skull of Yorick" was on display in one place and a smaller skull might be viewed for an extra admission fee—that of "Yorick as a child."

At any rate, if you care to see one of the spots where Thorwald was killed by the Indians and buried according to his instructions, you may take Center Street to the town landing, a neighborhood known as Bass Hole and called by the Indians "Hockanom." A small pine-covered hill beside the tidemarshes is the spot that has been chosen for this historic event. There are no crosses now, but one might throw out as a suggestion to Yarmouth that, inasmuch as Thorwald specified "forever-more" as the time limit, it would be in accordance with his wishes to put up a couple, one where his blond head might have been laid, another at his theoretical feet.

Here at Hockanom the Bray family operated a shipyard in 1750, one of the earliest ventures into shipbuilding on Cape Cod. They built fishing schooners of from 50 to 150 tons. No trace of this industry survives.

One evening in May, 1871, the *Register* came out with a piece of news that electrified the town of Yarmouth as few issues, before or since, ever have. "No Boston packet this year!" The packets —elegant craft of which Yarmouth had two, the *Commodore Hull* and the *Eagle Flight*—made the Boston run regularly, venturing out in any-thing less than a full gale; but with the railroad reaching Yarmouthport in 1854, the sailing be-came, financially, rougher and rougher. They could hold their own against the *Emerald,* the Barnstable packet which raced them regularly across the Bay, but the "cars" did them in. All that

remains as a reminder of these elaborate craft and
their mighty contests of speed is another piece of
poetry:

> *The Commodore Hull she sails so dull*
> *She makes her crew look sour;*
> *The Eagle Flight is out of sight*
> *Less than a half an hour.*
> *But the bold old Emerald takes delight*
> *To beat the Commodore and the Flight.*

A few years after the railroad came into Yarmouth, it attracted to this town the Cape "camp
meeting," an annual gathering of the Methodists
which has no counterpart in our own times, not
even in the evangelical hangovers that still break
out in the middle west.

The first Cape Cod camp meeting was held in
Truro. There, a scrappy congregation who had
had to nail their church together with one hand
while they held off their enemies with the other,
decided to set off the first week in August, 1819,
for a combination of activities which amounted to
roughing it with God. They slept in beds made on
the earth, and cooked their meals there in the clearing of the woods. The rest of it was prayer and
sermons.

The scene of the annual meeting, which attracted Methodists from other Cape towns, shifted
to Eastham, then to Orleans, and in 1863 to Yarmouth. A grove was purchased, a mile and a quarter from the railroad station, on the Hyannis road.
There the faithful gathered, to worship God and to
patronize the concessions that sprang up just outside the limits of the grove. At first they pitched
tents, and there was really something in it of a
return to nature—properly restricted, of course,

within the bristling bounds of Methodist morality. One who attended in the "tented grove" days described it thus:

"At night a curtain was stretched across the middle of the tent. The women slept on one side of the curtain and the men on the other. At 9:30 everything was quiet. There wasn't any cutting up didoes in them tents, I tell you. The bell at the stand rang at 9:30 and after that the camp policeman went on duty. Night lights were kept burning till well along in suncoming, too. If the watchman heard any noise—just any noise at all, you understand—or if a tent went dark, he'd come and pound on the outside." There the description ends, so that we shall never know just what the watchman did if there was no answer to his pounding, though I have heard elsewhere that the grove had a lockup for those who tried "cutting up didoes."

"Old Yarmouth" included what is now the town of Dennis, your next en route eastward, which was set off and incorporated in 1793. When Ichabod Paddock lived there, it was the East Parish of Yarmouth, and so to Yarmouth is given the credit for sending one of its native sons to Nantucket, a bit of New England history which to this day gives Yarmouth a chuckle and is somewhat embarrassing to the island. For, in 1690, Nantucket, which now prides itself upon being one of the world's greatest ex-whaling centers, sent for Ichabod Paddock "to instruct the people in the art of killing whales."

Of Captain Paddock's fabulous proficiency in his "art," the whalers of both the island and the Cape have heard accounts. Expurgating as I go,

I can give one version of a high point in the old whalemaster's career.

After years of slaughtering the great cows and bulls alike, Ichabod had at last met his match in the form of a giant battle-scarred "crook-jawed sparm bull," a monster who would make two hundred barrels of oil if he'd make a thimble. Time and again Captain Paddock had let fly at old Crook-Jaw from the small-boat, but never once had he made fast. Come at him anywhere, stem, stern or amidships, and your iron would either glance off like a dull axe on green pine, or shatter into a cloud of horse-nails.

A few years of the chase after Crook-Jaw, and the captain wearied of this business of wasted heaves and lost irons. He jammed his two good jaws together and vowed through his teeth he'd find out what kind of black conjury was upon the critter if it was the last thing he did at sea.

One day shortly afterwards he raised Crook-Jaw lolling in the choppy waters of Handkerchief Shoal, sound asleep and snoring like a sated sinner on Sabbath-day leave. Heaving to about a mile to leeward, Ichabod pulled off his long-leggers and plunged overboard. Straight up to the whale he swam, and then he waited. Half an hour he waited, treading water, and at last he got what he was waiting for. Crook-Jaw opened his great mouth and yawned. Wider, wider, like a cavern a-stretch in the quaking of the earth, went the whale's mouth, until the huge jaws stood apart so that a cart upon wheels might have gone into it. Then, arching like a porpoise, in dove Ichabod.

It was parlous close for air inside the whale, but once down below, the captain thought he saw a light, split-aglimmering, and started aft towards it. Sure enough, on squeezing through, he came into a snug lamp-lit cabin where, on opposite sides of the table, two people were sitting at cards. One was a betaking young wench with hair the color of Eastham corn, plum-blossom skin, and a hitherly glance in the five-fathom green of her eyes. The other was the Divil.

As Ichabod entered, the Divil slammed his cards on the table, and sparks singed their edges and sent little wisps of blue smoke curling upward.

"Divil take me!" he swore absent-mindedly. "Again I lose the hand!" And getting to his feet, he kicked over his chair and vanished in a huff.

"I'm very sorry, ma'am," Ichabod said. "I didn't come purposing to break up the game."

The girl laughed, and her voice was the ripple-wash of harbor waters on the bows of a shallop.

"The game was over," she told him.

"Your friend was mortal put out," Ichabod remarked. "Could a body inquire what the stakes might be?"

"Captain Paddock, *you* were the stakes!" And she stopped laughing and raised the brows above her green, green eyes, and added softly, "You might oblige me, sir, by bearing witness that I won."

And so it happened that Ichabod was quite given up for lost by his crew aboard the vessel; but at the coming of dawn they saw the waters of Handkerchief Shoal set a-dance by the arms of a returning figure, and Ichabod climbed wearily aboard.

Now, during the course of his little "gam," it had become evident to the captain that the green-eyed woman of Crook-Jaw had not spent all her life inside the whale's body; either that, or Ichabod himself had not been the first to venture through those gaping jaws. Hence, his queasy conscience being eased on certain essentials, the next evening, at the coming of sober-light, he pulled off his long-leggers and again plunged overboard, and was seen no more by his bewildered crew until the following morning.

This happened continuously until the vessel had to make in for a new fit-out, and again continuously, until the next fit-out. Ichabod was losing both his reputation as a whaler and a certain instinctive trust in which he had been held at home. He was also losing considerable of his usual color, and his men decided he had gone clean batchy.

The next time he came ashore, his good wife, a handsome creature not yet thirty, made him a gift —a shiny new whaling iron—which pleased Ichabod but also caused him a little pang, as a reminder of business which had been so long neglected. He was somewhat less pleased, when he went to sea again, to hear her insist that his father-in-law go with him.

A few days later, old Crook-Jaw spied the captain's vessel just outside the surf at Monomoy, and by this time the whale had come to regard Ichabod as a friend and guest, entitled to a certain amount of civility. He stood by, and Ichabod, standing on deck beside his father-in-law, watched him. When the old man began to exclaim at the size of the creature, and to beg Ichabod to lower for him, he could not properly refuse. Over they went in the small-boat, and with a mighty heave, the whalemaster sent his new iron whistling through the air at Crook-Jaw. He was confident that the whale would understand, and there would be no harm done, but to his astonishment, this time he made fast! The beast churned and thrashed the water, and finally died. When they cut him up, all that Ichabod Paddock found inside, where his cozy cabin had been, was a strand of seaweed which had bleached to the color of Eastham corn, a shell of plum-blossom pink, and two round sunsqualls, of pure emerald green.

As for the explanation of the killing of Crook-Jaw, I have not heard whether Ichabod's wife ever confessed to him what she had done. But the shiny "iron" she had given him as a present was made of pure silver—the only metal that could pierce the heart of a witch.

*Cottages and Beach, Provincetown, West End, 1940.* Etching by William Henry Bicknell. Courtesy of Josephine and Salvatore Del Deo.

*Grey Day on the Dunes, Provincetown, 1923.* Etching by William Henry Bicknell. Courtesy of Josephine and Salvatore Del Deo.

Untitled etching by William Henry Bicknell. Courtesy of
Josephine and Salvatore Del Deo.

William Henry Bicknell (1860–1947), a prolific etcher
and wood engraver, was born in Boston and trained at
The Boston Museum School of Fine Arts. Among the
numerous illustrations commissioned by publishers are
his nine etchings for Thomas Gray's "Elegy Written in
a Country Churchyard." For many years, Bicknell drew
landscapes and seascapes on the lower Cape. He died in
Provincetown in 1947.

Regional painting came into official favor during the Works Progress Administration years (1935–1943) under the sponsorship of the Federal Arts Project. Most major American painters were involved in the Project, and many were commissioned to do murals and easel paintings for display in federal buildings. Ross Moffett (1888–1971) and George Yater (1910– ) were distinguished WPA painters from the lower Cape.

In 1908 Ross Moffett left an Iowa farm to study painting, first at the Art Institute of Chicago, and later in Provincetown with renowned master of color Charles Hawthorne. During the WPA years, he painted murals for the Provincetown Town Hall, and for the Revere, Holyoke, and Somerville post offices. One of his paintings was chosen by F.D.R. to hang in the White House. Moffett's favorite subject was everyday life in Provincetown, especially in the Portuguese West End. His work is known for the bleak strength of his figures and the moody colors of his characteristically striated skies.

When he was eighteen years old, George Yater won a four-year scholarship to the John Herron Art School in his home state of Indiana. In 1932 he moved on to study with Henry Hersche at The Cape School of Art in Provincetown, and he has been painting the scenery of the lower Cape ever since. In the WPA years, Yater produced one landscape or seascape each week, and a supervisor would routinely appear to pick it up. The artist doesn't know where those paintings were displayed or what has become of them.

A George Yater retrospective was held at the Provincetown Art Association August 27–September 26, 1982. Yater is now living and working in Truro.

*Wrecked Schooners*, *1927*. Oil on canvas by Ross Moffett. Courtesy of Joséphine and Salvatore Del Deo.

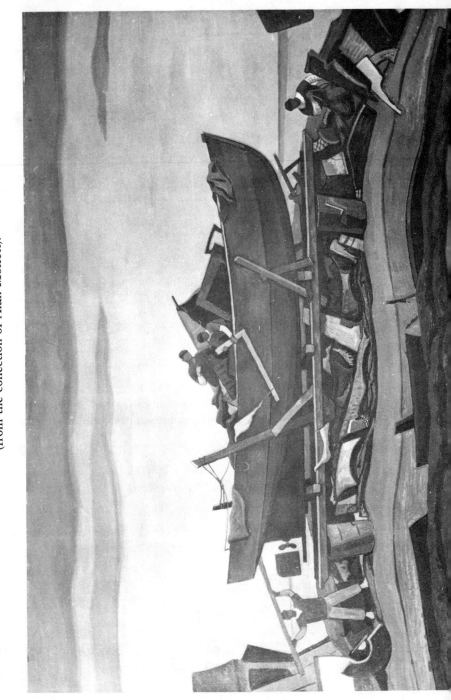

*Boatyard I, 1930*. Oil on canvas on plywood by Ross Moffett. Courtesy of Josephine and Salvatore Del Deo (from the collection of Alan Moffett).

*Oyster Shacks at Wellfleet.* Watercolor by George Yater. Courtesy of George Yater (from the collection of the Indiana National Bank).

*Fish Weirs off Truro.* Watercolor by George Yater. Courtesy of George Yater (from the collection of Diana Worthington).

# CHAPTER V

## DENNIS

*On U. S. 6, between Yarmouth and Brewster. Four miles between Dennis town lines.*

None of the towns has changed more completely, I think, than the group of five little villages that is called Dennis, after the Reverend Josiah Dennis, who agreed to settle as the pastor in 1725, when nobody else would. He preached for thirty-eight years, and all five villages perpetuate his name—Dennis, South Dennis, East Dennis, West Dennis and Dennisport—and this, it seems to me, is a very fair measure of immortality, coming at the rate of less than eight years of preaching per village.

"The adventure of the sea dies hard," and so it did in the town of Dennis, a land-name that rode high in the aristocracy of the sea wherever windships went; but when the "adventure" died, it made a thorough job of it.

There are still, to be sure, such pursuits as clamming, scalloping, lobstering, eeling. But these are the byplay of seafaring. Here, from these five sleepy villages, once went deepwater captains by the dozens; Grand Bankers set out, bound "down to the east'ard," for cod and haddock; great ships were built and launched, clippers with "masts so tall the sailors took along their wives when they went aloft to furl the skys'ls and sent down their grandchildren to say the job was done;" to these homes came more letters from Hong Kong, Shang-

85

hai, Calcutta, Liverpool, Bordeaux and the Mediterranean ports than from Boston or New York. To trade with the natives of the South Sea Islands, to be dismasted in an "Injy hurricane" or to fight off Chinese pirates was a part of the everyday business risks of these men whose descendants raise cranberries and hang out signs each spring, "Tourist Accommodations."

The logs and letters of Captain Joshua Sears reflect one of the most amusing personalities in the town's long line of skippers engaged in foreign trade.

In one of the letters bewailing his lot, he writes home: "I have never seen the need of a wife before so much as I have this voyage. But it will certainly take six months to get me tame enough to live with one."

From the log of the *Wild Hunter*, his Dennisport clipper, come these entries, of the year 1857:

*Saturday, September 5—That heavy swell keeps running from the west. Patience, patience—put your trust in God. Distance run 66 miles.*

*Sunday, September 6—Slow getting along— Thy ways, O Lord, are inscrutable.*

*Sunday, September 20—This is certainly very tedious, but I trust it is all for the best—J. Sears. Thy ways, O Lord, are past finding out.*

*Friday, September 25—Dead calm all this day. Current set the ship 20 miles due East. I never had such hard luck before. I feel almost discouraged.*

*Saturday, September 26—Commences calm, dead calm. Oh how disconsolate I do feel. Next voyage I will go down the China Sea and face all the typhoons that blows.*

*May 30—I am lonely, lonesome, disconsolate and low-spirited and have got the blues the worst kind —Oh for a cot in some vast wilderness, but on Cape Cod will do.*

Because he grumbled and groaned so much, and so artistically, my own belief is that Sears was one of the few who really might have *enjoyed* going to sea and relished the risks of the calling. His log notes and his letters home are generously spiced with lamentations over the lot of the seaman—so much so that one suspects the skipper of giving full play to that peculiar psychology of opposites which goes into the make-up of the "perverse Yankee."

Some years ago a Dennis man told of his experience when he went mate with Captain Sears on the *Wild Hunter's* maiden voyage. The ship was nearly a thousand tons and one of the finest afloat at that time, 1855. She was towed to Boston, rigged there, and sailed in January, 1856, for San Francisco, carrying a general cargo. She made the passage around the Horn in 120 days, then set out, in ballast, for Calcutta.

"Everything went smooth enough until we were off the Caroline Islands. We were running with the wind abeam when the cry of 'Pirates! Pirates!' was heard. We swung off the ship so as to bring the wind over the starboard quarter and all the stern sails were set. The ship went howling along at 15 knots. When we got time to look around, we found we were surrounded by Chinese pirates in 'proas,' sixty-foot boats with one lateen sail, carrying about 50 men each. As everyone knew, those Chinese pirates were the biggest devils ever sailed the seas. They had no firearms, but there were hundreds of them and they carried 'stink pots.' Once around a ship, they would heave these aboard, blind the crew, and then murder all hands, run the ship ashore and loot her.

"Captain Sears kept his course. He didn't budge an inch. As we approached, we began to fire both our small cannon and muskets. Well sir, I wish you could have seen those pirates! They opened a lane, and the *Wild Hunter* slipped through, belching fire and smoke. Some of the boys got down on their hands and knees and prayed. But Captain Sears and I stood at the wheel and kept her going right along. Some of the pirates jumped overboard, others committed suicide. One of our guns on the starboard side had clean cut away the mast of a big proa.

"Our muskets were mowing those rats down when hell suddenly broke loose certain sure. Some odd thousands of them threw stink pots at us and they were so fierce they yelled like mad. We held our breath, gathered up the stink pots and threw them overboard. After we got clear of the proas, we went back to our course, sent up Old Glory, gave them three cheers and a groan, and proceeded to Calcutta."

Spread a bit thick as this account obviously is, its essentials do not differ from those of many a story still known to Dennis, and of authentic record. There was Captain Benjamin Howes, in command of the barque *Lubra,* who was also overhauled by Chinese pirates, a day out of Hong Kong. Two men were shot down from the rigging, and one of the pirates shot and killed the captain as he sat in the cabin with his wife and infant. Captain Joshua Hall and his mate, Jabez Howes, of the schooner *Napoleon,* were murdered by pirates off Madeira. And as for gales, shipwreck and other assorted disasters, the town's share of these corresponded with its seafaring prominence.

They called at the West Indies ports for molasses—"Porty Reek long-lick"—which they took back in exchange for salt fish and other commodities. The Grand Bankers often took their trips there, instead of stopping at Portland, Boston or Gloucester. The Bankers took up another trade, too, which proved a bonanza while it lasted—"feather voyages" which supplied old New England with its highly prized "piller-bears."

These fishermen, having experienced several "broken voyages"—poor fares—were mending their gear off the Labrador coast one summer when it occurred to one of them to catch a duck that was roosting on the rocks nearby. The birds visited these God-forsaken shores by the millions, and at that season they were moulting and could scarcely fly. It was easy enough to kill them. With a broom made of bunched spruce-bows, a man could strike down as many as he liked. The fishermen could not get home quickly, and salted, the meat was no good. So they took the next best thing—the feathers. In Boston there was an enormous demand for them; and in Labrador and on the Bay de Chaleur, an enormous supply. The result was the widespread popularity of the "piller-bears"—feather beds so deep the children, to climb aboard, had to "rig up a jurymast and rattle down the shrouds." Barnabas Wixon and Ezra Howes of Dennis made their fortunes on feather voyages in the 1820's— until the ducks began to suspect that something was wrong with the Labrador Coast and stopped visiting there.

When you get far enough down-Cape to hear talk of "the Banks," you will doubtless hear frequent mention of Georges, but you are likely also to notice considerable disagreement as to just where Georges Banks are located. Provincetown vessels still go to Georges, and you have their authority for it that these Banks are about eighty miles due east of Nantucket. They are roughly 75 miles long, north and south, and 125 miles from east to west. And they are about as treacherous a place as a vessel can find herself, for the bottom is irregular, running from eight to fifty fathoms below the surface, with spots where only twelve feet keeps a vessel afloat. The "shoalest" of these grounds are ripped by strong, circular tides, and in any kind of gale, to stay on them means certain disaster. But that is where the big flounders feed and breed, and that is where the men of Dennis went in sailing ships of yesteryear when they were not making the longer trip down to the "Cape Shore" grounds off Nova Scotia, through the dread tides of Fundy, or the thousand-mile voyage to the Grand Banks.

Although nearly a century has passed since the tragic "gale of 1841," you will still find reminders of it on Cape Cod. Dennis lost many men, among them the crew of the schooner *Bride,* which came ashore on the Bay Side, her masts and spars gone. She rolled over on the surf-swept flats. There her crew was found next day—all five drowned in the cabin.

Such were their pursuits, such the hazards they faced. Today, one asks of a townsman:

"Did Cap'n Ben do well with his eeling this summer?"

"No, he ain't made anything but his expenses— and they ain't nothing."

Aside from the treasured logbooks and letters of the old skippers, most of the tangible evidence of Dennis's career at sea is now chiseled on the stones in her burying grounds. There you will find the markers of empty graves, with the brief statement, "Died at Sea," with now and then a doleful rhyme composed by some minister who had never seen green water. Sometimes their fate was never known; and sometimes they were buried "over the side" while the skipper read from his copy of the "Seaman's Devotional Assistant."

The incredibly prolific families of Howes, Hall, Crowell, Sears and Nickerson peopled the seven seas with these men. Thomas Howes, his wife, and a part of the next six generations of Howeses, lie in a one-family cemetery of 150 graves, the inscriptions dating from 1712 to 1918. To reach it, turn left at the triangle in Dennis, and inquire as you go from there.

Most of the epitaphs here are the usual expressions of sentiment. The composing of epitaphs, a Cape historian remarks, was a specialized business. The Reverend Timothy Alden, who preached so appealingly for his firewood, was one of these specialists, turning out a five-volume work on the subject. I have never heard him preach, but of his two attainments, I believe I should prefer that to his epitaphs. Here, for example, is one of his bravest offerings:

*Stop, passenger, and here view whatever is amiable and good summed up in the character of mrs. Cornelia Paterson . . . She was loveliness itself. The beauties of her person were exceeded only by those of her mind, which was adorned and dignified by a happy elegance of thought refined by virtue. She was delicately sentimental. Her manners were easy and engaging. Her temper was gentle, serene and sweet; her heart was meek, benevolent, virtuous. She walked in the path of religion, and lived for eternity. . . Go, passenger, reflect on thy own mortality, and leqrn to die.*

It is said of one Cape Cod widow, who had not got on too well with her late husband, that she refused to let the minister spread one of these tributes upon his stone. But something had to be written there, so the usual stock verse was chiseled on it, this too, against her wishes—

*As I am now, so you will be,*
*Prepare for death and follow me.*

She went out one dark night and scratched beneath it:

*To follow you I'll not consent*
*Because I know which way you went.*

There are other one-family cemeteries, among them the Paddocks', which is on your right, about a hundred feet from the highway as you go eastward. The oldest grave in the town is that of John Hall, in the burying ground at the head of the brook that runs westerly through the village of Dennis. He was buried in 1696, on ground that was part of the farm allotted him. He had nine sons, and in eight generations there were 235 families of Dennis Halls.

Another family of nine sons was that of Stephen Homer, who died in 1840. Seven of the Homer boys were 6 feet 3 inches or over, some of them 6 feet 6. I don't know how to explain the shortcomings of the other two. One of the Homers owned, as a keepsake, a bill of sale dated "Boston, Feb. the 20, 1776," which began:

*Received of my father, Benj'n Homer, of Yar-*
*mouth [Dennis] forty pounds and interest, in ac-*
*count settled in full for two-thirds of a negro man*
*named Forten.*

Fortunately for Forten, father and son never quarreled, at any rate not to the point of demanding an immediate division of joint property.

In some mysterious way—I suppose through the over-enthusiasm of townsmen aware of the tourist's demand for items of historical distinction—the notion once became current that Dennis's many little fence-posts were the work of Miles Standish himself, when the captain came down from Plymouth to lay out the town. The Cape has had some mighty whittlers, among its retired seamen and its depotmasters on the Old Colony Railroad, but never anything quite this prodigious; the best-seasoned fence-wood, furthermore, will hold up thirty years at the outside, in this climate.

There are other relics here, as elsewhere, without benefit of pedigree; for example, an old sea chest which is treasured in an East Dennis home, and proudly displayed to visitors. On the inside of the cover, it has this inscription:

*This chest was brought from England by Thomas*
*Howes in the ship Mayflower in the year 1637 and*
*has been passed down in the Howes family through*
*succeeding generations as follows:*

Below are written in eight generations of Howeses. The chest for years has been shown as "The Mayflower Chest." It is unquestionably quite old, being similar to the oak-paneled "Bradford Chest" in Plymouth, except that there are no handles. Here are the same wooden pegs, the spearhead iron hinges. As an antique, the chest is well treasured; and if Thomas Howes were not on record as being in Salem in 1635, and continuously in the country thereafter, it might be carping to deny him a 1637 *Mayflower* voyage.

A vantage point from which to observe the unique lay of the land, and from which to get all manner of impressions of the loveliness of Cape Cod and surrounding waters, is offered you atop Scargo Hill, which is ascended by motor, turning right off the highway at the small triangle opposite the South Dennis postoffice. The visitor to the Cape does well to take a map with him, and if the day is clear, he can get his bearings here at mid-Cape in relation to both Plymouth and Provincetown. The colors and all the rest of it I shall not try to describe, first because I can't, and second because they are always changing. The hill is only 160 feet high, the stone tower a few feet higher, but on this low-lying peninsula every foot of "up" means miles of "out." This is the highest point in mid-Cape.

Scargo Lake, to the eastward, figures in an oft-told Indian legend. So long ago that no tree-rings can number the years, Princess Scargo was the darling of her chieftain-father, Sagam of the Nobscussets. His favorite squaw, so the story goes, died in giving birth to the princess, and Sagam, stricken and bewildered, vowed that the innocent baby should never have to ponder the dark riddle of death, never have to face the intimacy of loss as he had faced it.

One day, among the gifts the distant tribes sent to Scargo, arrived one which snared her fancy as no other—a golden bowl carved from a pumpkin; water inside, and in the water, "little perch and dainty trout."

When the fish got bigger, Scargo made a little pool. They grew in number; then there came a dry summer. The streams failed, the pool dwindled, and some of the Princess's pets, "with gills wide opened, turned them on their sides to die."

The little girl had never heard of the thing called dying. But somehow she knew. Her grief was intolerable to Sagam. He called for signal fires, and drew to him all his warriors, squaws, even the papooses, for a mighty powwow. The tribe, he said, must dig a fishpond—one that would be so wide and so deep it would never fail—as broad across, in fact, as an arrow's flight.

The Princess picked the brawniest brave in the tribe to draw the bow, and stood him so the dart should have fair wind.

> *Scargo watched the arrow's falling,*
> *Placed a shell on either side,*
> *Cheated some on east and west lines,*
> *Got it longer than 'twas wide.*

For weeks in the broiling sun, the squaws toiled on, and the braves grunted. At last, in the autumn, it was finished; a great heap of sand, Scargo Hill, stood beside it. And the rains of October filled the lake to its brim. Of her beloved fish the Princess had saved a few.

> *Now she placed them in the pond,*
> *Watched them as they swam away,*
> *There they are, or their descendants,*
> *Swimming to this very day.*

*And on quiet summer evenings,*
*At the far side of the lake,*
*Calling gently, "Scargo, Scargo!"—*
*Then the echoes will awake.*

The legend has been told in several forms, but most published versions of it draw upon a long anonymous poem that was published in the *Cape Cod Magazine* in January, 1922, from which the above passages are quoted. The poem concludes:

*Where the shadows lie the deepest*
*Loving couples often pause.*
*They are listening to the echoes,*
*'Tis the grumbling of the squaws.*

I have never verified the frequent pausing of the loving couples, but the spot is not a bad one—and I presume this follows an evening at one of the two theaters located conveniently, just off Route 6.

In one of these, the Cape Cinema, is a mural painting which all guidebooks call to your attention because, so they declare, it is the "largest mural in the world," covering 6,400 square feet. I ask you to look at it in spite of the size, because it was designed by Rockwell Kent and Jo Mielzener, and they are credited by those who know with doing a thoroughly shipshape job of it. Worth a stretch of the neck.

The Cape Playhouse, which completes the frivolities of this sedate town, has shown the way to many other summer theaters, under the pioneering guidance of its founder, Raymond Moore. Moore began producing here in 1927, after some preliminaries in Provincetown. Robert Montgomery, Bette Davis, and Henry Fonda, among many others, were helped along their way in the Play-

house. The building that houses it was originally
the old Nobscusset meeting house.

Mr. Moore's residence in Dennis is one of the
oldest houses in town. A century ago, when it was
already middle-aged, it was the parish house of a
Dennis minister. Mr. Moore tells me it was built
in 1680. If you turn off the highway to your left
on Hope Lane, you will find it two-tenths of a
mile further, a "saltbox" type on the left side of
the road.

And now I jump, a bit abruptly, into something
I suppose I shall always regard as personal, though
there is no good reason for it, and I take the chance
that you will go all the way with me, or at least
far enough for the reward that awaits you.

Of all the cemeteries on Cape Cod, the one from
which I have carried away the deepest impression,
the keenest consciousness of the dignity of death,
and of the peace of death, is in Dennis. It has no
chiseled lace, no eulogies dragging in a rhyme by
the heels, no metaphysical abortions or neat slivers
of faith on ice. It hasn't even any gravestones. Its
single inscription is on a small slab of granite at
one corner of the gateless fence around it, reading:

> BURIAL GROUND OF THE NOBSCUSSET TRIBE OF
> INDIANS OF WHICH TRIBE MASHANTAMPAINE
> WAS CHIEF.

If you go there, you will find nothing but a
stone-posted iron fence, deep in the shadows of
ground-pine and hemlock; nothing but the earth,
thick-carpeted with fallen pine-needles; nothing
but a strange, half-intelligible whisper in the
boughs overhead. There is only a seclusion, a

silence deeper than the silence of chiseled words, warmer and simpler and more understandable than the accented emptiness of tombs.

One needs to know nothing about the Indians to walk out of this setting with all it has to give. They could be Dutch, or Hottentots, or even Yankees, lying beneath this ground, and it would mean the same—an earthy essay on the dignity of death.

To find this spot, stop at a house on the highway, at your right, named Scargo Villa, beyond the Sign of the Motor Car Inn, and go back around the house until you reach the stone fence.

The heavy timbers of old houses on the Cape are of two kinds—those that will "take paint" and those that won't. And those that won't are usually "salt-works timbers"—massive beams that supported the hundreds of vats in "works" which once lined the Cape shores "all up and down-along." As these sprawling plants were dismantled, Cape Codders, who never throw anything away, utilized the timbers in their homes, and because these are not the oldest dwellings, hundreds of such beams can still be identified.

The making of salt by solar evaporation of sea water was a major industry in almost every town of the Cape early in the last century, reaching at its peak in the thirties an output of well over half a million bushels annually, with 442 plants in operation. And according to local historians, it all began in Dennis.

Salt was wanted badly, for the preservation of fish, and during the year 1776 it was not easy to get, and fetched prices that made the fisherman groan.

Close to the Bay Side beach lived "Sleepy John" Sears, retired skipper and Yankee opportunist. When the British blockade sent the figure sky-rocketing, Captain Sears began to contrive. He contrived and he contrived, and finally he had a shallow trough, a hundred feet by ten, rigged with shutters that could enclose the big vat at night, or in thick weather. His first year he made only eight bushels, but he kept at it, and when a Har-wich man told him to use a windmill instead of his little handpump, for filling the vats, one of his greatest handicaps was removed. The rig of the salt vat improved steadily, and so did its efficiency.

When the neighbors saw what Cap'n John was up to, they thought he'd gone "whacky," and they called the contraption "Sears' Folly," and brought their friends for miles to see it. But they changed their tune in a few short months when they dis-covered that the Cap'n, whacky or not whacky, was making the sun shine him a fortune. Then they began building their own salt-works. These grew more and more elaborate. And the Banks fisher-men stopped groaning. The salt business paid at times as high as 25 per cent on the invested capital, which in the 1830's amounted to $2,000,000 on the Cape. From 1840 onward, the trade declined. Foreign mines uncovered new sources, tariff bar-riers were lowered, and principally, the salt-fish industry had begun its own long decline. The un-paintable timbers are the only remnants of the de-vice that snowballed profits for Cap'n John and his successors for nearly a hundred years.

A great many of the men who went to sea lived on Sea Street, in East Dennis. Here you will find

the long low white house with six windows across
the front, where lived "Sleepy John" Sears. The
house was built in 1758. Its interior makes a grand
display of hand-hewn timbers and panel-boards
of unmatched widths. Captain Joshua Sears lived
on Sea, too, and so did Captain Edmund Sears,
and a host of other Sears captains.

Captain Edmund was the proud owner of the
"first ingrain carpet" in town. At the time of the
Boston Tea Party, he was unloading his own vessel
in Boston Harbor. He rushed off to help in the
business of throwing tea overboard at the scene
of the "party," and then came down-Cape, arriving home in an exultant mood. He had been away
for many months, but the first thing he did when
he reached the house was to go straight to the
"bowfat," without saying a word to anyone, seize
the teapot and caddy, and heave them through
the window with a crash. Poor Mrs. Sears, watching him from a corner of the kitchen, turned to
the frightened children and whispered:

"Your poor father has come home crazy!"

The clipper ships of Dennis, proudest of all
Cape craft, were built in the yard on the Bay
Shore where, in 1850, Asa Shiverick and his three
sons, Asa, Jr., Paul and David, plunged into big
business. Old Asa had undertaken nothing more
daring than fishing craft, but Young Asa had been
to Boston, whence the long lean greyhounds of the
sea were racing 'round the Horn for big stakes—
and he had notions. In twelve years they built eight
full-rigged ships and barks, among them the *Wild
Hunter* in which Captain Joshua Sears set down
his doleful record; the *Hippogriffe,* a notoriously

"crank" ship, which ran upon an uncharted rock in the Java Sea, but which eventually sold for 7,000 rupees in Calcutta—more than she cost to build; and the *Belle of the West*. The *Wild Hunter* and the *Belle* were extreme clippers, the latter the sharpest of the fleet.

You may visit, if you like, the spot where these great ships were got off the ways, though you will find nothing there now but an abandoned guano plant and a tablet on a boulder, commemorating the works of the Shivericks. To reach it, turn left at the World War memorial tablet in East Dennis, and at the next crossroads take the right and continue towards the shore.

All trace of the scene once set here has vanished, and with it has gone from the Cape, for better or worse, the old feeling for ships. Daniel Webster, in a letter to a friend in West Dennis, said in 1851:

> *Gentlemen, the nature of your population is somewhat peculiar. I have often been struck by the very great number of sea captains as well as other mariners which the County of Barnstable and the neighboring islands furnish. . . . I was once engaged in the trial of a case in your district, in which a question arose respecting the entrance into the harbor of Owohyhee [Hawaii] between reefs of coral rock guarding it on either side. The counsel for the opposite party proposed to call witnesses to give information to the jury concerning this entrance. I saw at once a smile, which I thought I understood, and suggested to the judge that very probably some of the jurors had seen the entrance themselves; upon which, seven out of the twelve jurors arose and said that they were quite familiarly acquainted with it, having seen it often.*

Only a few old folks now have any more real feeling for sailing ships, any closer knowledge of a suit of sails than comes of having a print above the mantel. They must have winced, these old men, when they looked at a newspaper—a Cape Cod newspaper—and saw the two-column headline:

*SQUARE RIGGER STRIKES*
*IT RICH; BECOMES YACHT*

# CHAPTER VI

## BREWSTER

*On U. S. 6, between Dennis and Orleans. Eight miles between Brewster town lines.*

It is a long way to Brewster. My guidebook duties here become weighty and involved; for to go to Brewster my way, you must dig out your old *Bowditch,* your *Kedge Anchor and Young Sailor's Assistant* and your *Pacific Pilot,* and navigate a detour to a tiny island, two square miles rising steep-to out of the ocean between Australia and South America. This is Pitcairn's Island, refuge of the *Bounty* mutineers and home of their descendants.

Clara Freeman, daughter of Captain William Freeman, of Brewster, was the first white woman to go ashore at Pitcairn's. When her father took her there in 1883, she found a friend in Rosa Young. Rosa, born on the island, was a granddaughter of the Edward Young who, with John Adams, lived through the bloody days of conflict among the mutineer-settlers a few years after their arrival in 1790.

Clara Freeman made Rosa promise to write, and the Pitcairn girl kept the pledge. Her "letter" covers a period of six months, and is more like a diary than a letter. The original manuscript is kept in a Brewster home, and a copy may be seen in the Brewster Public Library. In it she refers to Clara's father as "the kind sea captain who frequently visits our lonely island." She tells, too, of the arrival of a trading schooner having aboard "two Tahitian women who are said to be the wives of the captain and the owner." The next day, Sunday, the Tahitians come ashore and go to church, and there Rosa sees them.

"Two very flashing looking ear-rings were in the lady's ears. Looking in the same direction again, I saw another face, much more homely in appearance, but sparkling with good humor. That face also was shaded by a very large hat. . . . Mother waited at the door, and when she bade them 'Yorana' — good morning — the Tahitian ladies were so pleased, and extending their hands, returned the greeting with hearty good will.

"If you could have seen them go into the boat," she continues, "it would have opened your eyes. Mr. Walker, the mate of the little bark *Oregon,* who was here when you came, took Mi-u-re up in his arms to lift her into the boat, but she wriggled and twisted herself about so as almost to throw them both down, but he held her fast and finally succeeded in getting her safely in. Marie, fearful lest anyone should take her up, kept at a safe distance and waded right into the water; then, seemingly without effort, she stepped right over the side of the boat and into it without any trouble, dragging about three yards of dripping wet garments after her."

In her next she tells of the passing of Mrs. Elizabeth Young—"the last link that bound us to the early days when this island was first inhabited. . . . Did anyone ever tell you, Clara, how her first husband met his death? Long ago when the little colony was young there was a day when the men

of that time went out in their canoes to fish. The
old people used to say for a fact that Matt Quintal's canoe—Matt was Mama's first husband—
usually carried two persons, but on that particular
day three or four attempts were made for two men
to go into the canoe but each time it was overturned, so that Matt was obliged to go alone. When
it was time for the fishermen to return, his boat
was observed to be resting on the water, but he
himself could not be seen. . . . How long it had
been so, no one knew, but it was supposed that he
had been seized by a fit, and getting out of the
boat, was drowned." Poor Matt Quintal was dealt
out a much more spectacular fate in the recent
versions given by the motion pictures and in popular fiction, by contrast with which his "fit" described here is a tame exit indeed. Thus do we
carry on our cultural advances.

On another day Rosa feels "a good deal vexed
on coming home to find that the pigs had eaten
several of my nice pineapples in which I take so
much pleasure and pride." On December 14, a
ship, *The Wandering Jew,* comes in, and the next
day, "we have been reading letters until we are
tired. I have not had time to read all I received,
the number being from 35 to 40. I got two from
Nettie, both written this year!" Rosa also is
pleased—as who would not be—by the fact that
*The Wandering Jew* brings her a Christmas card.
It was a merry Christmas for all on the island.
"After prayers were over I had the little girls sent
for, and distributed among them the contents of
the box sent from Wellesley College, and you
should have seen how much pleasure the little gifts
made. . . . We finished off at my home, where I

played on my old harmonium, *The Sweet Bye and Bye* and oh, how well it was sung as the full chorus burst from the lips of the young folks who seemed to sing with all their hearts!"

These descendants of the mutineers were exceedingly religious, and when the man-of-war *Constance* stopped there, Rosa wanted very much to meet the chaplain. She went aboard. "Whether he experienced the same feeling that I did I cannot tell, but I certainly thought that a more unchaplain-looking man was hard to find, and if words and manner are an index to a man's character, he certainly did not seem rightly fitted for a sacred office." Thoroughly shocked, she adds that "as we were about to leave the ship he said, 'Now we will have to sing *The Girl I Left Behind Me!*"

But Captain Freeman was not the only Cape Cod skipper to make in at Pitcairn's. One of the others, Captain Josiah Knowles, of the clipper *Wild Wave,* was wrecked on the reefs of Oeno Island.

"After remaining on the island [Oeno] for about two weeks," he reports, "I selected my boat crew . . . and set out in a boat for Pitcairn Island, about 100 miles away. I had upwards of $18,000 in gold, which I took with us in the boat.

"When we reached Pitcairn we found to our great surprise that the former residents had left for Norfolk Island, and notices to that effect were posted in many of the houses." Knowles' frail boat was stove in by the surf, so they built another, burning some of the houses to get nails and iron. "An ensign was made from the red hangings of the church pulpit, white cotton from an old shirt and the blue of a pair of overalls."

The Captain then stowed his gold aboard, and with two of the men, made the 1,500-mile sail to Nukahiva, where he was taken aboard an American sloop of war. He came back to Pitcairn fourteen years later, and despite certain unpaid items, was "kindly received."

You were warned that you would go a long way getting to Brewster. Our next detour is by way of Paris, to help track down the missing Dauphin of France. Everyone who visits Sandwich, Brewster, Falmouth, and other port towns all the way to the Carolinas and then to New Orleans, is confronted with this assignment, for in each of them he will be told that here was the *real* refuge of the vanished Dauphin. Audubon, say his biographers, was probably the Dauphin; but then, other biographies make out similar cases for their subjects.

From the fury of the French Revolution, the infant prince was whisked away in the arms of an American sea captain. On so much the legend always agrees, but each of the towns will supply you with its own captain who did the whisking. From this formidable array of whiskers, I give you Captain Davy Nickerson of Brewster because this town can at least offer you something tangible on which to hang the hoary tale.

Just before his sailing hour, on a day in the autumn of 1789, the story places Captain Nickerson in the gory streets of Paris, when suddenly "a veiled woman" confronts him, thrusts an infant in his arms, whispers, in broken English, a few carefully rehearsed words of pleading and instruction, and with a sob, dashes off before the Captain can stop her.

She has told Captain Nickerson to call the child René Rosseau, to take him to America, to bring him up there like any American child. And as Captain Nickerson's idea of how to bring up a child was exactly like that of any other Cape Codder of his day, he let René "do his teething on a belaying pin, swung his cradle from the spankerboom and turned him out to crawl the quarterdeck in a brisk no'theaster."

At any rate, he brought the lad up in the ways of the sea, and before he was twenty, the skipper's foster-son knew every sheave and fiddleblock, every pitch and heave of the crankest square-rigger that ever hooked mud in a foreign port. At twenty-three he was Captain Rosseau, master of his own vessel, and of navigation he already knew more than his teacher. The old man's methods were simpler and better—as long as they worked. Like others of his school, he could keep a dead reckoning with a piece of chalk on his stateroom door, and if it was lucky chalk, there was no cause for worry.

Young Cap'n Rosseau was new-fangled. So were his ways—his easting, his westing, his dev'ous summing and reducing. When Cap'n Nickerson would show him how to come to the same thing with half the fuss and feathers, a smile would come into his lean, dark face which infuriated the old man and made him go stomping out of the room. But let anyone else hint that the lad was pretentious in his navigation, and Cap'n Nickerson rose to the defense with fight in his eye. Let them ask him where he picked up the lad, let them question that furrin name of his, or the furrin look which showed plain simple in the cut of his jib— and the old skipper would shake them off with a minor explosion in his throat, a snort, and one or two well chosen platitudes about folks minding their own business.

Captain Rosseau was lost at sea, at the age of 25. Captain Nickerson's lucky chalk held out longer, but five years later he died at sea of a fever contracted at Prince's Island, in the Gulf of Guinea, while on a voyage in Elijah Cobb's ship, the *Ten Brothers.*

There is a burying ground behind the old First Parish Church in Brewster, and almost hidden from view of passersby, a memorial stone in the tall grass bears Captain David Nickerson's name. It was the custom of Cape folks to put the names of father and sons on the same stone, if all were lost at sea. And though the dark-eyed young furriner had a vessel of his own, and was lost in another part of the world, you will find on Cap'n Davy's stone another name—René Rosseau.

But the whole story of this far-flung village would require a volume to itself, with a Mercator's projection of the world for reference map. It must include the prudish adventures of Captain John Higgins in the Caroline Islands, where he put pants on the natives and taught them what they were for, gave them religion and instituted other "reforms" that helped bring on the spread of "white shadows in the South Seas." It must embrace the course around the Horn, Boston to San Francisco, where Brewster skippers drove their vessels recklessly and their crews insane, and where they encountered such gales as that which carried away Captain William Burgess's flying jibboom and split his sail-ends, and which he describes in his log as "brisk breezes from the south southeast."

As for home port itself, I would point out first that the record bears voluminous witness against Henry Thoreau for that oft-repeated quip of his, that the town was named after Elder William Brewster "for fear he would be forgotten else." In spite of the fact that in the Plymouth church he "taught twice every Sabbath and that powerfully," the picture that remains to us of old William is a warmer, friendlier one than that of many another *Mayflower* voyager. He was "tender harted, and compassionate of such as were in miserie." It is added, too, that "none did more offend him and displease him than such as would hautily and proudly carry and lift up themselves, being rise from nothing, and haveing litle els in them to comend them but a few fine cloaths, or a litle riches more than others." One of his daughters was named Fear Brewster, one of his sons Love Brewster and another son Wrestling Brewster. In the lean year 1623, William lived on shellfish and "gave thanks that he could seek abundance of the seas and of the treasures hid in the sands." When he died his estate consisted solely of books, 275 in all, of which 64 were "in the learned languages." And there, Mr. Thoreau, is old William Brewster, who has had so many descendants that some of them, though they know of William, have never even heard of the town of Brewster, Mass.!

The town did not take Brewster's name until
1803, when it was set off from Harwich, which lies
to the southward. Until then, Brewster was the
North Parish of Harwich, Harwich the South
Parish. Some wanted the separation, some didn't,
and when it was decreed, there was almost a miniature civil war. As early as 1752 the North and
South Parishes were having words, as indicated
by the expressed wish of the Reverend Edward
Pell who died in that year. He wanted to be buried
in the North Parish because, when the time of
resurrection should come, he was afraid God
would never think to look in the South Parish for
a righteous man. He was buried according to his
wishes, in the same cemetery where the stone for
Brewster's "Dauphin of France" is placed.
Whether or not the Reverend Pell will rise from
that ground as buoyantly as he had expected, he
may at least find the worms in the North Parish
a shade more class-conscious than those across-
Cape. Mr. Pell was a Harvard graduate.

On your left, a mile beyond the Dennis line,
you will see the Dillingham houses, two sensible
old homes, about one of which much nonsense has
been written. I have one guidebook which tells me
the house with the saltbox roof was built in 1660
by Isaac Dillingham, "who bought all the land
from here to the ocean for five pounds, five shillings and a red coat." Isaac Dillingham was running a tin shop in 1839, so that doubtless we have
here another proof of the remarkable longevity of
Cape Codders—for Isaac, 179 years.

John Dillingham, the settler, did indeed give
the Indians a grand hornswoggling here, but pre-

cisely the year in which his house was built cannot be determined now. Later owners have put the date, 1660, on it, but Dillingham didn't come to Brewster until 1668; on June 24 of that year, he bought the lot for this house from Thomas Prence. John came down from Sandwich after his neighbor, John Wing, had gone there and sent back word, saying, in effect: "There is a chance to make a killing here if you get in on the ground floor, John. With these Indians, it's like taking candy from a kid." John came, bought up everything in sight, and died at 85, the richest man in town.

Both Wing and Dillingham were Quakers. The Dillingham family's burying acre, where John lies with his three wives, among scores of other Dillinghams, is on the road to East Dennis, and is reached from here by turning right, directly opposite these houses, and then bearing left.

Because there was waterpower in West Brewster, the section you are now going over, it was once a busy place, an industrial center of the Old Colony. Religion and industry were the two principal interests of the early settlers, with religion, according to the ministers, getting rather the better of the two. Nevertheless, the town had a mill some two-score years before it had a church, and its moral alertness did not interfere with profits ranging up to several thousand per cent in certain lines.

Some time before 1662 Thomas Prence had a mill built here, to spare the Eastham farmers the long trip to Plymouth to have their corn ground. Possibly in an effort to stir up interest in the place,

some published works have pronounced it the site
of the first water-power grist mill in America,
though Watertown had a water-power grist mill
in 1635, Salem had one in 1636, and there were
probably half a dozen others. But the spot is one
of the most attractive on the Cape, with the water-
wheel of a later mill still intact; and without
trumping up history to induce you, I would lead
you there anyhow, turning off to right at the triangle just beyond Sea Meadows Inn.

Governor Prence's miller levied a toll, or
"pottle" as it was called, of three quarts to the
bushel, which was half again as much as the cus-
tomary charge. The miller quickly grew prosperous, and as he operated the only such facilities for
many miles around, gave American business one
of its first demonstrations of a principle that has
been hard to beat ever since.

Other mills and manufacturing establishments
were erected here in the century that followed, and
this part of Brewster came to be known as Factory Village. There were spinning mills, fulling
mills, looms, tanneries, iron works, and later the
cobbling business of Sidney Winslow which was
to grow ultimately into the vast United Shoe
Machinery Company. But the last echo of
Brewster's industrial boom had faded out years
before the country as a whole came into its right
as a nation of mechanized industry. There remains
one still wheel.

Stony Brook, the little millstream here, was bab-
bling consolation to the tribe of Sachem Wono
three centuries ago, after the chieftain and his
sons had been bamboozled out of their lands and

had come to live on the ground you tread now. They called it the Sauquatucket River, and they made their homes on its banks. They walked in slow processions, following it to the lower pond where, to this day, there stands near the water's edge a great isolated boulder, their prayer rock. They had need to pray. At one time they were a great people, but in the years 1612-1613 they had been tragically reduced by the pestilence—as one of our own early historians puts it, "an awful and admirable dispensation by which it pleased God to make room for his people of the English nation."

If you should come early enough in the year— the latter part of March—you would see Stony Brook so full of herring "running" for the pond that some of the fish are crowded onto its banks. These fish, called "herring" but really alewives, of the genus shad (*alosa tyrannus*) come up from the sea by the millions every year to spawn in the fresh-water ponds, and a proportion of them are caught in sluiceways, built at vantage points on the streams, or are seined from wider rivers, as in Harwich. Those which are allowed to get through to the pond stay there until midsummer, then go back to sea. The young fry go down to the sea in the fall, and do not return to the ponds for three years. By tagging experiments, the fact has been established that although these youngsters may travel thousands of miles in the Atlantic while they are growing, they return for spawning to the particular stream down which they first swam to the sea.

Salt herring is not the menu item it once was. Cape Codders used to cure them in the sun, smoke them and salt them in tubs of brine, string them through the gills to a stick, and sell them to each other, a dozen on a stick. A "stick of herring" was traditionally priced at ten cents. And there were some folks, it was said, who ate so much herring, and became so thoroughly inured to the many little bones it contains, that it was a day's work for them to get in and out of their underwear.

The towns claimed ownership of the herring streams, and the right to sell the annual privilege. Bidders came to Brewster and Harwich from far and wide when these towns auctioned off the rights. The privileges have sold as low as $150 a season on a stream yielding 1,000 barrels of herring. The record high was registered in 1920 on a stream owned jointly by the towns of Plymouth and Wareham—$11,000 for the season. It takes a lot of herring to bring back $11,000 and something for the work. The best account, to my knowledge, of that time of year when, for Cape Cod, "the herring are running," and of the homey, seasonal excitement that goes with it, is given by Joseph Lincoln in his book, *Cape Cod Yesterdays*. And Joseph Lincoln is one who should know. He was born and raised within a dog-trot of Stony Brook itself. Captain Freeman Lincoln's home, where the novelist spent his childhood, is on the highway, the little white story-and-a-half clapboarded house on your right, second beyond the A. & P. grocery.

The First Parish Church of Brewster, which in 1934 rounded out its first century, is "the new church," standing where Reverend Nathaniel Stone began preaching in the old meeting-house in 1700. Brewster was Harwich then, and this was the First Parish Church of Harwich, North Precinct. Across-Cape, in today's Harwich, stands its almost-twin, the South Precinct church.

Here in the North Parish, the Reverend Stone, who was a stickler for the moral proprieties, blazed away at the devil and groaned because his colleagues were too easy-going with the youngsters. The facts of life seemed only vaguely familiar to some of his fellow-ministers—men who blinked and shrugged when young couples, married but a few weeks, brought living proof into the world of their sin! Mr. Stone sighed for the old days, when such convicted sinners were taught at the whipping-post the ways of the righteous, and declared, "There is a sad failing in family government—a wicked practice of young people, which I have borne my public testimony against, and from the countenance that has been given by many ministers and churches to the openly scandalous vice of uncleanness in a neighboring pastor, namely Mr. Osborn." The Reverend Osborn, over in Eastham, was a gentle soul who counted not the months upon his fingers, but only smiled and exclaimed over the pink cheeks of the newborn. He was suspended.

Mr. Stone carried on his war against the devil and the boys and girls for fifty-five years, and the patient people of Brewster kept on going to church, and the generations of boys and girls seemed somehow to be very stubborn. But the fight was not given up with his passing. Writing in 1809, one of his successors, the Reverend John Simpkins, reports that "it is even at the present day considered as quite unfashionable not to attend the publick worship."

It is here, in the burying-ground behind the

church, that you will find Captain Nickerson's memorial stone, and also the grave of the Reverend Pell, who aimed his snub at the South Parish. There are many stones for the Brewster captains who never came back; of the 543 deaths recorded in this cemetery, fifty were "lost at sea."

Captain Elkanah Crosby, who died ashore and is buried here, was the father of eight girls, and seven of them married sea captains. The other died in her infancy. One of the sisters married a cousin, Captain Tully Crosby, who at 23 became skipper of the brig *Old Colony,* and who, in the clipper *Kingfisher* raced and beat Donald McKay's mighty *Bald Eagle,* picking up two days on her around the Horn and boiling into 'Frisco almost within hail of her. Captain Tully's stone is nearby.

At the north end of the cemetery, in the oldest section, is the Irishman, John Silk, who kept a small store, and whose widow married the postmaster, Edward O'Brien. The Widow Silk and Eddie O'Brien loyally worried through life together in Brewster, facing it out when the town clerk and the board of selectmen remonstrated against his appointment as postmaster, "he being a foreigner, a catholik and, in the opinion of the town, an alien."

Henry Kittredge, the Cape's historian, in recording this item, makes the comment: "Even today the old suspicion lives, and appears in the instinctively critical way in which every newcomer is scanned by the townspeople." As for the prejudice against Postmaster O'Brien as a "catholik," the heavy influx of Portuguese in the nineteenth century has robbed it of political meaning. But that it lives on was shown only a few years ago, in

Provincetown, when a division of the Ku Klux Klan was formed, with several of its "English-stock" businessmen wearing the sheet that should have been on little Junior's bed.

Another outbreak of religious conflict in Brewster was made note of in Benjamin Bangs's diary, and Benjamin, an innkeeper who died in 1769, also lies buried here. In 1744 he wrote, "Ye noise of ye war spoils us all, and we have civil war at home about a set of people called New Lights [also called the "Come-Outers"] who have been growing this year or two and now make a deal of disturbance all over New England. Some of them act very strangely." One of Benjamin's sons, who became attorney for the Commonwealth in Worcester County, is credited with the writing of "Yankee Doodle," and Benjamin himself admits, in one part of his diary, "getting all boozed." Save for these two lapses, the Bangses were quite respectable people.

Another respectable citizen of Brewster (for it was eminently respectable to smuggle rum into foreign ports, to bribe government officials, or to swing any little kindred deal at a respectable profit) was Captain Elijah Cobb. The Georgian type house, topped by a captain's walk, which this Yankee shipmaster built in 1800, still stands on the "Lower Road," where is also situated the cemetery where Cobb was buried. Leave the highway, turning left around the large tan house with the formal garden, and you will see it the second house on the right.

In his memoirs, Captain Cobb explains:

"On my return home I found that my pertner
in life's voyage had run me in debt for a cape Cod
farm; and as the place was distitute of a suitable
building for the accommodation of our little
family, it was thought advisable to proceed to erect
one the following season."

Cobb is remembered chiefly for his adventure
in Paris during the Reign of Terror, when, as a
24-year-old shipmaster on his first voyage, he saw
his vessel taken prize and her cargo eaten by a
starving populace. To recover damages, the persistent Yankee waited months, hacked through
mountains of red tape, and doggedly went to Robe-
spierre himself, performed the miracle of collection, and then threaded his way home, bringing
thirty packages of gold with him. To get his money
through the sluiceways of foreign exchange in
those times, he cut some financial capers that would
make our Wall Street dealings look like tiddledy-
winks.

As a demonstration of shrewdness, it was a spectacular job, but there is a side to Cobb, as he reveals himself in his *Memoirs of a Cape Cod Skipper,* that interests me more. This was his flair
for moralizing, his almost miraculous faculty for
appeasing a New England conscience while certain very profitable pieces of business were being
undertaken, to which that conscience might just
possibly demur. Other business men had it, in
Cobb's time, and have it today. But the shipmaster
who made a fat fortune for himself and settled
down in one of Brewster's spacious homes for the
rest of his life had it in unsurpassed degree. These
men could not make such fortunes out of their
salaries, which ran as low as $30 a month; their

money came through commissions, through big trading deals which the owners had to leave in their hands, and frequently through smuggling and other such channels. But however it came, the money was always accompanied by a religious platitude.

At the end of his account of the Paris episode, in which he recovers "damages" for his cargo of flour and rice at a profit of 200 per cent, Captain Cobb remarks:

"How often, my dear Grand Children, do we repine and murmer, when disappointment, affliction and trouble come upon us, and even distrust the goodness of our Heavenly Father when we, very frequently afterwards, realize that it was for our own good!"

Having brought a cargo of rum to Cork, Ireland, where the law at the time forbade importation, Cobb lost his ship, regained it, and afterwards had a little talk with the customs collector.

"The collector, observed to me when about taking leave, Capt. Cobb, I must confess, I think your usage has benn something rough here, I shou'd not blame you, if you were to help yourself a little, in the way of smuggling.—no Sir said I, but wou'd you not be one of the first to make a prize of me therefor—oh said he, I should have to do my duty —well Sir, said I, when you Catch'em you Hab'-em. God blesse you said he, and thus we parted, and the next morn' I sail'd; matters were, however, so arrainged, that between the Cove of Cork, and the Scilly Islands, that I hove overboard Eight hogsheads of N. E. rum, and a pilot boat sheer'd along side, and hove on board a small bag, which I found contained 264 English guineas—

and although I saw them pick up, and hoist on board 8 hhds of rum, I was satisfied."

But on one voyage, the Captain forgot business, and his letters reflect genuine grief. This was the trip of the *Ten Brothers* to Prince's Island, during which Davy Nickerson "took the fever" and died. Nickerson had been Cobb's mate on earlier voyages, and the disease spread to others aboard ship, including Cobb's friend and neighbor, Captain Isaac Clark, young Captain Joseph Mayo, and a cabin boy. All died before they could be brought home. Cobb himself had "a smart attack of the Nervous head ake," but he got over it.

The spelling and the wonderful things the Captain does with grammar in his "memoirs" are appealing, but the stuff itself is stilted and artificial, for the most part, suggesting that only at rare moments was he able to get away from the awful consciousness that he was "writing a book." Another of his better moments occurs when his "pertner in life's voyage" presents him with a daughter.

"After discharging my cargo in Boston, I visited my dear family, at the cape; where I found an additional pledge of affection, in a little black-eye'd daughter which we called Mary P, then 69 days old—it being night, and no light in the house, I hawled her out of Bed,and held her up to the window to look at her by moonlight."

For laying a devious course through barriers legal or otherwise, Captain Jeremiah Mayo runs a close second to Elijah Cobb; in fact, he was such a hand at sailing through hot water that a group of Napoleon's loyal followers offered him a commission, a month after the Battle of Waterloo, to

ship one slightly used emperor to America, if he
could see his way clear.

Despite the fact that such a cargo amounted to
very perishable goods at the time, Captain Mayo
saw a chance to show what he could really do, and
he snapped it up. Meanwhile, however, Napoleon
had surrendered himself. Kittredge, in his book,
*Shipmasters of Cape Cod,* tells of other adventures this six-foot-five-inch Brewster skipper had
at sea, his battle with pirates, his handling of a
very leaky ship, his blockade running, but most
amusing of all, the orders he received from his
owners when he had made in at Baltimore with a
cargo of flour, "to take no chances on running the
British blockade, but to load his flour on wagons
and bring it overland to New York." If you can
visualize a born adventurer with two long sea-legs,
squirming on the poop-deck of a four-wheeled tub
while the horses plod along with her, you may have
a fair impression of Jeremiah Mayo as he teamed
it northward. Mayo married Sally Crosby, and the
brig in which he was going to bring Napoleon over
was named the *Sally*.

Thirty years after Captain Mayo's "Irish
Armada" creaked its way up the Atlantic Coast
on the dry side of tideline, a member of his wife's
family, Albert Crosby, climbed aboard a prairie
schooner and set out for California, in the gold
rush of '49. Jeremiah was 63 then, and shorebound
for good, but I haven't any doubt he told Sally
just what he thought of a lubber who'd *choose*
"one of them bow-roofed democrats" for the voyage when there were ships aplenty making it
'round the Horn.

But Albert Crosby came back in a cloud of gold-dust. Jeremiah Mayo had lain in the churchyard twenty years when Albert returned, but there were other folks in Brewster who had had things to say about Albert when he'd set out—and Albert was going to show 'em. He showed 'em. He built a regular "show place," and to make certain sure it would have the best architecture in the world, he put a little of every kind into it.

Folks in Brewster sat around the postoffice stove and forgot to spit while Albert's hired man, Japheth Jenkins, told 'em about the plush chairs in Albert's new house, and all the gear in the Sunday parlor, made out of gold and marble and velvet, with rugs that made you think you was going to capsize every step you took. And the paintings! Albert had a "suit of paintings" in that house worth a hundred thousand dollars! And some of them paintings was gardens and flowers, and some was pictures of men, and some—well, you'd be surprised!

What Japheth didn't tell the boys was that in spite of the things folks had said of Albert, the town of Brewster was home to him; in spite of dreams of dwelling in marble halls, the straight, trim lines of an old Cape Cod cottage on Crosby Lane were ever before his eyes as he "rode the cars" eastward. And that was why, when Albert built the castle of his dreams, he built it around the plain little home of his boyhood, keeping the cottage intact. And whenever the plushes and the marble began to pall on him, or whenever he got homesick for Cape Cod, poor Albert would cross the polished floors, pass through the door to "home," and sit there and stare at the wide, uneven floorboards.

Crosby Lane is on your left as you go through East Brewster, just before you come to the railroad crossing. When you have reached what is left of the "castle," walk around to the rear for a glimpse of the secret weakness of Albert Crosby.

The Crosbys are dead; the $100,000 worth of art, which filled the windowless, skylighted wing, was auctioned off in 1929, "surprising" paintings and all; the "fancy gear" in the Sunday-parlor is gone too, gone for a song. The little Cape Cod cottage is still there.

One of the most important developments in the career of modern Cape Cod, now that we are a landfaring lot, is here in East Brewster. Opened to public use in the summer of 1937, Rowland C. Nickerson State Park is the first Commonwealth-owned park of Massachusetts.

If you have come down the Cape in the stern-sheets of an automobile trailer, you may have encountered some uninviting notices directed at craft like yours. But here is Trailer's Paradise. And if the State sticks to its original insistence on un-spoiled natural beauty, it will remain an attractive paradise indeed.

Rowland Nickerson was one of the Cape's "dry land skippers" who took a hand in building the great railroads of the west. As a pioneer in the development of the Atchison, Topeka & Santa Fe, he made his fortune and came back to buy up a summer estate and with it a slice of the Cape big enough to compare with the holdings of old feudal barons. It was the largest privately held forest acreage on the entire peninsula. Its ponds alone covered 328 acres. Its woods abounded in game,

the ponds in fish. But all of this was, in the mind
of its owner, exceedingly private property. The
Nickersons could not possibly use it all, but if they
couldn't, neither could anyone else. Cape sports-
men felt differently about it. A dispute arose over
public fishing rights, and Brewster stewed for
months in a thick statutory juice. A legislative
committee finally settled the argument—in favor
of the public.

In 1934 the railroad magnate's widow, Mrs.
Addie Nickerson, gave the park area to the State
as a memorial to Mr. Nickerson and to Rowland,
Jr., who died during the World War.

The park was at that time mostly a wilderness,
of little use to anyone. A CCC Camp was established by the government, roads built and reforest-
ation undertaken. In the first year, 88,000 red and
white pine and hemlock were added. A 400-acre
game preserve was set aside and the ponds were
stocked with perch, trout, chinook salmon and
other game fish. Accommodations for campers
and picnickers were laid out, including auto parks,
campsites, a bathhouse and all the rest of it. A
ruling has been made barring commercial concessions, and it remains to be seen whether the authorities will have enough good sense to stick by
it. Another ruling, which has been followed thus
far and which is just as vital to the maintenance
of the beauty of the park, is against all attempts
to improve on the design of nature. Swans, marble
urns and canned cupids will have no place here.

There are two other functions of the park, important to the Cape as a whole; first, it operates
as an area of pest control (tent caterpillars and
moths) and second, it constitutes an important fire

barrier. A fire tower has been located between Flax Pond and Cliff Pond, to supplement those in Harwich and Wellfleet, and fire-fighting facilities have been placed in many parts of the park.

To turn into the park, cross the railroad tracks in East Brewster on Route 6 and take the first right. As this book goes to print, Nickerson Park is still in its "honeymoon" stage, and there is only a nominal charge for the use of its facilities. Regarding this and the splendid intentions as to barring hot dog stands, concrete nymphs and other modern improvements, I have hopes, but I can make no guarantees.

If the seascape is more to your taste than park woodlands, Brewster is as good a town as any alongshore for clamming. The Bay Shore flats down the Cape are generously bedded, and by reaching them from a town landing, you have the right to dig in any part of the tidal area not restricted by local town ordinance or by state conservation rule. You may not get any clams, but nobody can legally stop you from digging. Your right is based on an old colonial ordinance of 1647, on which the Supreme Court based a decision in 1906.

According to this law, the holder of seashore property owns the flats, all the way to low tideline. If the owner does not want you to wade there, or swim when tide is full, he can come and drag you out of the water, or call upon the law to do it. But you, as the public, have certain rights on these flats regardless of ownership, and among them are "navigation, fishing and fowling." The clam is a shellfish. And so, if anyone chases you off his flats

for digging clams, you can fling back a citation at
him over your shoulder as you run—based on the
law of 1647.

If you do find clams, make the most of them.
There are three kinds—clams, quahaugs and sea
clams. You may steam or bake them, if they are
really clams; if they are quahaugs (pronounced,
God knows why, "ko-hogs," and if anybody asks
you how to spell it, reply that the quahaug was invented to be eaten, not spelt) take them to your
landlady, if she is a native, and tell her she may
have them. Then start talking about clam pie. Tell
her you have heard how good it is, but you think
the stories must be a little exaggerated. She won't
be able to resist baking one, and the chances are
you'll come off with all you can eat. And a cut of
clam pie is worth taking any chances.

If you have no landlady, sit down to your quahaugs and call them "little necks" or "cherry
stones," which they are, eat the small ones raw and
enjoy yourself. If what you have dug up is a mess
of sea clams, which is less likely, try similar ma-
neuvers to get your Cape Cod cook to build you a
chowder—offering to supply the clams, of course,
and a "junk" of salt pork. If this can't be engineered, restore your treasures to the sands whence
they have come. These sea clams are the big fellows, with necks a foot long, and with the ability
to spit ten feet to wind'ard. I have known Cape
Codders who could walk out barefoot over the
flats, and by the "feel" on their feet, determine
where to dig for one. I have tried it myself, but
nine times out of ten, after digging furiously lest
it get away, I have come up with a nice round
stone. Sea clamming is done commercially with

drags, towed along the bottom. Getting them that way is skilled labor, but by the foot method it is art.

If you undertake a clam bake of your own, you should make the most of that too, by building your bake correctly. To achieve this, you will require a good supply of stones as big as your two fists. You must have enough of these to fill in a circle, six feet in diameter, of two layers. On top of your stones build a fire of driftwood and race it for an hour, covering all the stones. *You* do the directing, and let the others in your party bring piles of wet seaweed, washed as clean as possible of sand. Rake the embers off your hot stones and pile the weed on to a depth of eighteen inches. Spread your clams over the weed, with your lobsters, potatoes, corn or anything else you want to bake. Keep everything well away from the edge, and bunched towards the center. Then cover with more weed, to a depth of three feet. Then batten all down with an old piece of sailcloth, tucking in the edges all around, to retain the steam, and on top of this pile plenty of sand. Your work is finished now, except for the hardest chore of all—to keep everybody else away from the bake for at least forty-five minutes, and to argue down those in the party who insist that half an hour is long enough, and they know because they tried it once on Long Island. Tell them this is Cape Cod. Explain that they do everything wrong here. That's why the baked clams taste so good.

*Old Water Mill, Brewster.* Photograph by Arthur C. Haskell,
for the Historic American Buildings Survey, courtesy of the
Library of Congress.

*Jonathon Kendrick House, Orleans, 1935.* Photograph by Arthur C. Haskell, for the Historic American Buildings Survey, courtesy of the Library of Congress.

# CHAPTER VII

## ORLEANS

*On U. S. 6, between Brewster and Eastham. One and one-half
miles between Orleans town lines.*

### ATTENTION VISITORS

*I have the largest assortment of bric-a-brac, old
books and other ancient articles to be found in
the place. Also dories and small boats of the
best makes at prices to suit.*

Drawn in by the wording of the advertisement,
I found the dories and small boats in the yard out
back. They were priced "to suit" their condition,
which, I found, did not suit me. So I went back
in and bought books. One was a scrapbook. Then
there were some charts and a couple of pilot books,
and a great family bible. Inside the cover of the
bible I read the name, J. Swift, and the date, 1844.

"Ah! Swift. A good old Cape name. Ought to
be a birth and death log in the back, with perhaps
some of those reverent or philosophical little
asides that are somehow thought to befit such occasions." So I turned to the back. In fancy scrawl,
across the columns reserved for the solemn record,
was this:

*I like fried mackerel better than boiled.*
*J. Swift.*

I asked my Orleans dealer in bric-a-brac and
small boats if he could tell me anything of interest
about the old bible or its owner. (You are tradi-

tionally entitled to at least one good story from the best second-hand dealers. For myself, I set it down as axiomatic that if I don't get a story along with it, whatever I've bought, I probably am not getting my money's worth.) But this time my friend shook his head.

"You've got me there," he said. "I'm sorry I don't know the feller. If I did, I'd give you a whackin' good yarn about him!"

They do have some "whackin' good yarns" in Orleans; one tale, still fresh in its memory, belongs in the history books, and you may be sure that when the rest of the world has forgotten, the children of this town will still hear the story of the *Perth Amboy.*

Joe Perry came from the Cape Verde Islands. In New Bedford, and on the Cape, Joe Perry's people are called "bravas," a dark race, part Portuguese and part African, descendants of the natives of the little island group off Senegambia. Joe met thousands of his own race, picked one for his wife. The Perrys came to Provincetown and Joe went fishing. The Perrys had a little girl, and Joe worked hard to make more money. He took out citizenship papers. Joe was reliable, and after many years at sea, in one pursuit or another, he was finally made captain of No. 740. No. 740 was a barge, and Joe liked her, and so did his wife and their daughter. They lived on her, they found life pleasant enough, and mainly, for Joe, it was nice because she was "so safe." His family was safe there.

At 1 A.M. on the morning of July 21, 1918, the tug *Perth Amboy* chugged into Gloucester Harbor with two barges in tow, and picked up No. 740 at the end of the line, as per schedule, bound around the Cape. Joe had aboard his "crew," which consisted of one man, and the "crew" had brought along his wife and child, for a cool ride on smooth waters in mid-July.

All went well until the tug and her fleet reached the entrance to Nauset Harbor, just off East Orleans. Mrs. Perry had cooked eggs and *linguica,* and was calling the others to mess. Joe sat on his "back porch" and smoked and looked across at the long gleaming sands of Nauset Beach, and tried to remember when he had last been to church. Suddenly a sharp *boom* startled him. It echoed through the Sunday morning quiet. Then another *boom.* Joe jumped up. He ran to the fore-end of the barge. And there, half a mile to leeward, he saw a low-lying gray form which he recognized from the pictures in the papers. A German U-Boat!

"All hands on deck!" Joe yelled. The others came running out. Joe herded them into the dory. They started rowing furiously for the beach. Their terror was dulled a little because they didn't really believe what they saw. They couldn't. And yet, the shots kept coming. They watched the explosions demolish the tug's pilot house. Then down went the barges, one, two, three. Joe cursed when No. 740 sank, and Mary wept. But some of the shells fell dangerously near their dory, and there wasn't time to pause for a last goodby to home. The submarine dove under, and was seen no more. In all, she had fired 147 shots, according to one count, and one of these came ashore—the first and last German shell to fall on American soil during the World War.

"Observers of the U-Boat gun-fire last Sunday,"
remarked the Provincetown *Advocate,* "were
unanimous in their criticism thereof. The German
marksmanship was downright poor."

Orleans, until 1797, was the South Precinct of
the mother town of Eastham. Why she was given
the name of Orleans nobody knows. The historians
have puzzled over it and given up, except one who
cites a local tradition that the town was named
after Louis Philippe, Duke of Orleans, who became King of France in 1830.

That explanation is possible, because, just a
month before Orleans became a town, the Duke
came to this country to join his two brothers, who
had been imprisoned since the Terror.

Here, at the inner crook of the Cape's elbow,
you enter what was once the country of the Nausets, tribe of Sachem Aspinet, who gave aid to
the shipwrecked company of the *Sparrowhawk* in
1627, and in a number of other ways showed
friendliness to the English. It was here too, that
Sachem Iyannough led Miles Standish in search
of the lad Billington, who had gone astray.
Standish, with ten heavily armed men, anchored
off Rock Harbor.

"The savages here came very thick amongst us,
and were earnest with us to bring in our boat; but
we neither well could; nor yet desired to do it, because we had less cause to trust them. . . . After
sunset, Aspinet came, with a great train; and
brought the boy with him, one bearing him
through the water. He had not less than a hundred
with him; the half whereof came to the shallop
side unarmed with him; the other half stood aloof

with their bows and arrows. There he delivered
us the boy, behung with beads; and made peace
with us; we bestowing a knife on him; and likewise on another that first entertained the boy, and
brought him hither. So they departed from us."

Shortly afterward Standish came again in a
shallop to this place, and while here made a prize
fool of himself over the theft of "certain beads,
scissors and other trifles," which Aspinet recovered
from the Indian who had taken them, after
Standish had rattled his sword and threatened to
"revenge it on them before his departure."

Sachem Aspinet, like Iyannough, was driven
into the swamp lands by Standish in 1623, there
to die of disease.

But the Nausets were a forbearing people. In
the winter of 1627 the *Sparrowhawk,* bound for
Virginia, lost her course "either by ye insufficiencie
of ye maister, or his ilnes; for he was sick and lame
of ye scurvie, so that he could be lye in ye cabin
dore, and give direction."

The vessel, her nose knocked about in a driving
winter storm, struck a bar near the entrance to
Nauset Harbor. The great waves swept her inside,
where the "many passengers and sundrie goods"
were saved, but the vessel herself could not be
floated again. The Indians met the little company,
and addressed them in English, offering "to bring
them to ye English houses, or carry their letters."
They guided two of the men to Plymouth, with a
message for Governor Bradford, who set sail to
bring them aid.

"It was noe season of ye year to goe without
[outside] ye Cape, but understanding where ye

ship lay, he went into ye bottom of ye bay, on the inside, and put into a crick called Naumskachett [Namskaket] wher it is not much above 2. mile over land to ye bay wher they were."

While the crew of the *Sparrowhawk* were trying to mend their vessel, another fierce storm broke over her, tore her away again, and pounded her into a hopeless wreck. She was abandoned then, and the sands piled over her in storms through the years. She disappeared from view and almost from memory until 1782, more than a century and a half later, when a lashing gale swept the sand away to bring her to light again.

Nobody did anything about her, so Father Neptune tucked her back in the sand and kept her there for almost another century. Then, in 1863, when she once more emerged, she was examined, and it was reported that she was "well built of oak, still wholly undecayed, the corners of her timbers being sharp as when new." Two years later she was dug out and taken to Boston, where she was exhibited on the Common, and her rudder was then sent to Pilgrim Memorial Hall, in Plymouth, where it is still on display. The dune on Nauset Beach under which the *Sparrowhawk* lay is still known as "Old Ship."

The *Sparrowhawk,* though by no means the first wreck along the back-side of the Cape, begins a long list of lost ships, identified and recorded. Your general direction changes here, as the map shows you, from east to north. On your left is still Cape Cod Bay, but on your right, and across the Cape, instead of the more merciful waters of Vineyard Sound and Nantucket Sound, the surf rolls in unchecked from the ocean itself, over shifting sandbars, treacherous shoals.

"Nauset Beach, "Kittredge says, "which stretches along the whole coastline of Orleans and Eastham, holds in its fatal sands the shattered skeletons of vessels from half the seaports of the world; while farther north, the outer shores of Wellfleet and Truro have gathered in the hulls of a thousand ships, driven helplessly upon them by northeast gales." In a northeaster, this back-side of the Cape is a lee shore, and in a strong flow tide, coursing towards its shoals and bars, few sailing vessels could keep away. No cable was stout enough, no anchor they were capable of carrying could hold fast against that pull. The tide off Monomoy is so swift that lightships have many times been cast from their moorings, and these vessels are equipped with mushroom anchors weighing from 5,000 to 7,000 pounds, held by a length of chain of nine tons.

A map has been made of the approximate locations of Cape wrecks down to 1903. So many tragedies are crowded in with the tiny numerals on the map as to leave it barely legible.

With the decline of seafaring depression came to another major industry of the lower Cape— "wrecking."

As in most commercial arts, there were amateurs and professionals in wrecking. The amateurs were often heroes—men whose one interest was the saving of life; and the story of heroism is a long one on the Cape. The professional wrecker had a number of interests, and the order of importance, as between life and property, was not quite so definitely established.

The stories, the dark hints, the baleful traditions, are hotly denied. There was no such thing, the Cape says today, as "mooncussing," yet the term has come down in a country where Keeper Collins, of Nauset Light, "found obstinate resistance on Cape Cod to the project of building a lighthouse on this coast, as it would injure the wrecking business."

"Mooncussing" now means simply the search for whatever the tide carries in. But the origin of the word, and its ancient meaning, are well known to this day on the Lower Cape. On a dark night a skipper unfamiliar with the back-side shoals and beset by wind and tide might easily have been led by a lamp, swung slowly through a wide arc, in the belief that he was following some man better informed than he. If such a lamp were swung from ashore, he would thus be lured into waters from which there was no escape. But this could not be accomplished in the light of the moon. Hence—mooncussers.

The Reverend Enoch Pratt, writing his history of Eastham early in the last century, said, "The law requires that this should be done [reporting of a wreck to the town clerk] yet it cannot be denied that it was frequently evaded, and the property found appropriated to private use, which has often been the case since."

The laws of salvage, since that time, have become so complex that there are men in Boston and other coast cities today who make a very good thing out of convincing the court a certain way on one day and the opposite way the next. But the

unwritten law of the professional wrecker was simple enough—finders keepers—and was compli-
cated only when the wrecked crew showed up
alive to mar the even tenor of industry. There is
an old tradition, mentioned by Kipling and many
others before him, that it was worth a man's life
to reach the shore of Truro, or of "Helltown"
(Provincetown) in a wreck, for the chances were
he'd be "met by a wrecker's wife with a brick in
her stocking." And Provincetown still talks of certain leading citizens who were over on the Back
Shore with a relay of drays, the day after the Portland Gale, in '98, and who came off with enough to
insure a comfortable old age.

But there never has been proof enough to con-
vict on a charge of "mooncussing," and if you ask
a Lower Cape surfman of the Coast Guard if he
ever heard of a case, the chances are he'll tell you
"no, all that stuff comes out of books." So don't,
for heaven's sake, believe all you read in books!

If the newspapers come out with a story of a
new sea serpent, discovered on or off Nauset
Beach, don't believe all you read in the newspapers
either. The finding of a sea serpent, his skull, his
tailbone, or his tracks, is almost an annual phenom-
enon along this coast.

A report of the first such discovery on record
in Cape waters was made by B. Franklin, uncle
of Benjamin:

> Boston, Sept. 28, 1719—On the 17 Instant there
> appear'd in Cape-Cod harbour a strange creature,
> His head like a Lyons, with very large Teeth, Ears
> hanging down, a large Beard, a long beard, with
> curling hair on his head, his Body a bout 16 foot

> *Long, a round buttock, with a short Tayle of a yellowish colour, the Whale boats gave him chase, he was very fierce and gnashed his teeth with great rage when they attackt him, he was shot at 3 times and Wounded, when he rose out of the Water he always faced the boats in that angry maner, the Harpaniers struck at him, but in vaine, for after 5 hours chase, he took to sea again. None of the people ever saw his like befor.*

And so, another big one gets away. A down-east shipmaster, in a statement made in 1818 and "sworn to before a justice of the peace of Kennebec County, Maine," gives us another noble specimen, in an even more dramatic pose:*

> *At six o'clock in the afternoon of June 21st, in the packet Delia, plying between Boston and Hallowell . . . Captain Shubael West and fifteen others on board with him, saw an object directly ahead which he had no doubt was the sea serpent . . . engaged in a fight with a large hump-back whale that was endeavoring to elude the attack. The serpent threw up his tail from twenty-five to thirty feet in a perpendicular direction, striking the whale by it with tremendous blows rapidly repeated, which were distinctly heard and very loud for two or three minutes. . . . They went down for a short time, and then came up to the surface under the packet's larboard quarter, the whale appearing first and the serpent in pursuit, who was again seen to shoot up his tail as before, which he held out of the water some time, waving it in the air before striking, and at the same time, while his tail remained in that position, he raised his head fifteen or twenty feet, as if taking a view of the surface of the sea. After being seen in this position a few minutes, the serpent and the whale again sunk and disappeared, and neither were seen after by any on board.*

"Professor" George Washington Ready, of Provincetown, outdoes either of these accounts with the most spectacular varmint yet placed on

*Rev. Henry T. Cheever, *The Whale and His Captors,* New York, 1864 (p. 122).

the record. I shall give his story when we get there. But Orleans, Eastham and Wellfleet are still shooting at his mark. Thus, in 1936:

### THERE ARE SEA SERPENTS OFF CAPE!—CARCASS PROVES IT

Orleans, Jan. 17—Somewhere in the briny deeps that wash the Nauset strand, Orleans Coast Guards swear sea serpents with tongues shaped like fish tails, swivel-jointed necks and 200 teeth mounted in cavernous jaws stalk their prey. Surfman Fred Moll found the remains of such a critter on the beach below the station yesterday. All that remains of the marine mystery is a grinning head with a few inches of what appears to be a snake-like body attached.

One week later a biologist came along to spoil the story:

Chatham, Jan. 24—It was only a dolphin after all, according to Ed Taylor, John Nickerson and Everett Eldredge Jr., after two days of research to identify the snaky skull picked up on the beach below the Orleans Coast Guard Station a week ago.

The Coast Guards, during these long wintry afternoons, seem to develop a strange preoccupation all down the Cape with phenomena in the animal world, and they break into print with discoveries even more wonderful than Surfman Moll's dead sea serpent. In the same year another Orleans surfman adopted a "light-fingered crow," and the bird's criminal record on the Cape— thieving milk off doorsteps—was a matter of public interest for weeks. He became Feathered Enemy No. 1, until the morning the Cape read that he had tackled a bottle and found it to be sour milk, whereupon in chagrin he had committed suicide. And there was Joe (biologically Josephine) the duck mascot of the Monomoy station, who went on a sea food diet exclusively and hatched out a brood that would not swim in fresh water.

But if it's yarns you want, look up old Charley Mayo in Orleans—Charley F., for there are half a dozen Charley Mayos in town—or perhaps by the time this book reaches you, a dozen. Charley, who will be a hundred in 1950, is a walking encyclopaedia of fishing lore of the Cape. He went to sea as a "salt-passer" when he was 12, and he has been to the Banks on a score of vessels that have long since gone down or gone out. But the chief claim to fame of this grand old white-mustached Bankerman was his record as the fastest mackerel splitter who ever sailed from a Cape port.

One day they held the watch on Charley, down at the wharf, about thirty years ago. A vessel was in with a fare of mackerel fresh out of Barnstable Bay. There was talk of splitting fish, and there were arguments and finally there was money placed. In sixty seconds Charley split 69 mackerel, and money changed hands. But he wasn't satisfied. "Time me again," he said. "I can do a mite better. There was a soft one in that bunch." That time he split 71.

Orleans sent out many a man like Charley Mayo, but not on her own vessels, for the harbor here was against her as a deep-sea fishing port. But with her miles of in-reaching waterfront, Orleans has had clams, scallops and other shellfish, and while neighbor towns were reckoning values in terms of bushels of corn, Orleans' unit was a barrel of clams. The Reverend Pratt reported, nearly a century ago, that a man could earn at the business as much as seventy-five cents a day. Today, the story goes:

## SCALLOP RENDEZVOUS
## OFF ROCK HARBOR IS
## OCEANIC GOLD MINE

### $20 a Trip per Man Is
### Expected From
### New Bed

You can go to Rock Harbor by taking the Skaket Road from the traffic signal in Orleans Center, and following directions at the fork, where one route goes to Skaket and the other to Rock Harbor. If scallops are to you just so many reefs taken in the hem of a petticoat, the short drive will still be worth making. If you are on the Cape after October 1, you should see the scallopers go out. Look up in your Farmer's Almanac the time of flood tide, and be on hand on any calm day.

What the fish dealer calls a scallop is only part of a scallop—the part that the scalloper calls an "eye." And what the scalloper calls an eye is not an eye at all, so that by simple inquiry it is very difficult to find out what a scallop really is. He is a shellfish, shaped somewhat like a clam but with ribbed or fluted shells which he opens and shuts to propel himself along. He works on the principle of the rocket, without getting as excited over it. And what the scalloper calls the "eye", and the only part of him that is eaten, is the single large muscle that opens and shuts the doors. So much of the scallop is wasted that the fishermen have asked the Government, please to try and discover some use for the 25 tons of scallop meat thrown away each week in the season because nobody knows what else to do with it—though "art studios" buy the shells by the barrel, decorate them, and sell them to tourists as ashtrays.

You do not need a permit if you scallop for yourself. You may pick yourself up a mess if you can find them at low tide in shallow water along the flats. All you need is a bag to carry them home in. When you pick them up, they will clap their shells together, and by this single round of applause, squirt water on you. When you get them home, use a flat, dull, round-pointed knife to open them. Hold the scallop with the darker shell up, in your left hand. Stick the knife in at the right, near the hinge, and sever the muscle from the lower shell. That is Stroke One. To make Stroke Two, holding the eye with your thumb, pull away the mess of real eyes and gills around the mouth of the shell, leaving the clean muscle attached to the upper shell. Stroke Three cuts the muscle free. You may require several extra strokes on the second phase, but for the professional scalloper, three is bogey. A practiced hand can cut out a gallon an hour—there are 800 to 1,000 eyes in a gallon—and 32 a minute is the record.

A full-grown scallop is about three inches across. He grows an inch a year, approximately, and the rings on his shell mark his years. It is illegal to take him if he wears no ring. It is also illegal to soak him in fresh water, with a little soda added, to swell him up, if you are going to sell him. And it is distinctly illegal to sell pieces cut out of a skate, as scallops. Both these devices have been tried. There are other strict regulations governing the industry. The season is closed from May 1 to October 1, and commercial scalloping must be done with permit. The permits usually are denied "off-Capers." There are also restricted areas and

limits, and scallopers are nearly always getting
fined for something.

At Rock Harbor lives the Lamplighter of
Orleans, old Josh Northup, who took the job when
the church ladies—the Sewing Circle and Female
Samaritan Society—organized the Orleans Street
Light Club in 1911, and who for years went up
and down the streets, armed with ladder, oil and
matches and listened to the complaints of the
townsfolk with a philosophical nod. "I'd start on
one end of my beat quite a while before dark and
folks there would get all set up at the spectacle of
me burning oil before sundown. By the time I
reached the other end, it was after dark, and they
kicked because they weren't getting their money's
worth." The lights were not to be lit on what the
calendar called a "moonlight night," whether a
moon showed up or not, so that the most dangerous
time to be abroad probably was on a scheduled
moonlight night. Josh Northup stuck to the calendar.

The unusual house on the Skaket Road (at left)
with Ionic columns and an enclosed captain's walk
to top it all, was the home of one of the Cape's
most famous shipmasters, Captain Eben H. Linnell. The captain built it along the lines of a house
that had taken his fancy in Southern France.

Sailing a full-bodied ship, the *Buena Vista,*
Captain Linnell raced Levi Stephen's clipper, the
*Southern Cross,* San Francisco to Calcutta in
1851, and made the voyage in 60 days, only four
days slower than the clipper's time. As his reward
for proving that he could drive a good old-fash-

ioned hooker pretty near as fast as these new fancy-cut clipper ships, his owners placed him in command of a clipper. Later he sailed the speedy *Flying Mist,* and in 1859 he gave a grand ball aboard that vessel while she lay at Hong Kong, which several sea captains attended with their wives. Captain Joshua Sears, of Dennis, was in Hong Kong, with his *Flying Hunter.* He went to the ball and wrote home to Mrs. Sears:

> *I should like to have had you and Lulu there, for crinoline was very much in demand, as there is only about fifteen ladies in port, and some of them have got such d——d jealous husbands that they cannot let them dance with anyone out of their sight.*

At the shoreline on the Bay, in December of 1814, Orleans stood up and defied England, and by virtue of her impossible marine approaches, won the "Battle of Rock Harbor."

The British had been patrolling the coast with their ships, and demanding ransom money all alongshore, threatening to destroy the saltworks if they were refused. Eastham paid $1,200 and Brewster slavishly dug up $4,000, taxing her poor, principally, to preserve the large saltworks that belonged to her wealthier townsmen. But Orleans stuck out her chin and told the British frigate *Newcastle* that she could, in effect, go to hell. She very nearly went there, grounding on the sandy bottom off Rock Harbor, and losing some of her spars and rigging before she could clear. The townsmen of Orleans stood on the shore and hooted, which annoyed the commander of the *Newcastle,* whose position was undignified enough without all this. He dispatched a barge into the harbor to seize a schooner and three sloops. Two vessels were burned, two taken prize. An Orleans man, impressed to pilot one of the prize craft, ran her aground at Yarmouth.

Your visit to Orleans should include a jaunt down the Chatham road (Route 28) as far as South Orleans, though you will be retracing this short drive on your way back. Following the first settlement of the town, in 1644, the Indians were slowly crowded out of their lands and into a part of this section known as Potanumaquut. A meeting house was built for the "praying Indians"—those who were Christianized—and a graveyard laid out beside it. The Indian church had disappeared before 1800; in 1890 the burying ground was still marked, but all trace of it is gone now. These acres were used for truck gardens, and Orleans folks say that many a man living today owes the nourishment he got from home-grown vegetables to the last of the Nauset Indians.

Next door to the Episcopal Church, at the left, there is a relic of "mooncussing days"—the deck-house of a wrecked ship, which is now used as one room of a gift shop. The vessel, now of disputed identity, came ashore in 1858. For a time the deck-house served as a cobbler's shop, and later as part of the town clerk's dwelling.

A quarter-mile south of the South Orleans post-office, on the right side of the road, a Cape Cod cottage nestles behind a tall Labrador spruce, nestles and smiles to itself, no doubt, over some of the yarns that have been spun around it.

Built by Captain John Kenrick a few years after the Revolutionary War, this little cottage is a well nigh perfect example of Cape Cod architecture at its best, and it has been photographed several times to illustrate magazine articles and other literature on the subject.

The house is all that the writers have claimed for it—pictorially—and on such grounds it deserves your attention, in spite of all the misinformation that has been printed about its builder. I have two guide-books which call Captain Kenrick "the first American commander to circumnavigate the world." He was not the first to try it, and what is sadder, he didn't do it. Kenrick was sent out by a Boston group in 1787 on a highly speculative venture—the opening of the northwest fur trade. His 83-foot vessel, the *Columbia,* set sail accompanied by a sloop, the *Lady Washington.* Their projected route lay around the Horn, northward past California to the Oregon coast, where the furs were to be taken aboard; thence to China, where they were to be traded for silk; west through the China Sea, across the Indian Ocean, and then around the Cape of Good Hope and northwest across the Atlantic to Boston.

Thus poor John Kenrick's course did lie around the world—in a sadly under-provisioned and under-equipped little vessel. The miracle of working indefinitely without food was expected of her crew by the ruthless Boston speculators who employed them, and before she had rounded the Horn, the crew came down with scurvy. She finally arrived in Nootka Sound, Vancouver Island.

"At this point, the Captain's character began to disintegrate."* When he had obtained a full load

*Henry C. Kittredge, *Cape Cod, Its People and Their History,* (p. 239 ff.)

of otter skins from the Indians, he turned his ship over to Captain Gray—who had commanded the sloop *Lady Washington*—and sent him on over the projected route. For himself, he took the sloop, and proceeded on a series of madcap adventures in the Pacific—fights with the natives, crossings to China, loafing at Hawaii, and finally, having "abandoned all idea of returning home," purchasing a great tract of wild land on Vancouver Island and building a house there.

Captain Kenrick's exit was as spectacular as everything else he did. On one last voyage over the Pacific, the sloop encountered a British vessel, and in salute fired off a blank charge. The Englishman fired to return the courtesy. By some mischance her gun was loaded, and the American skipper was blown to bits.

Cape Cod's main contribution to the architecture of homes is simplicity. The principle seems to be, roughly, that the looks of a house are not enhanced by any "gadget" or trick which does not in some way add to its function as a shelter; and conversely, if the need for shelter is perfectly fulfilled, and the structure best designed to meet the elements where it stands, its looks will take care of themselves—will be good looks. There is nothing new, of course, about the principle; but there is plenty of evidence that it is not always followed. The Cape Cod cottage adheres faithfully.

The type is the "story and a half," with a large chimney in the center. This generous piece of masonry is important not only for the draught, but as a mainstay for the entire structure. A large chimney, a well shaped mass around it, and a few carefully placed windows, are main requisites. The windows are small-paned, and they go up near the eaves. Any form of dormer is incongruous. The ceilings are kept low, and the usual design places one square room on each side of the front door, a large kitchen across the rear, with a "buttery" at one end and a small bedroom at the other. From the entrance hall in front, a narrow stairway, which is sometimes called the "chicken ladder," goes steeply to the attic, slanting towards the front of the chimney. Upstairs there are usually two rooms and a bath. With this design as a base, ells can be built on, and were built to keep up with the expanding family. Piazzas go poorly.

The foundation of stone, set dry, provides for plenty of ventilation. In the fall, many old Cape Codders "banked up" for the winter, filling a trough around the base of the house with seaweed to stop the draughts. The salt air of the Cape will very soon bring the shingles of a new house around to a beautiful silver gray. Inland, they turn brown or dark gray, but here, if a house is shingled with white cedar, it will lose its schoolgirl complexion in a couple of years and weather to the color of its century-old companions.

A trellis or two and the conventional white picket fence, from eighteen to twenty-four inches high, are the only bits of "running rigging" your craft needs out of doors. Even the fences had one function to perform, suggested by the woman who "could count the missing pickets in her neighbor's fence quicker than she could mend her own." The condition of the fence, on the Cape, is as important as the state of a flight of white steps in Baltimore.

The earmarks of an old house are several. If the door to her brick oven is wooden, she probably was built before 1800. If her window panes are twenty-four, she is older than if they are twelve. If her shingles are of white pine, add a century earlier than cedar. If they are split or "rived," instead of sawn, do the same. If any of her floor-planks are more than two feet wide, she has heard talk of the British on our shores, and her timbers may have been to sea. If she has a round-cellar, she deserves respect, or has succeeded to the site of one that did; but for such veneration, she should also have a "summer beam" in her kitchen, she should face south, and there should be a mark upon her floor under one of the windows, for the telling of time on sunny days; under her attic steps there should be a cat-hole; there should be a little grooved rain-trough on her threshold, and she may have a millstone, perhaps, as her doorstep. She is at her best if her fireplace in the kitchen is large enough for her mistress to walk in and do the cooking, and for the children to sit at the ends and look up through the chimney at the stars. The high child mortality rate that attracts the notice of wanderers in Cape cemeteries probably owes much to the colds caught in the fireplace.

In the village of Orleans you pass a large house that was once the old Higgins Tavern, a stagecoach stop where down-Cape travelers put up for the night with a prayer that their craft would not capsize in the deep sand on the morrow. It is the building at the left just before Sherman's Garage. Here Thoreau, on his journey down-Cape, paused, feeling "very much as if we were on a sandbar in the ocean, and not knowing whether we should see land or water when the mist cleared away." The Tavern was built in 1829, but it was a tavern in a very mild sense, for Orleans had gone dry three years before, and even the use of tobacco was discouraged in concerted campaigns here. "The cause of temperance," writes the Reverend Mr. Pratt, "is very prosperous in the town." In 1837 a professional reformer, the Reverend Charles S. Adams, came down from Boston and read an original poem before the Temperance Society and the Anti-Tobacco Society.

> *Popes, kings and legislatures all combine*
> *By excommunication, threats and fine,*
> *To stay its march, to break its iron rod—*
> *It conquers still, and triumphs like a god:*
> *This nauseous weed, despite of all their laws,*
> *Still holds its throne between the human jaws.*

It ran for twenty-four pages.

"Hysteric fits," Thoreau said, "are very common in Orleans, Eastham and towns below, particularly on Sunday, in the times of divine service. When one woman is affected, five or six others generally sympathize with her; and the congregation is thrown into the utmost confusion." His explanation for all this was the fact that "a large portion of the population are women whose husbands are either abroad on the sea or else drowned, and there is nobody but they and the ministers left behind."

Two of Orleans' churches played the parts outlined by Messrs. Pratt and Thoreau—the Universalist, which mothered the famous Sewing Circle, and the Methodist, and both have been dutiful in the safekeeping of local history. In the Chapel of the Holy Spirit, Episcopal, you will find a Fifteenth Century Della Robbia plaque, and a bit of altar lace that dates back more than 200 years, when it was used in a church in Southern England.

On the way around Town Cove is located the cable station of the Compagnie Francaise des Cables Telegraphiques, terminus of a line running across the Atlantic to Brest. The cable makes in at Nauset Harbor, runs along the bottom of Town Cove, and up into a small white cottage.

Despite the advent of transatlantic wireless, the cable line is still one of several reasons why the government stresses the war-time importance of the Cape Cod Canal. In the great Portland Gale, of 1898, when land lines were down throughout the Cape region, the schooner *King Philip* of Taunton was lost, presumably somewhere off Cape Ann. The freak violence of this storm brought all that was left of her to the Bay Side beach in Brewster—a small steam pump, with a serial number on a brass plate, through which the vessel was identified. A newspaperman in Brewster took down the number, but could not notify Boston by regular channels. He cabled it via France, Ireland, Newfoundland and New York. It was the only evidence on which the widow of Captain Duncan of the *King Philip* was able to collect his insurance.

Throughout this country's participation in the World War the station was closely guarded by a company of Marines. Again, at a crucial stage of the Italo-Ethiopian War, it was bringing in widely awaited bulletins, and at that time Captain James Van Amburg of the fish dragger *Andover* was working in Cape waters when his net and steel lines became snared in the cable. The only way he could recover his gear, which is no small item in a fisherman's equipment, would have been to cut the cable. And the reason he didn't do that was that he knew the whole western world was waiting to hear of the fortunes of war in Africa. He sailed away minus several hundred dollars worth of dredging gear.

In East Orleans you are brought to the shore of Pleasant Bay, and close to Pochet Island. Probably, as you look across the inlet, the waters out beyond Nauset Beach are rolling inward with the lazy rhythm of summer surf. On a wild night of April, 1717, roaring mountains of white water heaved and guttered beyond the bars under a northeaster that overtook a great ship, whisked her like a toy boat onto Nauset shoals, a few miles further down-Cape, and pounded her to pieces. She was the proud London galley *Whidah,* fallen into bad hands, and her wreck ended the rocketing career of young "Black Bellamy" under the "skull and bones-across." The beach was strewn for miles with wreckage and the bodies of all 101 of Samuel Bellamy's crew. And at the same time, here at Pochet Island, landed one of his "prize ships," the pink *Mary Anne,* with seven of Bellamy's youthful freebooters and three captives on board.

The *Mary Anne,* Andrew Crumstey, master, was an Irish craft, bound for New York with a cargo of Madeira wine. The *Whidah* took her near Nantucket Shoals, put seven young men aboard with Alex Mackonachy, the *Mary Anne's* cook, John Dunavan and nineteen-year-old Tom Fitzgerald, the mate, and added her to the fleet of prizes she was collecting, as Bellamy headed northward.

Then came retribution. The northeaster drove the *Whidah* and her prize off their course, and the pink *Mary Anne* rocked and groaned in her timbers and acted as if she would pitch-pole over the shoals.

"For God's sake, let us go down into the Hould and Die together!" Tom Fitzgerald cried. And he no sooner left his trick at the wheel than she struck. Below, the bungs were pulled from Crumstey's Madeira as all seven pirates decided that if they must go to hell now, they might as well go drunk. But at the coming of dawn, ten thick-tongued mariners blinked and saw the sands of Pochet Island beneath their vessel's riven keel.

Cook Mackonachy scared up a "mugup," with fine Madeira to wash it down. And then a canoe came out from the mainland, and John Cole and William Smith, townsmen of the South Parish of Eastham, who knew nothing of the capture of the *Mary Anne* by Bellamy's men, offered to row them all ashore, and suggested, too, that it would be much safer to ballast the canoe well with casks of the Madeira.

Under these conditions, John Cole was eager to show his hospitality when they reached his house on the Bay Side, and again the *Mary Anne's* cargo was broken out. The seven of Bellamy's men were now well on their way to a fine "offing." All at once Alex Mackonachy, the cook, stood up and with remorseful streams down his cheeks, declared the seven were naught but a scurvy pack of pirates, "Bellamy's men, so help me!" and no more would he drink with them!

Little Johnnie Cole, who had often been scared into good behavior at the mention of "Black Bellamy," was eavesdropping. He ran like everything, and finally he ran to the house of Justice Doane. The Justice, a late sleeper, was annoyed, but at mention of the cargo of fine Madeira, he sprang up, gathered a posse and started for John Cole's house. At their approach, the pirates scurried out, went leaping over the headstones in the burying acre, and struck out up the highway. Justice Doane and his men went into the house.

The next day, staggering up the King's Road, were two befuddled parties. The pirates were still too drunk to do anything but reel up-Cape on foot, and the posse was too drunk to do anything but reel after them. But at last the law triumphed. The fugitives were taken to Barnstable jail, kept there through the summer, and on the fifteenth of November, six of them were hanged in Boston, among them John Brown of Jamaica, who listened to Cotton Mather's preaching until he went mad and gave back "blasphemes and Oathes." By that time, the cargo of the *Mary Anne* was judiciously divided and resting in the cellars of the law-abiding townsmen of the South Parish of Eastham.

At the north end of Pleasant Bay another pirate hoard, so the townsfolk say, still awaits a resurrecting spade. One end of Hogg Island is traditionally known as "Money Head" and there are recollections of actual digging undertaken there. History is hazy on the details of Captain Kidd's wanderings, yet I would definitely not subscribe to the theory, advanced locally, that it was Kidd who put a "box of gold" on Hogg Island. Kidd's "bagg put into a box, lockt and nailed, corded about and sealed," was left in many places, among them "on Gardiner's Island, at the eastern end of Long Island"; but the treasures of Pleasant Bay are plentiful enough, as she stands.

Your way around Orleans should lead you to Tonset, for a view of the harbor. Two miles from the intersection of the Tonset and East Orleans roads you pass an ancient little house bearing the inscription:

> HERE LIVED JOSHUA CROSBY, WHO COMMANDED
> A QUARTERDECK GUN ON THE FRIGATE CONSTI-
> TUTION DURING THE FIGHT WITH THE GUER-
> RIERE IN THE WAR OF 1812.

The house was a century old when Joshua lived in it. One of its tenants landscaped it with the bones of a whale.

There were two Cape Cod lads, as a matter of fact, aboard the *Constitution* in that fight, and one, a son of Harwich, gave a version of it which is included in the Chamber of Commerce booklet, *Cape Cod Legends*. This young man came back declaring that the brave fight was really won by "a bar'l o' merlarses."

"So sure was the *Guerriere* that the fight was theirs, that they placed a barrel of molasses on deck to be made into 'switchel' (a mixture of molasses, ginger, rum and water) with which to 'treat' the Yankees whom they expected to defeat. 'Switchel' was what was known as a 'landlubber's' drink and to be offered it was a supreme insult to the manhood of a tough jack tar in 1812.

"But good marksmanship raked the deck of the *Guerriere* early in the engagement. By good fortune one of these shots smashed the barrel of molasses. Over the deck the sticky mess ran, and, mixed with blood and water, it made the deck so slippery, it was almost impossible to obtain a foothold and man the ropes of the *Guerriere*. This was a serious handicap in maneuvering the ship, and so *Old Ironsides* won the fight 'by a bar'l of merlarses.' "

The improved Orleans-Provincetown highway, smoothing your course from this town to the Cape-end, cuts through a spot, about a mile beyond the village, long known as Jeremiah's Gutter. It was once, traditionally, owned by Jeremiah Smith. At this point, one of the narrowest parts of the "Narrow Land," your course turns northward.

When Bellamy's *Whidah* broke up off Well-fleet in 1717, there was a wild scramble all alongshore for her treasures, and the pickings were talked of for years. Henry Thoreau, walking the beach in 1849, picked up a French crown piece dated 1743, from a later wreck.

Cape folks living on the Back Side allowed no hundred-year tarnish to gather on silver coins before they set out a-wrecking. At the time of the *Whidah's* wreck, the Governor, knowing their habits, at once despatched a King's representative to the scene. Cape folk chuckled. But Captain Cyprian Southack set sail, anchored in Provincetown Harbor, and then scratched his head. He wanted a horse. Provincetown could offer him a whaleboat, but there was not a "shipshape" horse in town. So he took the whaleboat. He set out over the Bay, intending to take a horse at Orleans.

When he came to Boat Meadow Creek, on the Bay Side at Jeremiah's Gutter, the tide was still high. It was higher, in fact, than it had ever been known to flow before. The Captain kept steering. From Boat Meadow Creek he steered through Jeremiah's Gutter to Town Cove—to Nauset Harbor! He had—by the grace of God!— he had crossed the Cape in a whaleboat!

When he got there, he sat down, scratched his head again, tried to think how the devil you spell "excellency," and then wrote a letter to Governor Shute.

"At my Coming their I found the Rack all to Pices," he reported, "North and South, Distance from one a Nother 4 Miles. Sir, whear shee Strock first I se one Anchor at Low water, sea being so Great Ever sence I have ben here, Can not Come to se what maye be their for Riches, nor aney of her Guns."

Cape folk chuckled and hooted. When Captain Southack did finally "Come to se what maye be their for Riches," he found the *Whidah's* bones picked clean.

# CHAPTER VIII

## EASTHAM

*Provincetown for beauty,*
*Wellfleet for pride,*
*If it wasn't for milk cans*
*Eastham 'd' a' died.*

The poetry, anonymous and of aesthetic interest only to the Cape Cod schoolboy of another generation, had a point nevertheless. In the days when salt hay contented the cows and the customers were not too picky, every up-Cape train took on a cargo of milk from the Nauset dairy herds.

The youth of neighborhoods where local rivalry exists usually has its jingles, and the nameless young bards of Cape Cod have left several to posterity. To the milk can quatrain the Eastham lads might fling back:

*The Cape Cod girls they have no combs,*
*They comb their hair with codfish bones;*
*The Cape Cod boys they have no sleds,*
*They slide downhill on codfish heads.*

"Cape Cod," in the sense used here, referred to Provincetown, and up only as far as High Head, North Truro. There were other gems in the repertory, referring to Wellfleet residents as "Bible-faces," and to the good people of Harwich as "Hairleggers."

Even with her milk cans, Eastham was only a shadow of her former self, for in Old Colony times she had embraced Wellfleet as the North Parish and Orleans as the South. When she lost Orleans, in 1797, she was sheared of her most populous section, and it happened at a time when she was having thin years of her own, with an eroding soil and depleted forests. But the parting from Orleans was a parting for good; only the other day I ran across a newspaper story:

Orleans, Feb. 5—A fight to the finish with Eastham over ancient legislation governing control of the shell fishery was promised at the Orleans town meeting yesterday. . . . The assembly cheered when Moderator John Kenrick donated his $25 moderator's fee as the nucleus of a "fighting fund" to repel Eastham attacks on the Orleans town charter.

Yet Eastham makes many demands upon your attention. She is small, but her fourth dimension—time—stretches back to embrace teeming tracts on the unseen maps of history.

If I were judge of a beauty contest and the fifteen towns of Cape Cod were marched before my eyes, I think I should give the prize to Eastham. Her hard old features are not regular; her complexion is lumped and full of scars from her everlasting duel with the sea, and there is no "pose" in her smile, which comes grim and sparing through the wrinkles of centuries. But you will not have to look long to find "character" in this old townface, and like our Cape Cod landlady of another chapter, I would point out that there is nothing in the world like the bareness of her "back side."

Beyond admitting that I am in love with her, I shall not try to list the colors of her dunes or paint you the surf and the sunset. The sailing ships that Thoreau watched are now gone beyond all horizons, but the thirty-mile beachscape which he sketched is otherwise little changed. To tell you to read Thoreau, for such description, would be far wiser than to expect you to read me; but to tell you to go see, and hear and smell and feel the beach, is wisest of all. While surf rolls up to break on sand, this will ever be so.

The pear blossoms blow each spring over a spot in Eastham, just as they were blowing soon after a band of Plymouth adventurers had left their "poore church, like an anciente mother, growne old and forsaken of her children," to come to "a place called Nawsett." And in the flowering of a tree in that place, a story is kept alive from the time a little ship, well named the *Fortune,* sailed into Plymouth Harbor.

Thomas Prence was in his beginning twenties when he stepped ashore in 1621. Most of the *Fortune's* people were "lusty yonge men, and many of them wilde enough, who little considered whither or aboute what they went," but Thomas Prence was neither wild nor reckless. Like the others, he had neither "pot nor pan to drese any meate in," but unlike them, his eyes were on a single star, which shone coldly bright and was un-clouded by either fear for himself or pity for others.

Perhaps for love, or perhaps with an eye on the star, he moved auspiciously from the beginning, chose his friends and courted and married the preacher's daughter. "August 5, 1624—The ninth marriage at New Plymouth is of Mr. Thomas Prence with Mrs. [Miss] Patience Brewster."

Thomas was quite as religious as was required of him by his father-in-law's "singuler good gift of prayer," but "ye parsimonie of ye adventurers" aboard the *Fortune* was still fresh in his mind and "ye conceit of greate returne" brought out a strange hardness at times which Patience did not find it easy to understand. Thomas was not a simple man. Patience lived to see him take his place quickly among the leaders, and to celebrate his election as Governor of the Colony before he was 35. But she died in the interval between election and the day she would have become the little colony's First Lady.

A year after the death of Patience was added to the "sorrows, troubls &c." of old William Brewster, Thomas married again. Also, about that time, he began dubiously comparing his fortune in the new world with the dream-castles he had brought with him from the old. And at the end of ten years, 1644, he followed Edmund Freeman down the Cape, but not to stop at the settlement in Sandwich, nor in Barnstable nor Yarmouth, but on to a land of "richest soyle, for ye most part a blakish & deep mould, much like that wher groweth ye best Tobaco in Virginia."

The land at Nauset had already been "bought" of the Indians—at the wonderful prices our ancestors paid to these people—but Thomas Prence, John Doane and the other shrewd young men saw more open fields to the northward, and inspiration came with the view. They went to the Indians, demanding of them "who laid claim to Billingsgate [Wellfleet]." The red men looked at them. They thought of the Pamets (in Truro) who hunted and fished in "Billingsgate" when it pleased them; but so did they, the Nausets, hunt there.

Still hazy about the white man's use of this word "owned," the Indians answered that there was not any who *owned* it. "Then the land," said the young men, "is ours." And the Indians nodded and for lack of anything more illuminating to add, replied that "it was."

The young men went back to Plymouth, and there was plenty of time on the way to unite on a story. On their return, they told the other ambitious colonists that Nauset "would prove so straite, as it would not be competente to receive ye whole body, much less be capable of any addition or increase."

But half of Plymouth still shared Thomas Prence's hopes of enrichment and insisted on going with him. The April thaw had softened Nauset fields when the company arrived. There was time to plant corn and beans and to build snugly for the next winter. And there was timber for that in abundance. The rich soil needed only to be dug, and trees hewn.

Nauset prospered and in 1651 was named Eastham. Thomas Prence built his house near Fort Hill and one day, after a journey up-Cape, brought to his new wife, Mary, a little pear tree which some ship had fetched from the old country. He planted it near the house, and Mary cared for it.

Seven years after his removal to Cape Cod, Thomas was again elected Governor of the Colony. But if this must mean leaving Eastham, the Governor-elect, now middle-aged and well settled, declared he would forego the office. There was

nothing the General Court could do but to let
him govern from Eastham. It was a feather in the
cap of the Lower Cape. There he served for seventeen years, until his death in 1673.

Among his numerous children, the Governor
had two beautiful girls. Down from Sandwich,
one day, came a young man who fancied one of
the Prence girls, and under a pear tree whose
blossoms flickered silver on a clear night, a troth
was plighted. The young man went home and told
his brother about a girl and a pear tree, a marvelous clear night, and blossoms of silver. He said
the girl had a sister. And so, down from Sandwich
hurried another young man, and under the now
riotous flowering of the tree, a second troth was
plighted. The names of the young men were Edmund Freeman Junior and John Freeman.

You will find this note in Henry Thoreau's
book:
"There was recently standing, on what was once
his [Prence's] farm, in this town, a pear tree which
is said to have been brought from England, and
planted there by him, about two hundred years
ago. It was blown down a few months before we
were there. A late account says that it was recently
in a vigorous state; the fruit small, but excellent;
and it yielded on an average fifteen bushels. Some
appropriate lines have been addressed to it, by a
Mr. Heman Doane, from which I will quote,
partly because they are the only specimen of Cape
Cod verse which I remember to have seen (ah,
lucky Thoreau!) and partly because they are not
bad." One of the passages he quotes:

> *"That exiled band long since have passed away,*
> *And still, old Tree! Thou standest in the place*
> *Where Prence's hand did plant thee in his day,—*
> *An undesigned memorial of his race."*

But as you pass that place today, you will find on the spot where Thomas Prence set down his sapling, a pear tree flourishing still. For the link in the story that Thoreau missed, in his preoccupation with the poetry, was a cutting from the old tree, after it had been blown down in the gale he mentions.

The Doanes of Eastham, who owned the farm in Thoreau's time, were like other Cape Codders; they wasted not the good things of the earth— particularly when such things had a place in the tradition of a household. And so, a pear tree, descendant of English stock and the work once removed of the Governor's hand, still is on the Eastham farm where Thomas Prence lived. In South Eastham you will find an old cemetery at the right of the highway. There is a fork about three-tenths of a mile beyond this burying ground. Bearing right, just a few feet from the fork you are brought before a small white house, the home of a man who is in his eighties at this writing, and whose name is Abalino Doane. On Abalino's acres stood the Governor's house, and a few rods northeast, in a field, the pear tree still stands.

Abalino is a descendant of Deacon John Doane. Of the Deacon it is written that he lived to be 110 and had to be rocked in a cradle in his old age. However, the patient members of the family who had to rock him through the years got their satisfaction at long last—they buried him standing up!

The Deacon had left a brother, Daniel, in Plymouth. When Deacon John saw Eastham prosper, he sent for Daniel, who was a physician. One of Daniel's descendants (possibly in payment of an overdue doctor bill) acquired the Prence homestead. Abalino Doane inherited it a few generations later.

Timbers taken from the Prence house went into a barn, which stood as Eastham's oldest building until another northeast gale swept across the duneland and took it apart like the wonderful one-hoss shay. The stone doorstep was given to Provincetown for the Pilgrim Memorial, and is set at the base of that structure today.

About the time that Thoreau stopped at the Doane place, Captain Lincoln Dawson had just returned from a voyage in his trading schooner to Italy. Captain Dawson, a down-easter, had married a Doane, and when he came to visit at Eastham, he told all the folks about an opera he had attended abroad. It was a grand tale, and a grand, grand opera, and he wasn't certain of the title but he said it sounded like "Rosemandel and Abalino." And so, the first two grandchildren born after the Captain's return—conveniently a girl and a boy— were Rosemandel Doane and Abalino Doane.

On the hill hard by the site of the Governor's house once lived the Reverend Samuel Treat—he of the frightening religious doctrines and the still more frightening vocal chords. When, upon a calm summer day, the ridgepole of the Prence home began to creak and quake in sudden strain of a thousand vibrations through the rafters, as if struck by a "hauricane" sweeping over the hill, little Prences would stare in awe and gravely tell each other, "Mister Treat is laughing again!"

In the pulpit Sam Treat was as completely devastating as he was at home, though the nervous systems of the "praying Indians" were less subject to breakdown than those of the white neighbors. His voice, which "could be heard at a great distance from the meeting house, even amidst the shrieks of hysterical women and the winds that howled over the plains of Nauset" pleased his darkskinned congregation, and they seemed to take philosophically the dread world which he said awaited most of them.

"Impenitent sinners will writhe in hell," he boomed in brave crescendo, "with a thousand devils rending and tearing and mascerating them throughout all Eternity!" Then, sliding into diminuendo, "Some think that sinning ends with this life; but it is a mistake. The creature is held under an everlasting law; the damned increase in sin in hell. Possibly,"—to the Indians—"the mention of this may please thee. But remember, there shall be no pleasant sins there; no eating, drinking, singing, dancing, wanton dalliance, and drinking stolen waters;" and crescendo again, *"but damned sins, bitter, hellish sins; sins exasperated by torments, cursing God, spite, rage and blasphemy!"*

Yes, the Indians liked the "little father," and shrewdly they divined a warm heart under the breast that heaved with warnings of hills of brimstone and the clouds of sulphur. And when Sam Treat died in 1717, a thousand red men gathered around the little house on the hill. It was the winter of the "Great Snow," which heaped the drifts to impassable heights about the knoll—until the

praying braves had tunneled through so that Sam
Treat might be borne to the burying acre.

So says the historian. If you come to Cape Cod
in the winter and stand on this spot after a February northeaster has left all Nauset Sea a vast "kit-
tle-boil;" if you hear the booming of the breakers
as they carry over the Nauset Plain and echo with
a terrifying nearness from every sandpocket; or
if you are walking through the winter-quiet streets
of Provincetown and hear the roaring surf two
miles across the dunes, and if you mistake the
sound for the down-Cape train pulling up to Bradford Street—then you will have some apprecia-
tion of the sermons that could make an undertone
of the Atlantic; and you will not dismiss lightly
the words on a headstone that stands in the country
of the Nausets:

> *Here lies the Body of the Late Learned and Rev-*
> *erend Samuel Treat, the Pious and Faithful Min-*
> *ister of this Church, who, after a very Zealous Dis-*
> *charge of his Ministry for a Space of 45 Years and*
> *Laborious Travail for the Soules of the Indians, fell*
> *Asleep in Christ, March 1717, in the 69th yr. of*
> *his Age.*

The red-skinned Americans were not long in
vanishing, after their champion's death, and the
church also began to lose its white following. One
of his successors, the Reverend Mr. Shaw, found
it hard sailing indeed, and Peter Walker, the
"rhyming blacksmith of Eastham," sang his own
version over the anvil:

> *A learned Treat, a pious Webb*
> *And Cheever—all no more,*
> *Mister Shaw then took the helm*
> *And run the ship ashore.*

A quarter-mile from the highway, on a hill near the Prence homestead, a tall square mansard-roofed house looks across the slope and jealously guards its store of treasures—relics of the sort usually described as "priceless." These particular treasures are priceless principally because there is no active market; but they are treasures nevertheless. For the house is that of the Pennimans, and the strange collection that crowds its gloomy wall-space goes back to whaling days.

Seafaring Cape Codders were one and all afflicted with a mighty itch for souvenirs. In voyages to strange parts of the world, it was natural that they should come down with this infirmity, and the symptoms remain scattered throughout the Cape to this day. They brought home little souvenirs and big ones, huge ones, impossible ones. They brought some that would keep and they tried to bring some that wouldn't. And the oddities that the Cap'n fetched home to Marthy were stood along the mantel, hidden in the corners, stowed in trunks in the attic, and in the sheds out back. But they were saved somehow, no matter how many. They were "kept in the family," and keeping-in-the-family was an inescapable duty on the Cape.

"These are the very try-pots your grandfather Atkins had on the *Tilly H*," was the explanation many a Cape Cod child heard as he gazed at huge iron vessels that took up nearly all the play-space in the front yard. The most remarkable such keepsake I have run across was the collection of "blowed eggs and things" a Harwich woman showed me, which filled two rooms of her home. Her brother was a naturalist, and the "blowed eggs and things" consisted of more than a thousand stuffed birds, all the way from hummingbirds to condors; several alligator and snake skins; and an enormous assortment of blown birds' eggs, catalogued and kept in great chests. The whole was encased in glass, and I believe it deserved to be in some museum, but the lady on Gorham Road was "keeping it in the family," and probably her children will do the same.

In the Penniman collection are huge whale's teeth, the "baleen" of the right whale, ten feet long, and brought home somehow by Captain Edward Penniman from his voyages in the *Europa* and other barks. They are in the parlor. There, too, are scrimshawed whalebone and carved ivory, scores of little knicknacks that were laboriously cut and polished while the lookout searched in vain for spouts.

Pie was a great breakfast item in those days, and the "pie-rimer" with a little jag-wheel to make the marks was a favorite manufacture of the "scrimshanderer," though I don't see how the poor ladies could have made enough pies to wear out the rimers that were provided them. There are pie-rimers in the Penniman collection that only a fierce love for the pastry could have inspired.

On one of Captain Penniman's voyages his first mate was drowned, and at the next call of "Blo-o-ow!" he went in one of the boats himself. He had his wife and small son with him on that voyage, and they were left alone to keep ship. Watching the skipper make away on a doubtful chase, Mrs. Penniman suddenly saw a huge whale pop up in the lee of the vessel. She rushed to hoist the flag as a signal to the captain, and in her haste, hoisted it Union down. The skipper, seeing it, cried, "My God, the boy is dead!" and raced back. The whale waited to see the fun, was killed, and made $10,000 for the ship. Mrs. Penniman was forgiven.

In the Town Hall, in Middle Eastham, the story of an ancient and formidable land trust—the great Eastham Herbage Company—is kept "preserved" within the covers of three mottled volumes, records that start with the doings of the "77 Eastham Proprietors" in 1744. And these old books will never give up the secret of the land trust, because the "records" of its most important proceedings have been left blank.

Just as Thomas Prence, Deacon Doane and their colleagues recognized something for nothing at a great distance, so did the "77 Proprietors," whose purpose, it seems, was to lay claim to everything in sight and then go to court if necessary to fight it out. Anything that could be clawed away in this manner was to be sold for the best possible price, and the proceeds divided seventy-seven ways.

The project, conceived in delusions of grandeur, began auspiciously with what amounted to a declaration of a stock dividend. On July 19, 1744, it was voted "that each proprietor's name should be writ on a pees of paper and put in a hat and the number of each lot or meadow on another pees of paper and put in another hat." The simultaneous drawing of name and number was to determine ownership of the lots. David Doane and Joseph Smith were appointed tellers.

In this manner the land not under documented claim was divided. Anything else that looked easy also was appropriated. The land trust flourished. The 77 wizards had found the magic key which their forefathers had sought so diligently! It might even be possible to claim Harwich, or Barnstable, or even Plymouth, Boston, and rest of New England. Seventy-seven men of Eastham tossed on their beds, fevered out of all sleep by the bewitching lure of land.

Then the South Parish became a town, and it was discovered that almost all of the worthwhile holdings of "the 77" were now in the town of Orleans. Orleans formed her own "Proprietors," and they too joined forces and went to court. The "Orleans Canal Proprietors" came armed with plans for cutting a Cape Cod Canal through Jeremiah's Gutter, a project which previously had been spiked by the Eastham claims to the land at that place. The canal was never cut, but in a legal battle participated in by every amateur corporation lawyer on the Lower Cape, Orleans sued Eastham and won the verdict—$64.16.

The bubble was burst. The "77 Proprietors of Norsit" became the "Eastham Herbage Company," with grass to sell at Sunken Meadow. Dreams of annexing Boston went floating into spoondrift over the dunes. Shares of the great land trust plummeted to 88 cents. Seventy-seven men of Eastham slept unburdened for all time of the restless vision of every man a king.

I have touched on the strange and wonderful accomplishments of mascots in our Coast Guard stations, and the astounding findings of the surfmen in the field of zoology. But I was reserving a few notes on the business end of this service for Eastham, for here you have an opportunity to see a modern station, accessible by motor.

An appealing picture is usually made of the Massachusetts Humane Society and its work, beginning "as early as 1776" for the aid of shipwrecked sailors. These chroniclers usually skip the fact that the freezing gales of a hundred years had been taking their toll of shipwrecked sailormen before that time. Nothing was done to provide havens for them, and when, at last, sparing outlays were made for shelter, these rude shacks were "but a stage to the grave." Thoreau is authority for this, and his book (Chapter IV) gives the only contemporary glimpse at the other side of the picture.

"Far away in some desolate hollow by the seaside, just within the bank, stands a lonely building on piles driven into the sand," he writes, "with a slight nail put through the staple, which a freezing man can bend, with some straw, perchance, on the floor on which he may lie, or which he may burn in the fireplace to keep him alive. Perhaps this hut has never been required to shelter a shipwrecked man, and the benevolent person who promised to inspect it annually, to see that the straw and matches are here, and that the boards will keep off the wind, has grown remiss and thinks that storms and shipwrecks are over; and this very night a perishing crew may pry open its door with their numbed fingers and leave half their number dead here by morning."

There was plenty of heroism, of course, on the part of men who made up the life-saving crews. A vivid account of the rescues and the tragedies that took place along this coast in the last years of the Nineteenth Century, the days of the four-masters, is given in a book now out of print, *The Life Savers of Cape Cod,* by John W. Dalton. Dalton died many years ago, but mariners generally recognize the authenticity of his book, which is full of first-hand accounts and photographs he made while he was covering wrecks of Cape Cod for the newspapers.

On the north shore of Nauset Inlet still stands a little gray shack, the boat-house of the old Humane Society. The rescue of five men and the captain's wife from the British schooner *Walter Miller* in 1897, after she had run aground on Nauset Bars in heavy surf, wrote a heroic finis to the career of this station, which was the last on the Cape. The shack is still used as a boat-house, privately owned, and the station itself is now a home in East Orleans.

In 1872 the U. S. Life Saving Service had finally been established, and in 1915 this branch was combined with the Revenue Cutter Service, to form the Coast Guard Department. Thus the work of the Coast Guard now combines saving of life and property with prevention of smuggling and other irregularities, and the entire force is also kept adaptable to other uses in event of war.

The service in time of peace is under control of the Treasury Department. One peaceful day in the summer of 1935, Secretary of the Treasury Henry Morgenthau was visiting the Cape. His party was picnicking on Nauset Beach, when a sudden thunderstorm overtook them. The Commander-in-Chief knew where to run. He led his friends into the old Nauset Coast Guard Station, took possession of the galley, and had the picnic indoors. Visitors were welcome at the stations, but littering up the galley with banana peels and sardine cans was strictly against the rules. Boatswain Nickerson promptly told these nervy strangers as much. The Secretary said he wasn't exactly a visitor, and when he introduced himself to the bo'sun, the banana peels were all right.

The bo'sun took Morgenthau's party through, on an inspection of the plant, which had been in use more than sixty years and was then one of the oldest units in the service. He showed Morgenthau where the tides had eaten away the bank, too, so that only 30 feet remained in front of the station, where there had been 160 feet when the building was erected. He said it wasn't very stable. And Morgenthau, who had dabbled a bit in stabilization, nodded thoughtfully.

A few weeks later from Washington came authorization of a new station at Nauset.

The way to the station leads off the main road a short distance beyond Town Hall. From the tower room you can see both shores of the Cape, and below you will find the newest equipment in the business, including the improved beachcart trailer with big tires; the modern Hunt gun which shoots a line aboard a stranded vessel, and the breeches buoy which follows; and you may inspect the surfboat, the signalling apparatus, and the inside wind indicator. There is some equipment in the gun closet in the keeper's room which is brought out only on special occasions.

You can hear the boys tell you about beach patrol too, and what good clean fun it is—when you don't have to dig sand out of your face. And sometimes they may tell you of their adventures when they are "home good"—which means on leave.

To see them in beachcart or breeches buoy drill, which follows regular schedules, is a nice summer diversion; but to see them at work, in a February gale, offers thrills of a wholly different sort. The Nauset station reported giving major assistance in four cases for the year 1936; one life saved; 29 persons on board vessels assisted; 42 instances of "miscellaneous assistance;" and valuation of property saved $79,450.

A man on beach patrol from Peaked Hill, farther down-Cape, fights his way through driving snow, sees a liner heading, through some miscalculation, towards the deadly bars offshore. He fires his Coston signal, the ship answers with a rocket and clears off. The man trudges on, having saved perhaps hundreds of lives. And the incident goes down in the book as one instance of "miscellaneous assistance."

On a day in February of 1936, seven lads of the CCC camp in Brewster went on a lark. Great sheets and blocks of ice overlay the Bay. There was a novel thrill in climbing over the frozen crust of the harbor. Other kids had done it, and when water-wise Cape Codders had chased them off, they had come back and told what fun it was. Out these seven lads went. Hours later, horror spread through the camp, and wires shot out the news that seven CCC youths were adrift on a fugitive ice floe "somewhere on Cape Cod Bay."

That night crowds of helpless boys stood on the shore and built fires, shivered in the ten-degree blasts that raked the beach and prayed that their fellow workers could be reached before they were frozen to death or drowned. And that night Coast Guard forces were mobilized from end to end of the Cape; planes were called for; the Coast Guard cutter *Harriet Lane* set out, despite the fact that she was not built for icebreaking; and newspapers took the story over the nation that seven young lives were balanced on a cake of ice off the Massachusetts coast.

Twenty hours later, after all hope had been abandoned, the *Harriet Lane* was still grinding and crashing her way through the ice.

"Visibility was less than half a mile that morning," says Chief Boatswain Feddersen, who was skippering the cutter. "A thick snowstorm had turned into rain and sleet. By daylight we were about a mile and a half off Wellfleet, when a plane circled over the ship. The flyers waved and pointed to the east and south. We followed that course, and about 8 o'clock I raised the boys through high-powered glasses in the pilot house.

"At first I sighted five of them, all in a clump. They were moving up and down, which told me they were still alive and not bad off. Then I saw the other two boys about a mile to the southwest. Then we ran into some extra bad ice, up to ten feet thick, and piled up six to eight feet high. Finally we got within a quarter of a mile of the five boys, and the other two started walking towards us.

"I ordered a dory over. I did not know what condition the boys were in, suspected they would be much worse off than they were. While they were dragging the dory over the ice, we managed

to get the ship out of a bad jam and work her
to a point within twenty yards of the boys.

"My men walked the lads—all except young
Fitzsimmons, whose feet were frozen—back to the
*Harriet Lane,* to keep them active. They brought
Fitzsimmons in the dory. The crew rubbed ice on
his feet; that's the cure for frostbite.

"The boys were crazy with joy as they climbed
over the rail. They ran around and around the
deck, shouting and punching each other like school
kids. Lucky for those boys that the wind changed
from south to nor'west, or they would have been
swept out to sea before we could reach them!"

On that same Monday morning, a Washington
newspaper columnist was sitting in his office. And
while the seven boys were punching each other
and yelling for joy, his fingers were punching the
keys of a typewriter:

> *Treasury and Postoffice bills carry bigger allowances*
> *this year—partly natural growth and partly fancy*
> *trimmings like airplanes for the Coast Guard.*

The career of the Coast Guard as a marine de-
tective force to fight rum running and other smuggling is a dramatic continued story—continued to
this day—but it is kept as far as possible from the
public eye. Now and then it does pop into the
news, and of course rumors are always afloat.
There is a whole new category of modern sea yarns
on Cape Cod, half legend, half fact, spun around
the "hot cargoes" of prohibition times and the
years since. When you get to Provincetown, where
most of the rum running went on, you may hear
a few.

Nauset Light, a mile from the Coast Guard station, has been shining since 1838, with a new tower set up each time the sea bowls the old one over. The present tower was once one of twin lights of Chatham, and now these two bright-eyed old ladies of the beach exchange quick glances across the strands of Nauset.

Seth Knowles' windmill has turned modest in her later days, hiding behind the houses that line the highway across the road from Town Hall. When she was in her prime she was a grand worker, and even now she can crush a lively bushel if the wind is right. But in those days—when she sat on a hill in South Eastham and was fed by farmers for miles around—nobody passed her by, as thousands of tourists have been doing lately. Kids watched her in awe as the sails filled to a brisk sou'wester and majestically cut great circles out of the sky; and they stood for hours waiting for Miller Seth to haul taut on his brakes and heave to; for then, if his "dispepsy" wasn't ailing him too bad, he'd let 'em go aloft, up in the cap, and see her great fan-shaft—bigger timber, it was, than a Grand Banker's mainboom—her giant hand-hewn gear and the massive spindle that turned the stone down on the grist deck.

All this machinery is still here in the old mill, and on Saturday afternoons in the summer time, if there's a fit breeze of wind, Miller John Fulcher sets his sails, swings her into the wind's eye, fills the hopper and gives the lift-wheel a spin. Miller John, now nearing eighty, sits at the helm and gravely dips his thumb into the trough to test the "grind." He has the "miller's thumb;" he is the

last of a proud list of "dry-land sailors" of Cape
Cod.

Almost to 1900 the Seth Knowles Mill was a
going business, ready to take any man's grist at a
"pottle" of two quarts to the bushel, and promising
to have it ready on next grinding day. Then the
business fell off, and Miller John turned to selling
hay. The mill was idle many years, until at last
the town of Eastham bought her, just to "keep her
in the family." And now Miller John takes the
helm in the summer time—when the wind is right
—to show off-Capers "how they did it in the old
days."

Folks stop when they hear her grinding. The
old windmiller has put her through her paces before crowds of up to a thousand at such times.
Yet the best that is in her—a glimpse of the seven-
foot hand-made peg-wheel, the homely old stones,
the smell, the weathering of her oaken frame—
these things are any man's for the asking. If she's
closed and locked, the key is across the road, in
Town Hall.

To me, this old mill is an historical exhibit of
the first rank—a bit of the dead past which lives
and breathes still, which sings at her work and
is close, endearingly close, to the earth and sky
together. I have a copy of Blunt's *American Coast
Pilot,* which aided the mariners of a hundred
years ago, by listing landmarks. This 1833 edition
notes "a windmill on a hill over the salt mills
which is near the shore at Eastham."

The date 1793 is nailed into a board inside the
mill, but this might have been placed upon her
arrival in Eastham, and does not necessarily mark
her real age. The history of the individual wind-

mills of this type is not clearly set forth, and accounts of the Eastham relic vary. The truth is that nobody knows on good evidence when she was first built or where she came from. She is of the type that Millwright Tom Paine designed. Millwright Paine was an Eastham man, and he was wanted all over the Cape by towns that clamored for mills. You could buy a mill then for £75— something less than the price of a new Ford car today; but nobody could build a mill as taut and trim as Tom Paine's. In 1683, he put up two such plants in Eastham. The mills were bought and sold, "dismasted" and moved, traded back and forth. For all we know of her, these old timbers may have braced older machinery, that once was grinding corn for the "sumpy" on a great table around which sat Sam'l and Eliza Treat and their eleven children.

Continuing Bay-ward from the mill, the Samoset Road leads to a slight rise by the beach, and a tablet here marks the "First Encounter" the *Mayflower* company had with hostile Indians. Let William Bradford tell it at first hand:

"But presently, all on ye sudain, they heard a great & strange crie, which they knew to be the same voyces they heard in ye night, though they varied their notes, & one of their company being abroad came runing in, & cried, 'Men, Indeans, Indeans'; and wthall, their arrowes came flying amongst them. Their men rane with all speed to recover their armes, as by ye good providence of God they did. . . . The crie of ye Indeans was dreadfull, espetially when they saw ther men rune out of ye randevoue towourds ye shallop, to recover

their armes, the Indieans wheeling aboute upon
them. But some runing out with coats of malle on,
& cutlesses in their hands, they soone got their
armes, & let flye amongs them, and quickly stopped
their violence."

Bradford also explains, though the memorial
tablet doesn't, that the reason the Indians were
hostile was that "one Hunt, a mr. of a ship" had
been there six years before and had seized twenty-
four of the Indians and carried them to Spain,
where he "sold those silly savages for rials of
eight."

There is a story, too—a long and involved one
that has taken on much verbal avoirdupois in the
telling and retelling—about a schooner that went
aground on the nearby flats during the War of
1812.

The vessel was one of the prizes of the British
ship-o'-the-line *Spencer,* Richard Raggett in command. Other prizes were an Eastham skipper,
Hoppy Mayo by name, and two barrels of rum
that had been taken from his whaleboat. Commodore Raggett, every other inch a gentleman, liked
the simple, forthright cut of the Yankee's jib, and
Hoppy's innocence and the Commodore's own
liquor invited confidences.

For these bloody silt-harbors, the Commodore
said, a man wanted a pilot who knew the shoals
and the deeps. How the devil was a man to carry
out orders when he couldn't make in close enough
to land a two-pound ball? Hoppy nodded, sympa-
thy beclouding his round face. Another drink, and
he offered to pilot the schooner.

She left Provincetown, with Hoppy Mayo and

twenty-three Britishers aboard. So was Hoppy's rum, and to pass the time, he broke it out for Lieutenant Fotheringay, who was in command of the prize. When Hoppy had drunk the Britisher under the table, he took a couple of pistols, heaved the rest of the ship's arms overboard, battened down the hatch on twenty-one sailors in the fo'cs'le, took over the helm at gunpoint, and steered the schooner for home. On the Eastham flats he grounded her, and when a crowd of townsmen came out to the aid of a stranded Marblehead schooner, they were greeted by neighbor Hoppy Mayo with twenty-three infuriated British prisoners.

Northward again on the highway, you are going through the asparagus country—acres of the "Truro grass," as Cape Codders call this vegetable, which has become an important source of income in Eastham's later days. All sorts of truck gardening are done in Eastham, but asparagus is the big crop. You can get a field of asparagus under way in three or four years, at a cost of about $500 an acre. I have read that the returns after that may run as high, in good times, as 25 per cent on the investment. But every time I have talked with a "Truro grass man," I have been told that times were "still pretty bad." On the acres which are now spread with commercial fertilizer, the Indians once spread fish—principally horseshoe crabs, chopped up—and seaweed and sometimes oyster shells. When the land "ran out," they let it grow to timber, then burned it off and started all over again. Their crops were the "corne & beans of various collours" which the needy Pilgrims found cached.

A short distance north of Eastham Center the
highway passes a cemetery, where one of the
hardest-driving shipmasters of the Cape has gone
to his just reward. When Captain Freeman Hatch
took his clipper ship, the *Northern Light,* out of
San Francisco on a return voyage to Boston in
1853, he had been offered a new suit of clothes if
he could beat the *Trade Wind,* which had sailed
three days before.

Captain Hatch not only won his suit of clothes,
but reached home in 76 days, 8 hours, a sailing
record never equalled. When he arrived in Boston,
he admitted that he had "strained the ship dread-
fully." He said nothing about straining the ship's
people, nor does the stone in this cemetery have
any word of the crew, in its commemoration of the
"Astonishing Passage," an "Achievement Won By
No Other Mortal Before Or Since."

# CHAPTER IX

## WELLFLEET

*On U. S. 6, between Eastham and Truro. Eight miles between Wellfleet town lines.*

> "I've thought, if I ever met a learned man I should like to ask him this question. Can you tell me how *Axy* is spelt, and what it means? *Axy*," says he; "there's a girl over here is named *A'xy*. Now, what is it? What does it mean? Is it Scripture? I've read my Bible twenty-five years, over and over, and I never come across it."
>
> "Did you read it twenty-five years for this object?" I asked.
>
> "Well, how is it spelt? Wife, how is it spelt?" She said, "It is in the Bible; I've seen it."
>
> "Well, how do you spell it?"
>
> "I don't know. A-c-h, ach; s-e-h, seh—Achseh."
>
> "Does that spell *Axy*? Well, do you know what it means?" he asked, turning to me.
>
> "No," I replied, "I've never heard the sound before."

This passage occurs in the chapter of Thoreau's *Cape Cod* entitled "The Wellfleet Oysterman." I have an old second-hand copy of this work, which I bought of a down-Cape dealer, and in the margin alongside the passage, I find, in a faint and trembling hand:

"Judges, I, 13, the old fool."

The lower-Cape gibes at Wellfleet's "Bible-faces," like most schoolboy apocrypha, stemmed from truth. There were fishing captains of this town, a century ago, who ordered strict observance

of the Sabbath, and who went wild-eyed in an
agony of inner conflict as they read the Scrip-
ture to their crews while some godless Gloucester
craft lay in plain sight off the starboard bow, haul-
ing up a full fare of mackerel or cod. But there
may have been some satisfaction for their regretful
ghosts in the case of a man whom we will call Joe
Crocker—because he is still a neighbor—and who
once ran an establishment with a name something
like "The Fisherman's Haven & Handy Outfitter."

One Sunday afternoon Joe was strolling down
the beach when he came across a school of stranded
blackfish—"puffin' pigs," as they were called. The
sparm oil man, who "tried out" the heads of these
creatures, would pay as high as four dollars for
the "melon" under the skull. According to the law,
the man who first cut his initials in a "beached pig"
was the rightful claimant.

Joe got out his knife and worked like fury,
"wishing his name was Ira so's he wouldn't have
to bother cutting the jibboom on the J." He was
finishing up the last few fish when Pastor Williams, the little old white-haired Methody minister, overtook him.

"Working on the Sabbath, eh, Mr. Crocker?"

"No such thing, Pastor," said Joe, taking his
knife by the blade and letting fly to flick out a
period in the last fish. "Just playing mumblety-
peg."

The Pastor raked him crossways and departed
with a last warning:

"Laugh me off today, Joe Crocker, but you'll
have the devil to pay tomorrow!"

Early next morning Joe was down at the try-
works to sell his fish. But the sparm oil man handed

Joe a copy of the newspaper. There, on the front page, was a long piece about new oil discoveries in Pennsylvania, and about how they were sure to scuttle the whale-oil market. The sparm man was buying no more!

Two days later a committee of townsmen called at the Fishermen's Haven. They came to tell Joe he'd have to clear his blackfish off the flats. He refused, pointing out that the fish were there of their own accord; he had not gone to sea and driven them ashore.

Next day Joe's fish turned "real severe." The wind had shifted to the s'uthard, bringing some relief to the town, but now delegations began coming in from towns further up-Cape. And they were furious. It looked like civil war. Then Pastor Williams stepped in. He declared Joe Crocker was responsible; the fish were his, they bore his mark.

Finally, Joe had to give in. He hired twenty men and half a dozen flounder-draggers to tow his fish out to sea. Joe Crocker, for one, had learned it paid to keep the Sabbath holy.

Anything that "might come in handy some day" found its way into the Cape Codder's attic; and for most of the gimcracks thus disposed of, "some day" has not yet arrived. Here is the story of Arthur Rogers, and one gimcrack that had to wait forty years to have its day.

The first horseless wagon was yet to chug down the King's Road. Arthur Rogers, known for miles both ways as the "buggy-man of Wellfleet," was behind his orders. Old Cap'n Bearse was clamoring for his sulky in time to enter her in the races up to Harwich, and there was Seth Chipman's "democrat," that wanted a deal of tautening up. Arthur stood in his carriage yard, wondering where to begin, when a stranger opened the gate and pushed in a wheel-barrow—an "Irish locomotive," as the seamen called it. The barrow carried a general cargo of boxes, bags, and other dunnage, but she was making heavy weather up the shell-path.

"Got to have a new wheel," the stranger said. "Can you fit me out?"

"I can do it in a biding time," Arthur answered. "You can see what I've got ahead of me here."

"I'm in a hurry, mister. And I'm broke, too. But I tell you what. You put me on a wheel, and I'll give you this here fiddle in pay. It's the only thing I got that you'd want just now."

Arthur shook his head. "Don't play," he said.

The stranger kept after him, and gave him a long, sad story. Finally, to get him out of the way, Arthur fitted him out with a wheel, and the fiddle was stowed in the attic. The stranger went up the highway and was seen no more.

Forty years later, Miss Una Rogers sat in her home on Main Street, Wellfleet, and read in the paper a fascinating story about old violins. She remembered something that looked like the case of a fiddle, stowed away in the attic, and went to dig it out.

Inscribed in the case, but readable only in a good light, was the legend:

ANTONIUS & HIERONYMUS FR AMATI
CREMONEN ANDRAEA FIL F 1622

And now, a quotation from the encyclopaedia:

*Amati (the brothers) Andrea and Nicolo. They were the first of a great Italian family of violin makers and the founders of the Cremona school. Their instruments are now esteemed of priceless value. Andrea was succeeded by two sons, Antonio and Geronimo, whose services to the craft were also signal. . . . From Nicolo Amati, son of Geronimo ("Hieronymus") the art of violin making was carried on by an apprentice in his school, Antonio Stradivari.*"

Wellfleet has recently lost an island. The ocean, like an indecisive sculptor, putters around with Cape Cod, chipping off here and slapping on there, to suit its mood of the moment; and the recent disappearance of the island of Billingsgate is one of its most striking changes in the design.

Half a century ago there were more than thirty houses, a school and a lighthouse on Billingsgate, and people not only fished there; they tilled the soil as well. But when southwest breezes began to salt the clam-pie and the cod muddle with sea-spray, they moved to the mainland. A Boston doctor bought the island for a summer home, and built a clubhouse for gunners. When he sold it to another Bostonian about twenty years ago, only five acres were left of it. Still later the Federated Bird Clubs took over the shrinking remnant as a refuge for wildfowl. In 1935 high tide began to cover the mudflat—all that now remained of Billingsgate. And when a tax exemption form was sent to the Bird Clubs to fill out, it was returned with a letter explaining that the Clubs had made of Billingsgate Island "a gift to the Commonwealth of Massachusetts." I do not know whether the Commonwealth ever acknowledged the "gift." The tides acknowledge nothing.

"Billingsgate—abusive, violent invective (from the scolding of fishwomen in Billingsgate market)."

The fish market near London Bridge began business in 1558, and was well known to our own Pilgrim fathers. They called the whole Wellfleet region after the place in London, and Wellfleet Harbor they called Grampus Bay, because of the blackfish they saw stranded there.

In 1763, when Billingsgate set itself off from Eastham, as a town in its own right, it was a busy settlement of fishermen, many of whom were concerning themselves entirely with oysters. So important was this branch of the trade that when they came to name the new town after some village of old England, they chose Wallfleet, celebrated for its excellent oysters. But they were more expert with their oyster rakes than they were with their quill-pens, and Wellfleet was the nearest they could get with their spelling.

Seven years later the native oysters of Wellfleet had all died—possibly of mortification at being named after a bed of off-Cape furriners—and from then on, oysters were shipped from the south to be planted in Wellfleet Harbor. In late years the business found hard going, and the final blow came in 1936 with the shutdown of D. Atwood & Company, "Wellfleet oyster growers for the last thirty years." This has probably meant the end of the Wellfleet oysterman in any commercial capacity. The thing that finished the modern industry was a tiny parasite, known as the "drill," which works its way through the shell of the oyster, and for which an effective exterminant has not yet been found.

Wellfleet has found the sea a capricious mistress indeed. The town has been a center of fishing, ship-

building, whaling and coasting. But always the
sea-ways changed, each time leaving Wellfleet's
industries hard aground. Men who went to sea for
a living would give up in disgust—with the resolve
to walk inland, like Odysseus, with a pair of oars
"until somebody asks what they are for."

The Wellfleeter can still rake up a mess of
quahaugs, and with her neighbors the town shares
in a fair amount of lobstering. A summer visitor
once asked "why all those chickencoops were
stacked along the wharf;" and after such an insult,
the lobstermen declared, it wasn't any wonder that
no lobsters would walk into the pots for a month
after!

But within the lobstermen's own circles, a question still burns, open to fierce argument on both
sides. If you can state and prove which way a
lobster goes into a pot—bow first or stern first—you
will be doing the trade a vast service.

Debate on this point can go on in a shanty for
hours. One stove-side orator declares that he has
hung over the rail and watched lobsters in two
fathom of clear water, and the smaller fry have
shot in bow-first in their fright when a bigger fellow approached. But his dory-mate counters that
the big fellow went in stern-to. I have even heard
a compromise held out for—a combination entrance, with the lobster sliding into the anteroom
head-on and then reversing to get into the bait-
chamber. And at this point there is usually another
round of Portygee prune whiskey.

People who live near the Cape Cod Canal have
found a simpler way to catch lobsters. At low tide,
just before the New York boat goes through and
stirs up the water, they lower a bait and stand by

with an eel spear. The law forbids traps in the Canal—which is trap enough by itself—but there are plenty of lobsters there, and spearing a salad is no great chore.

No one has yet determined how large a lobster can grow. It seems to depend mainly on how long he can go on living before he is caught. One has been preserved in the Museum of Natural History in New York, with a live weight of 34 pounds. Aboard the Coast Guard cutter *Faunce,* which often beats in Cape waters, there were preserved the claws of a 25-pounder, which measured a yard from tail to clawtip. A Cape fishing vessel presented him to the cutter one day, out of gratitude for the loan of a pilot.

Across Wellfleet Bay, and adhering to the Cape by a narrow thread of beachway, lies a deserted fragment of land which the historians seem to have overlooked. The place is called Great Island, and though it has been reached by a few hardy motorists, there is no road. The ruins of a building— some ancient structure with a stockade around it— have been buried in these outlying sands, a discovery so unexpected by the townsmen who chanced across it that they started excavations, thinking perhaps it was once a Dutch trading post. They have been puttering with it ever since.

The building was found to have been 100 feet long, the walls of planking caulked with clay, and the windows heavily leaded. On the site, a collection of knives, forks, spoons, clay pipes and pewter buttons has been unearthed, plus one English coin dated 1723.

The local historian recalls that these islands west

of the present townsite were chosen for earliest settlement, particularly Billingsgate, Great Island
and Bound Brook Island. As long as they keep
their heads above tidewater, I should think the
latter two would offer fair possibilities to the treas-
ure-seeker—unless his interests are confined wholly
to pirate gold. On searching for the latter, I have
no more practical hints to give here than I had at
Orleans—though Wellfleet, too, has run temperatures from this same fever. Wellfleet's "pirate
gold" lies somewhere on the ocean shore. There I
shall let it remain, at least until we get there.

I have heard that it is witch-haunted, this
ground on both sides of the town line as you enter
Wellfleet from the south.

Although several witches have been mentioned
as haunters of the place, investigation reveals only
one with proper credentials—the Sea Witch of
Billingsgate—but she has a number of exploits to
her credit. They pop up through several centuries
of local lore, suggesting almost as many lives for
this creature as for the cat who was one of her
ever-present "familiars."

Her main interest appears to have been in the
marine phase of the business—contriving for the
souls of lost sailors and such—but she has taken
many a flyer among landlubbers too. Wherever she
may show, you can spot her by her heels. They
were a weakness with her, those high red heels,
and she affected them even at the risk of being
frequently betrayed. Also, if business should ever
take her abroad o' nights again, you will know her
by her familiars running alongside—a cat and a
gray goat with one glass eye.

Frankly, the chances are against meeting her. She has become inactive over these half-dozen decades just past. For one thing, business at sea has fallen off; and then, these Portuguese people have brought over effective countercharms from the Old Country. We know now that if any witch should start cutting up didoes around our house, we can drive her away once and for all by sticking pins in the heart of a calf and dropping the heart down the chimney.

But the science of preventive conjury was unknown here in the heyday of the Sea Witch of Billingsgate. Some said she was a red girl, some said she was white. In her time, it is clear, she was both. Having heard something of the talents of these creatures, I would not begrudge her a Scot's plaid.

But her color or her form at a given time depended on the soul that was "betaken" by her at the moment. The notion that there was more than one witch operating in the territory is grossly unfair to the Lower Cape towns. It is a libel, an old wives' tale. And I should firmly refuse to believe anything—except, of course, that there was a Sea Witch of Billingsgate, and that her familiars were a cat and a gray goat with one glass eye.

Among the poor souls that were "betaken" was pretty little Goody Hallett of Eastham. Goody was only fifteen, and no more knowful of the black arts than a babe in swaddlecloth.

One spring night in 1715, Goody was seduced; and the following winter she was apprehended, lying in a barn, with a dead baby in her arms. She was at once whisked into the village, seized up to

Deacon Doane's fine new whipping-post and given a lashing as a sort of preliminary to the real punishment that awaited the outcome of her trial for murder. Pending that, she was clapped into Eastham Gaol.

The poor girl asked only that she be allowed to die, and while the town fathers were inclined to oblige her in this, a little writhing first, they thought, might serve as a valuable warning to others of the godless younger generation of their day. The gaoler was cautioned against bringing Goody any victuals that wanted cutting with a knife.

One afternoon, while the girl was beating wildly against the bars of her cell window, a stranger sauntered up to the wall and stood looking in at her. He was dressed in fine French bombasset, and he carried a gold-tipped cane. Something about his gaze quieted Goody and kept her spellmoored. One of the iron cell bars stood between their faces. He reached out, took it lightly between his thumb and finger, and flicked it away—clean out of the window-frame—as if it were no more than a stray bit of ryestraw. Then he smiled and slowly shook his head.

"Ah, these stiff-necked hymn-bellerin' Yankees! I tell ye, sometimes they make me feel like the rawest greeny ever went on the account!"

The words meant nothing to little Goody Hallett, but in the man's voice there was something smooth and wisterly, something that tautened the spell.

"Now, my girl," he went on, flicking another bar out of the window, "I'm going to play ye fair and square, cross my—er, by yer leave. Ye're

young, but ye've showed old enough, sartin, for
the employment I can get ye. Ye can forget all
this, child," and with a gesture, he tossed away still
another bar from the window. "Yer life's still before ye. 'Tis all in the future— yes, hmm!"

Soothingly, softly, he went on talking to her, but
once he had led up to it properly, he made no bones
about who he was. And as he spoke, from time to
time he punctuated his remarks by taking out the
bars from the window, until all were gone, and
Goody Hallett's way to freedom lay clear. Also,
the while he spoke, the girl felt bitter against those
who had not let her die; and beguiled into venge-
ful thoughts, she listened and nodded.

At last he took a paper from his waistcoat.

"Can ye write, Goody? Well, no matter. A
mark's as good. Just put it there, where the line's
broken into small grains." He touched a gold quill
to his tongue, and as Goody took the quill, she
observed that the tip glistened scarlet. She was
about to make the mark when he caught her arm.

"What! Tricks, is it? So soon?" His eyes were
suddenly like fiery drills, and his fingers bruised
her. But after a moment, he smiled again. "Young,
aye! I forget ye're but a child, Goody Hallett. Go
on and make yer mark; but if it's to be two lines,
ye'll oblige me to make 'em slantindicular, like an
X—not any other way."

Goody understood. And that night she disappeared from Eastham Gaol, and before her case
could come up in General Court, the town of Eastham found that locks and bars could not hold
Goody Hallett. No one seems to have thought of
using silver "darbies" on her wrists—which would
have done the trick—or else no one in Eastham

was willing to give Deacon Doane's gaoler the loan of the silver. At any rate, Goody was finally "warned out" of Eastham town; and so she crossed into Billingsgate, where she lived in a lorn hut on the poverty-grass meadow, and where etarnal-strange capers were cut each night before cock-crow.

It is said that she, like Ichabod Paddock's lady-friend, took up quarters in a whale, and that she went cruising about, with a ship's light hung to the creature's tail, luring unwary mariners on the shoals. She dealt also in tempests, dabbled a bit in hurricanes, and now and then singled out some skipper who caught her fancy, to take him out at night, whisk him from the deck of his ship, bridle him and ride him up and down Cape Cod, and then send him back before morning, worn and creak-j'inted from the cruel exertions. Now and then she selected a strong, good-looking young fo'mast hand for other kinds of "divarsion." For Goody, in her later years, had become a deep-dyed sinner, whom you would never have taken for the blossoming maid, once the pride of the hymn-sing-ing Halletts of Eastham town.

Now, it has been said that the man who ruined Goody on that moonlit occasion under an old apple tree in 1715 was Black Bellamy himself. But I suspect that the tale grew of the fact that the pirate happened to be in Eastham in that year, and was wrecked two years later in the waters hard by. I have no doubt that Goody had a hand in brewing the April hurricane that brought on disaster to Bellamy's ship, the *Whidah*. But if she did, she was merely cooperating with her employer as she

had done in a long string of other shipwrecks in
the territory.

As the record shows, Sam Bellamy was a simple,
blustering windbag of a fellow, and a furriner at
that; and I doubt if he was capable of the un-
common finesse it wanted, to trick the prettiest girl
in a Cape Cod town. It wants a mite of doing to
win one of these creatures, and in the version which
I have heard of Goody's first fall, it seems to me
the native touch was present.

The last official appearance of the Sea Witch of
Billingsgate was as an Indian, living in the north
end of town. On the record she is set down as
Delilah Roach, and Delilah is described by the
historians as the "sole survivor of the tribe of
Nausets."

Well, Delilah herself insisted on having it that
way. When the suspicion got around town that she
was the Sea Witch, she marched right into the
town clerk's office, to straighten the thing out—the
way she wanted it straightened. And the town
clerk, though he knew very well that Delilah's
late husband, Simon Roach, had been the last *real*
Indian, was not the man to cross Delilah. Her
black eyes burned with the Unholy Powers as she
stood over his table and commanded him to write,
and as she commanded, so it was written. Delilah
Roach was set down as the "last Indian." And as
she flounced out of the office, the town clerk stole
a glance at her. Beneath the hem of her skirt, which
just missed sweeping the floor, his eye caught a
brief spot of scarlet, now on the left side, now
on the right.

Other townsfolk, even to the selectmen themselves, knew the importance of avoiding a "black conjury;" and in 1802, it was voted in town meeting "to repair the Indian's house and make her comfortable."

You will pass the spot where Delilah lies buried —or so we all hope—and I shall call it out to you, but by your leave, I shall describe it as the grave of the last Indian of Wellfleet.

Meanwhile, if you turn east from the highway at an intersection near the South Wellfleet depot, a dirt road will lead you through Goody Hallett's nocturnal stamping ground, to the sea.

Here it was, on the shoals a few hundred yards offshore, that Bellamy went aground in the *Whidah*. When she capsized, broke up, and left the bodies of 101 buccaneers alongshore for Captain Cyprian Southack to bury, she carried in her strong-chests such cash on hand as Sam had come by in a short but lively career. Captain Southack duly found the dead, but not the money, which is said to have been in gold coins, filling a great iron pot. It may still be in the neighborhood; it may be scattered to brighten the abode of the groundfish just beyond the low tidemark; it may have been taken off by the mooncussers, or it may have been recovered by those two red-coated strangers who came in the night to Gull Pond with pick and chart, and who then were seen no more.

A few paces beyond the road's end, on this beach, you will find the concrete foundations of a wireless station, the first in America to transmit across the Atlantic. Four high steel towers were erected here

in 1902, under the supervision of Guglielmo Marconi, and early in 1903 President Theodore Roosevelt led off with greetings to King Edward VII:
"Taking advantage of the wonderful triumph of
scientific research and ingenuity," etc., etc. The
message actually got there. The station was dismasted in 1920, after others had taken over its
work.

The fire tower further along the highway in
South Wellfleet is open to such visitors as are willing to go aloft under their own steam. There is a
pair of good binoculars up there, and perhaps you
can get the towerman to tell you about the time
they saw smoke, smelled smoke, but had trouble
finding the fire—until they discovered it right
under the tower! And if the crow's nest is not
too crowded, he may even spin you the yarn about
the government fellers who tracked down two public enemies through the names that were written
in his registry.
It seems that when these two strangers came
aloft, they seemed uncommonly anxious to get a
glimpse at the Atlantic ship lanes to the eastward,
and they had brought their own high-powered binoculars. When the fire lookout asked them to sign
the register, they balked at first, but decided they
had better put down something. The aliases helped
later in their capture.

On the way into Wellfleet's trading center the
highway treats you to a Joseph's garden, set in a
triangle to your left. I have heard them called
Joseph's gardens, these retired dories which are
filled with earth and made to serve as flowerboxes,

but the particular Joseph who was in command of this craft of many colors remained unknown until Elizabeth Reynard's book, *The Narrow Land*, tracked him down in Falmouth. You will find Joseph's gardens up and down the Cape, and that hapless shepherd of souls, the Reverend Joseph Metcalfe, was their originator, according to Miss Reynard's legend.

The parson, a gentle soul whose little salary had to be stretched in support of ten daughters, had carried in the warmth of his heart two secret, earthly wishes, which an all-knowing Providence had seen fit to withhold from him for many years. The one was for a wig to replace the mouldy adornment he had already worn long beyond its time, so that it was "gnawed by silver-boterflies;" and the other, "a boat in which to take mine ease on the deep."

At last the poor parson came into an inheritance. The first thing he did was to cancel a debt of £60 salary arrears owed him by his church. And the next was to buy a wig and a boat. About the latter, he was as eager as a child with a new pet. But, alas, his boyish enthusiasm was not shared by his flock! When they heard that he had bought a boat, head-shaking elders told him if it was fish he needed, they would see that he was given fish; but it was unseemly that the parson should buy himself a boat. And so, when the boat was delivered, it lay unlaunched in the parsonage yard.

That night a tempest blew up, and Joseph went out in the morning to care for his stricken brethren. The wind had uprooted the rose trees in his garden, but some were lying in the boat when he returned from his work.

Joseph Metcalfe knew his flock. He straightened
the rose trees in the boat, and covered the roots with
soil. And there, after his death, the roses were left
to bloom where the parson's dream of finding his
ease had died a-borning.

A tale with which Wellfleeters are more familiar
begins with a strawberry festival some years ago,
at which Captain Simeon Attwood's little girl,
Martha, was expected to sing. Little Martha had
sung at many a church sociable. Everybody knew
the child "had talent;" many thought she "showed
promise;" and some even went to Cap'n Simeon to
tell him that "something ought to be done" with
her.

"No harm in singing," the Cap'n agreed, "but
I can't see as there's anything to do about it but
sing. She can sing all she wants—so long as she
gets a decent schooling and learns to keep house
shipshape."

But at this strawberry festival, Martha suddenly
decided she didn't want to sing. That had never
happened before. Martha's mother waved a finger
and used an expression thousands of other mothers
resorted to in that day.

"We'll have no prima donnas in this family,
young lady!" And when Martha held out stub-
bornly for the right of free silence, Mrs. Attwood
took her across her knee and rendered a staccato
number that left part of Martha matching the
ripest strawberries of the festival. "Now, then,
Martha, get up there and sing!"

Martha rose, caught her breath, gave her dress
a smoothing down and between sobs managed to
blurt out the gay verses beginning:

"Who will buy my strawberries?"
Probably you have guessed the rest, possibly
you've heard of her. Her debut was in Siena, as
Mimi in "La Boheme," and when Tullio Serafin
heard her, he engaged her for the Metropolitan.

Martha Attwood's first husband was Reuben
Baker, son of Captain Lorenzo Dow Baker, of
Wellfleet. Captain Baker, bringing back his trading schooner from a voyage to Jamaica in 1870,
carried on board a couple of stalks of green bananas. When he dropped anchor in Boston they
were ripe. The demand for the bananas was so
clamorous that a year later, instead of bringing
home another cargo of bamboo, he came loaded
with bananas. These, too, were snapped up, and so
were all the later banana cargoes he could fetch
up from the tropics. He formed L. D. Baker &
Company, which later became the Boston Fruit
Company, and eventually the vast United Fruit
Company.

Wellfleet and her neighbor town, Truro, had
their great whaling days, but the Revolutionary
War dealt both towns such a blow that neither
had capital enough left to fit out anew for the
business. You will not find many reminders, therefore, of those old days as you visit Wellfleet now.

Whaling made Elisha Doane one of the richest
men in Massachusetts, and it did almost as much
for Jesse Holbrook. Our old historian, with fine
Yankee reserve, describes Captain Jesse as "a
strong, athletic man, weighing 350 pounds." In one
voyage he killed 52 whales. Some of them he may
have simply got aboard and sat on till they suffo-

cated; but like Ichabod Paddock, Captain Jesse
was so skillful with the iron that he hired out as
a professor of practical whaling, in the employ of
a London firm. He taught twelve years.

If you fancy reading what their survivors
thought of these old whalemen, you should
turn off the highway at Commercial Street for
Chequesset Neck, where you will find the oldest
"Judgment Lot" in town.

In the surrounding woods, too, there are several
small old cemeteries, some of them "pox acres."
These were where the Old Colony buried its victims of the dread smallpox—far from the settlement—and where Cape folks continued to bring
the bodies of such unfortunates until late in the
Nineteenth Century.

Hidden away in many wooded parts of Cape
Cod, the "pox acres" are avoided to this day by
many an old-timer who remembers what they were
for. I have succeeded in getting them to tell me
where the lots are located, but not in getting them
to go with me. "I know there ain't been no burying
there for forty year," one of these old men explained to me, "but I jest don't never go there
anyway. It's a notion I have." And if you care to
read of the ravages of the pox in centuries past,
you will understand why the Cape still has "a
notion."

The road to Bound Brook Island, which is an
island only by virtue of an uncertain little creek,
leads off the highway to the left, in North Wellfleet. My five-foot map of the Cape, dated 1858,
shows at least two dozen houses on Bound Brook
Island, and a school as well. Today there are not

more than half a dozen in the section proper.

When Cape Cod families moved, they went into the business wholeheartedly, whenever possible taking the house along as the principal item of their luggage. And sometimes they took along church, schoolhouse and all. That was done usually for an economic reason, or because the village streets were being washed away from under their feet. But the practice of moving houses carries down to this day; only recently the Clifford house, an ancient landmark on the highlands between Chathamport and West Chatham, was rolled up the South Shore across four towns to a spot in Englewood, West Yarmouth. Dozens of others have had similar travels.

If you have not yet found Sam Bellamy's pot of gold, your last chance at it comes on Gull Pond Road, marked at the right, where, failing in gold, I can at least show you a great green-rimmed cauldron of silver with a sheen beyond the powers of all the smiths of India.

Ben Eaton's place, the last house at Gull Pond, is the spot where "two red-coated strangers" tethered their horses one night long ago and held a chart up to the moonlight while a scared little girl held her breath and peered at them over a window-ledge. They dug a hole here, but whether they had any more luck than you might have, nobody in Wellfleet knows. The tale has come down through generations of folks at Gull Pond, which was something closer to a wilderness then, and curiously the story seems to have escaped the embroidery that hangs in festoons over most of these local traditions. It never reveals whether the strangers really found and took away the gold.

The wreck of the ship *Franklin* is several times mentioned by Thoreau, who saw Cape Cod wreckers along the beach, working on the remains of her cargo. In his book he also makes a note of many fruit trees which had been washed ashore from her, all nicely tied up and labeled. When Thoreau arrived on the scene, they were already growing in a Cape Codder's garden. They had been consigned originally to a "Mr. Bell," who was "importing the nucleus of a nursery to be established near Boston."

At Gull Pond, next to Ben Eaton's house, lives Walter P. Rowell, in whose orchard stand four sturdy apple trees. Their fruit is different from the Cape apples—something like a Baldwin, but livelier, snappier, juicier. And that, the neighborhood agrees, is because they are "Franklin apples" —from saplings that were tossed up by the sea, out of the wreck in 1848.

Across the pond, the outlines are visible of the house where Thoreau spent the night with his "Wellfleet Oysterman," the old patriarch who kept dolorously insisting that he was "a poor, good-for-nothing crittur, as Isaiah says," but who, when bedtime came, took a great pride in exhibiting his legs. "We had never had the good fortune to see an old man's legs before," writes Thoreau, ever the inquiring scientist, "and we were surprised to find them fair and plump as an infant's."

On the highway, near the Truro line, there is a gasoline station. On the roadside opposite was buried Delilah Roach, the "last Indian in Wellfleet."

# CHAPTER X

## TRURO

*On U. S. 6, between Wellfleet and Provincetown. Eleven miles between Truro town lines.*

"It's shutting in thick over the whole of the bay," Cap'n Eldad told the lad at the wheel, who was a green hand and off-Cape at that. "Better let her go for home." And he started down the companionway.

"But what course shall I steer?" the youth called after him; for "home" was in Truro, and the vessel was in the middle of Cape Cod Bay.

"Follow the gulls," replied Cap'n Eldad. "They'll take you straight into Pamet Harbor."

The skipper turned in. He awoke six hours later —long beyond any reasonable running time—came on deck, and found the vessel off the Back Shore of the Cape. What in 'tarnity's name, he wanted to know, was his helmsman trying to do—go a furrin viage?

"I've been following the gulls, like you told me," the lad replied.

"Why, you fog-brained farmer! You've been following Chatham gulls, not Truro gulls!"

They say the gulls of Truro won't dive for fish on the Sabbath. I cannot say whether it is the birds that keep the Sabbath holy or the fish. It may be both, for although the stern old town of Truro has been seduced into milder forms of piety in her later

days, her grim hills still hold ancient churches
against the sky.

There are ghost towns lined with mouldering
houses, long abandoned by the living, and there
are ghost towns where the pine-smoke still curls
from solid chimneys, while shadowy citizens peer
in through the panes of great-room windows at
dear, familiar hearths, and then turn away bewildered by the talk of an alien host. Such a ghost
town, abuzz with scandalized whispers of the pious
dead, is Truro.

The "Hill of Storms," where much of the old
town's past was enacted, is bare now, save for rows
of gravestones. Luckily, the yarn has been spun,
the book written. Townsmen who sleep on the hill
still live in its pages; but even there they live pre-
cariously, for the book has long been out of print—
the history written by grand old Shebnah Rich,
with its four-masted title, *Truro, Cape Cod, or
Land Marks and Sea Marks,* and with its overwhelming array of quotations from forgotten poets.
I sometimes suspect old Shebnah of slipping those
countless pieces of poetry into his own text just to
show, by contrast, how well he could write!

You will find a copy of Rich's history in many
a Truro home, on the shelf beside the family Bible
and the log of grandpa's last voyage; but these
three books you are not expected to borrow. You
will find well worn copies in the Cape public li-
braries too, but the covers are labeled with the
warning, in large letters, "NOT TO BE TAKEN
AWAY."

Sometimes acknowledging the debt, more often
ignoring it, Cape writers have all gone to old
Shebnah. If you have leisure on Cape Cod, I can

offer you no better direction to Truro than the pages between those worn green covers—with the suggestion that you skip the yards of poetic jewelry, which must have taken the old man days and days to dig up from God knows where.

The South Truro road is a left turn from the highway, a short distance beyond the Wellfleet line. Upon a barren hill in South Truro, the austere Methodist meeting-house stands like a sentinel of virtue—which virtue has forgotten to relieve. I don't know whether Historian Rich regarded this structure, built in 1851, as one of his "landmarks" or "seamarks," for it can be seen upon its hill from far out in the Bay, and many a fisherman has steered by it. It looks more austere from the water, but it makes a picture from any point. It was closed to use a few years ago, but I understand that instead of letting it go to ruin, the people of Truro are taking steps in its behalf.

Eastward across the road from this building is the Methodist burying ground, and on this site once stood a church that was built "in spite of hell and high water," after Methodism was shunted away from Provincetown.

With plans for a house of God, the Methodists came to Truro in 1794—whereupon a town meeting was promptly called, and it was voted that "there shall not be a Methodist Meeting-house built in this town."

They brought the boards and shingles with them from Provincetown, but the historian says, "a mob destroyed the timber and tarred and feathered the preacher in effigy and threatened to serve him the same. But by keeping guard at night, and keeping their weapons by them while at work, in about four months they erected a chapel, with songs of praise."

There was no plastering or finish, he adds, and for twenty years "the swallows flew in and out at pleasure, building their nests on the rough open beams and feeding their young during divine services."

The Methodists throve like the swallows, and their preachers were about as nimble. One of them took as his text, "The world, the flesh and the devil," and in announcing it, said, "I shall touch lightly upon the world, hasten to the flesh, and pass on to the devil, when I will give it to you hot as you can sup it."

If you have turned off the highway to see the South Truro meeting-house, continue northward on the same road to the Pamet River. Here, near the railroad station, were the wharves, fish-packing house, sail-loft, and outfitting store, the salt works, bridges and breakwaters, banks and insurance companies. Here were the shipyards, rushing new craft down to the sea, and making old craft seaworthy again to the ring of the caulker's maul.

Where the gulls wheel now over a silted harbor and the dry weeds crackle on the salt meadows, Truro boomed a century ago, worshipped on the hill, toiled along shore and sent her young men to sea. In 1930 there were 500 people in Truro; but in 1850, there were more than 2,000. At Pamet River they built the Union Wharf, moving "an immense tonnage of sand." The fifty stockholders, each owning one share, wheeled the sand themselves—one-fiftieth of the work for each—while a committee stood by "to see that there was no shirking."

Then came the Union Company Store, an elegant outfitting establishment that later was to crash and bring down with it the last of Truro's hopes for an industrial future. Also belonging to the heyday was the Boston packet, the *Postboy*—the "finest specimen of naval architecture afloat in Bay waters." She had solid mahogany furniture and silk draperies. Captain Zoheth Rich, her master, called her the "Pizby." Although she sailed about once a week, people were anxiously inquiring every day, and to all these queries, the skipper's reply was ever the same—"tomorrer."

The generation of Cape Codders who could remember the packets is gone. But the story of Elnathan Annable, the stammering sailor, survives the ages. According to the legend, the skipper of a Truro packet falls overboard while the vessel is scudding before the wind, and only one man is on deck to witness the accident. But poor Elnathan Annable stammers, and when he is excited, cannot speak a word. Elnathan is a good singer, however, and can overcome his stammering by singing the reluctant words. He manages to call all hands on deck, but cannot tell them what has happened. At last one of the crew shouts, "Sing it!" And Elnathan, pale and horrified, sings out:

> *O, you'll forgive these tears,*
> *For now you all must learn*
> *John Nickerson is overboard*
> *Half a mile astern!*

If there is a blue haze over the Bay as you pause at Pamet River, and the Pilgrim Monument

in Provincetown across-harbor has lost her masthead in the mist, look for a phantom sail far beyond the Cape-end. She is Cap'n Zoheth's "Pizby"
—lost out there in the spindrift, waiting for
"tomorrer."

Turning right, you can follow the "Pamet River
North," making a loop in your route. Back on the
highway, go up the hill beyond the library and
turn left around the Catholic church for the "Bell
Meeting House." This old structure, the white
church near Town Hall, has been Truro's pride
since 1827.

The big fleet of Banks vessels was usually ready
to sail about April 1, and on the Sunday before,
the churches would be crowded to hear the good-
bye sermon to the Bankers. It was on such a Sunday, in 1843, that the Reverend Boyter—poor, mis-
guided off-Caper that he was!—chose to address
the big congregation in the Bell Meeting House on
"Fishermen's Luck."

"Unquestionably he gave much wise and practical advice," Rich writes, "which the fishermen
might well have heeded; but the spirit and appli-
cation of his sermon was unfortunate. . . . He declared emphatically that there was no such thing
as luck, and warned them to banish it forever from
their households, vessels and vocabularies." He
also advised them to bait their hooks with red
flannel. "Mr. Boyter," the history succinctly adds,
"moved to Orange, N. J."

Before you continue out to the Bay Shore, pause
in the " 'tarnity acres" here on the hill. There are
things to ponder among these old stones.

The tragic "October gale" of 1841 hit the little village of Truro hardest of all the Cape towns. Seven of her fishing vessels went out before the storm struck. Six were never seen again; and the seventh, the *Pomona,* was found bottom-up in Nauset Harbor, her crew drowned in the cabin. In this cemetery, the marble shaft "sacred to the memory of fifty-seven citizens of Truro," tersely tells the story. The names of the "citizens"—most of them in their twenties, nine under fifteen and one only eleven years old—are inscribed.

A writer who recalled the storm had this to say in the Provincetown *Advocate*:

"We saw a father who had two sons among the missing, for days and weeks go morning and evening to the hill-top which overlooked the ocean, and there seating himself, would watch for hours, scanning the distant horizon with his glass."

The shaft, placed here the year after the gale, bears as its last line a poignant quotation:

"MAN GOETH TO HIS LONG HOME, AND THE
MOURNERS GO ABOUT THE STREETS."

Another old church stood by the Bell Meeting House on this hill. A few years ago, a Truro artist, one of the growing community of artists and writers in the town, bought it and moved it into the valley. There he has converted it into a studio, installing skylights and posing his models on a platform where the pulpit once rocked with denunciations of the flesh.

On the "Hill of Storms," which the highway traverses a little further north, are the town's oldest graves, but they are hidden among more recent ones. Within that cemetery stood the first meeting-house, where for 120 years Truro came to worship and to accomplish a number of other things. For, close at hand were at that time the "parade ground," the stocks and whipping post, and the "Lyar's Bench." A Sabbath going-to-meeting was an all-day piece of business, with plenty of variety to fill the hours.

They came from many miles around, some on the family horse, "loaded like a dromedary, and badly sprung amidships," and some afoot, the girls wearing their old shoes and stockings and carrying their new ones in their hands until they arrived at the meeting-house.

When the meeting-house was completed in 1709, the first thing the town fathers did was to vote the purchase of a cushion for the pulpit and an hour-glass. The cushion was for the protection of the minister, and the hour-glass, timing his sermon, for the protection of the flock.

Here the Reverend Jude Damon, "cautious in all his statements, always allowing for a margin on the safe side," pondered and solved the age-long problem of how to ask God for a wind. During the summer, Banks fishing vessels were sailing and arriving at the same time in Pamet Harbor. A west wind was fair wind for those departing for the Banks, an east wind fair for those returning. To pray for either east or west was to put a breeze dead ahead for half the fleet. "Mr. Damon soon understood this, and his benevolent heart thus shaped his prayers:

"'We pray, O Lord, that thou wilt watch over our mariners that go down to do business upon the mighty deep, keep them in the hollow of thy hand; and we pray thee that thou wilt send a side-wind.' "

In the long "noonings"—periods between the morning and afternoon services—the Lyar's Bench was held down by Uncle Hut Dyer, "Prince of Yarners," who would light his pipe and hold the youth of Truro spellbound as the pastor never had. Hut could spin 'em so tall their mastheads scraped the under-side of the golden streets and made the angels set out rat-traps. He could sing, too—on a weekday—and he knew the songs the Grand Bankers sang:

> *Up jumped the mackerel*
> *With his striped back—*
> *Says he, reef in the mains'l and haul on the tack,*
> *For it's windy weather,*
> *It's stormy weather,*
> *And when the wind blows, pipe all hands together—*
> *For upon my word, it's windy weather.*

That one only had twenty verses\*, but Hut knew some long ones too.

The hunt for Indian belongings has been kept up more or less steadily on Cape Cod ever since the Pilgrims set the precedent on Corn Hill in 1620. From the finds that are being made to this day, it appears that the whole lower Cape, down to High Head in North Truro, is dotted with Indian burying grounds, only a fraction of which have been unearthed and only one or two of which have been examined scientifically.

---

\*Of this song, Rich says that it was an old one which he had "supposed local," but which is quoted complete in Thomas Hood's works. "It is related in his (Hood's) life that during one of his visits to Brighton, his favorite resort, he became acquainted with an old lieutenant of the Coast Guards, from whom he learned this odd song, in which he delighted, and which was the only one he was ever known to sing."

The Pilgrims were not wholly unscientific when they dug into the Indian graves and caches in Truro. But they were after food rather than material for a doctor's thesis, and if they had not "gott seed to plant them corne ye next year," they probably would have starved. The Corn Hill Road in Truro leads to the crest "wher latly a house had been, wher some planks and a great ketle was remaining, and heaps of sand newly padled with their hands, which they, digging up, found in them diverce faire Indean baskets filled with corne, and some in eares, faire and good, of diverce collours, which seemed to them a very goodly sight." They took all the ears and filled the kettle with loose corn, which two men carried on a staff. "Besides, they that could put any into their pockets, filled the same." Doughty Miles Standish, he who later was to rise in such wrath against the Indians over the theft of a few trinkets, was a leader of the party, as the tablet at Corn Hill will inform you.

An exciting discovery was made by a second *Mayflower* party on a hill further inland, but there is no marker there, because nobody has solved the mystery of the yellow-haired man. These people came upon "a place like a grave," and digging it up, they found two skeletons, one a man and the other a little child. "The [man's] skull had fine yellow hair still on it." Strings of fine white beads and bracelets were on the child's legs and arms, and "there was also by it a little bow, about three-quarters long, and some other old knacks."

Where the yellow-haired man came from has been a mystery ever since. Believers in the Norsemen's presence on Cape Cod would have to explain how, after six hundred years, there remained "some of the flesh unconsumed." They have grappled with this problem, and have made their Norsemen very tough indeed in an effort to get around it.

In 1935, experts of the Peabody Museum of Harvard undertook some digging in Eastham and brought out several Indian skeletons, and some burial paraphernalia; but since then the activity has shifted back to Truro, and on a farm which you can see from the highway, to your left just beyond the juncture of Long Nook Koad, many unusual items have been uncovered.

A "kitchen midden" or community kitchen, is indicated by the discoveries here. Unfortunately, all efforts to have a real archaeologist supervise the digging have thus far fallen through.

A field dug up by the home-grown archaeologist is really less enlightening than no field at all; for he not only contributes his bit of misinformation on the subject, but he is sealing for all time the source of possible knowledge. Private collections of arrowheads, knives, pottery and the like have been jealously guarded in Cape Cod houses for years— until some heir comes along who neither knows nor cares anything about them and clears them out along with Uncle Isaiah's pipe collection. The archaeologists seem to be waking up a bit now, however. They are eager to get at such finds before they are spoiled or lost. Recently a ten-year-old girl of Chatham went into the backyard to bury her pet hen. Digging in the yard, she uncovered a human leg bone. She brought it into the house, and later a skull and other bones were found there. Phillips Andover Academy promptly got in touch with the family, and acquired the discovery for its studies.

A favorite spot along the Back Shore for swimming and beach-picnicking can be reached over the Long Nook Road, which branches from the highway to the ocean shore. There are many old houses along this road, some built as early as 1710. They are now owned for the most part by wealthy "summer families," and only a few are occupied through the year. The rugged old houses are being coddled as they never have before; the neighborhood has become conscientious about such matters as the preservation of ancient garbage pails; and the width of the old floor planks is something of a measure of social status.

What may be of more importance to the nation's future than the spot where the Pilgrims dug up corn is an unpretentious building a mile or so north of Corn Hill where no brass tablets are allowed and where publicity has gone uncourted. Beyond the juncture of the Long Nook Road, the highway drops into a hollow, which is known as Whitmanville. A road turns out left at the bottom of this hollow. It goes to the Bay Shore, where is located the Marine Experimental Station of the Lankenau Hospital Research Institute, of Philadelphia. Specialists have been working in this laboratory since 1930, their main line of investigation being the biological basis of cancer.

The research, supported by the International Cancer Foundation, is under the direction of Dr. Frederick S. Hammett, who is known internationally for his studies of this disease. These men are attacking the problem of cellular growth, as a basic approach to the more specific study of the disease itself. The "spade-work" that has been accomplished is already widely recognized. Leading scientists come from all parts of the world to observe its progress.

Marine life is especially well suited for the experiments, and the Bay waters are free of factory pollution and other conditions that would tend to throw the tests off.

What comes of this work may be of tremendous interest eventually, to a public that cannot follow the technical processes now. Visits to the laboratory are only by appointment.

Lighthouses go back to the most ancient times, in other parts of the world, but on Cape Cod, with its most perilous of shoal waters, we took all of a hundred and fifty years in getting the first lighthouse up.

The idea of building special land-guides for sailors was not taken seriously on the Cape until a Wellfleet minister began agitation for the High Land Light. If the thought of safety at sea occurred to the Cape at all, the profits of "wrecking" were an effective soft-pedal.

"That mountain of clay in Truro seems to have been erected in the midst of sand hills by the God of Nature for the foundation of a lighthouse, which, if it should be obtained, in time no doubt would save the lives of thousands," wrote the Reverend Levi Whitman in 1794. And knowing his people, he added that it would save "millions of property." This was the first word put in for the beacon here on Truro's "Clay Pounds," the pe-

culiar cliff with the stratum of bluish clay running
through it.

Thus, the "High Land" was the spot chosen in
1797. Because this is the first landmark picked up
on the transatlantic route to Boston, a primary light
has been maintained here ever since. The road to
the High Land branches off the highway to the
right.

Cape Cod Light, as this beacon is known officially, will continue to be an important marker
long after the usefulness of many other Cape lights
is outgrown. Already some of these have become
superfluous and have been sold to private owners.
The Canal cut-off has diverted the traffic, but even
more important, the radio beacon now gives ships
at sea their positions. Small fishing vessels still steer
by the lights, but many of these craft are also
equipped with radio compass, by which they can
pick up flashes sent out periodically from a series
of stations, and thus reckon their positions.

The radio beacon is in fact the modern-world
replacement of the picturesque white tower. It is
more efficient, more dependable. The usefulness of
Cape Cod Light itself is now eclipsed by the radio
compass station that squats beside it.

A U. S. Naval radio station was established at
High Land in 1904. Up to the World War it was
engaged largely in commercial work. In 1917, with
our entrance into hostilities, it became a point of
great importance, and during the war years was
closely guarded by a detachment of Marines. At
this time the station began to concentrate on work
with the radio compass, just then coming into general use. At present it devotes itself exclusively to
this work, receiving more than a hundred calls a

day from ships within a radius of several hundred miles. There are similar stations at Bar Harbor, Portland and Nantucket.

With the development of the radio beacon, however, as a part of the lighthouse service, the radio compass has lost much of its old importance. Radio beacon and radio compass operate on the same principles, and with similar apparatus, but they are, so to speak, the reverse of one another. A ship using the beacon tunes in her radio compass to pick up the flashes sent out periodically and automatically every twenty minutes from a series of stations. By a process of triangulation, she can determine her position at sea every few minutes, without being under the necessity of calling radio compass stations and asking for her true bearing from each of them.

The radio beacon station at High Land is the master station of the series which includes Boston Lightship and the station at Vineyard Haven. Every hour, at precisely ten minutes after the hour, signals are flashed in rotation by these three stations. The High Land station begins by sending out the letter "Q" every two seconds for the period of a minute, and then falls silent as the Boston Lightship sends out "Z" for the following minute. Then "W", the call of Vineyard Haven, goes out thirty times during the next minute.

This rotation, governed by synchronized automatic clocks, continues for ten minutes. Again at twenty minutes to the hour, the beacons begin to operate in the same rotation for another ten minutes; so that a ship equipped with radio compass can take her bearings every twenty minutes.

The lighthouse now standing at High Land was
built in 1857, replacing an earlier structure. Up to
1931 it burned oil. Now, with electricity installed,
it burns a single 1,000-watt bulb, of 2,500 candlepower. The huge bullseye lenses stretch this out to
an equivalent of 4,000,000 candlepower. Under
normal conditions, Cape Cod Light can be seen for
twenty miles, and beyond that by reflection.

The plant operates an electric foghorn, audible
fifteen miles out. Among mariners a strange phe-
nomenon is often mentioned, upon which there is
wide agreement. It is known as the "blind spot,"
which sometimes develops around a fog station,
and which no technician has ever been able to explain; for this strange disability does not seem to
come of a change in the wind's direction. Failing to
hear the signal from a nearby station over a long
period, a vessel will sometimes question it, yet the
same station may get complaints from ten miles
away, that people living ashore have had their
sleep disturbed by its groans.

A lighthouse cannot check the force of vicious
tides or square the northeasters about, and to the
end of sailing days such craft as were caught off the
lee shore here had a losing battle of it. A mile offshore, northeast of the Clay Pounds, the surf
breaks over Peaked Hill Bars, a crowded corner
of Cape Cod's graveyard of ships. Only by standing on this shore after a winter gale has whipped
up great marching seas beyond the outer bar can an
inlander realize what forces had to be withstood by
those hapless wooden hulls. We have seen many
headlines announcing the crashes of air liners in
recent years, but for every one of these, Truro and

Provincetown have heard a score of times the dread cry, "Ship ashore and all hands perishing!" The largest of the sailing vessels to come ashore at Peaked Hill was the British ship-of-war, *Somerset*. In a November gale of 1778 she struck on the outer bar near Dead Man's Hollow, rode over on the high tide, and beached herself for all time. Four hundred eighty of her survivors were taken prisoner and marched all the way to Boston. While the up-Cape towns jeered them and made merry, Provincetown and Truro were too busy to do much celebrating.

"There is wicked work at the wreck, riotous doings," wrote General Otis, who was sent to take charge of the situation. "The Truro and Provincetown men made a division of the clothing, etc. Truro took two-thirds and Provincetown one-third. There is a plundering gang that way." A Provincetown historian more delicately puts it, "The laws of *Meum* and *Tuum* were being disregarded."

Like the *Sparrowhawk* at Orleans, this ship buried herself in the sand and emerged a century later; "her massive timbers and six-inch live-oak planking told plainly that it was the almost forgotten wreck of the *Somerset*."

Her reappearance in 1886 created something of a stir through the country. The *New York World* carried a story on May 16, describing the excitement in Provincetown and Truro, and the rush for the beach by eager townsfolk, who apparently had changed no more in the hundred years than the *Somerset* had.

"Above her charred and crushed timbers, old ocean had piled a cairn of sand thirty feet high. The wiry beachgrass grew rank above it. The gulls made their nimble tracks across it; the men of the life-saving service trudged over it daily. . . . There is much local excitement about the ancient wreck. Everybody in town has visited the 'back side' to see the exhumed frigate and to secure some relic." The old-time mariners fought the war over again in the ship-chandlers' shops, and "if they cannot tell you exactly how the *Somerset* was wrecked, they can at least inform you how she should have been wrecked. The amateur wreckers and relic-hunters are swarming the beach from near and far, and seem resolved upon carrying away the whole hull in sections. . . . They come to the beach well equipped with saws, axes and shovels, crowbars and wedges."

The ship's doctor aboard the *Somerset,* incidentally, had escaped arrest somehow, had come ashore and had married a Truro girl, raised a family and built up a local practice. Among the interested spectators a hundred years later were many of his descendants.

Fishermen who lay their trawls on "the Middleground," a stretch of shoal twenty miles northeast of the High Land, often snag their hooks on something that lies on the bottom there—something that has been there since the "Portland Gale," that freak hurricane of 1898 which left one of the major disasters of marine history in its wake.

Just where the sidewheel steamer *Portland* went down, with three hundred passengers and crew, nobody knows. Having booked a large Thanksgiving holiday crowd, she was kept to her schedule in the face of storm warnings. She sailed out of Boston in a driving snowstorm on the evening of November 27. She was never seen again.

The gale registered ninety miles an hour at Nantucket, and death rode afar that night over land and sea. The toll was five hundred lives, and more than a score of ships. The wreckage that came ashore next day showed that these vessels had been blown many miles off course—so many miles, in some instances, that it seemed as if the long arms of some malignant giant must have felt through the darkness for them, up and down the coast, to drag them back into the roaring cauldron of Massachusetts Bay.

Most mysterious of all was the fate of the *Portland*. She was bound for her name-port, yet some of her wreckage was found the following night by a surfman of the Peaked Hill Bars life-saving station; and then the bodies began drifting ashore all the way from Peaked Hill to Monomoy Point, in Chatham.

Nobody knows to this day where the *Portland* went down; but the fishermen still snag their hooks on the bottom at the Middleground—where something has lain since 1898.

Bayberry, beach plum, beach pea and blueberry make up the mottled jacket which the lower Cape wears under its great-coat of pine and oak. For hundreds of years the Cape people have made candles of the bayberries, jelly of the beach plums, and breakfast of the blueberries. Thoreau's Wellfleet Oysterman liked the beach pea too—"cooked green," and you will find an abundance of the small pods still growing near his home on the Gull Pond Road.

I know a lad in Provincetown who lives "up-back" among the dunes, and who makes his living selling blueberries in the summer time, for from twenty to thirty cents a quart, and who "goes wooding" in the winter. When the wind is northeast, he carts off all the driftwood he can carry, for then the tide is generous with its treasures; when the wind is southwest, he stays home. The hard wood of old wierpoles burns many hours to a stick, and the sea has treated it chemically so that it flares in blue, green, red, yellow and many beautiful shades between. Wierpole wood in fireplace lengths brings a big price—once you get it cut. In season my small friend sets traps, too, and sells his skunk and muskrat pelts to the mail-order houses for fifty cents a skin. And so, what with his "blueberrying," his "wooding," his "skunking" and his "ratting," he gets along. But if the blueberries don't "come good" in their short season, or if the summer people don't do likewise, he goes in the fall to Truro and picks bayberries. And if he should tell you what he gets for picking bayberries, I know you would join me in hoping that the blueberries "come good."

There is a bayberry candle factory near the fish freezing plant in Pond Village, directly across the Cape from the High Land. In the candle factory they will show you how they cook the berries in water, skim off the wax, refine it and then dip the wicks. The business is an ancient one. Thoreau gives us this excerpt from the "History of Virginia" which Robert Beverley wrote in 1705:

"At the mouth of their rivers, and all along upon the sea and bay, and near many of their creeks and swamps, grows the myrtle [bayberry], bearing a berry, of which they make a hard, brittle wax, of a curious green color, which by refining becomes almost transparent. Of this they make candles, which are never greasy to the touch nor melt with lying in the hottest weather; neither does the snuff of these ever offend the smell, like that of a tallow candle; but, instead of being disagreeable, if an accident puts a candle out, it yields a pleasant fragrancy to all that are in the room; insomuch that nice people often put them out on purpose to have the incense of the expiring snuff. The melting of these berries is said to have been first found out by a surgeon in New England, who performed wonderful things with a salve made of them."

Practically everything the Pilgrims did, even down to the pilfering of graves, has been marked with a tablet by their descendants. Here at Pond Village they made their "rendevous" the night of November 16, 1620, "making a great fire, and a barricade to windward of us; and kept good watch, with three sentinels all night." One historian says they sank the iron kettle (the one they had taken from Corn Hill) in this pond because it was too heavy to carry further, and another says they put it there "for safekeeping." I suspect they did it to hide the theft from the Indians. At any rate, sunk the kettle was; and there history leaves it.

Still another Pilgrim marker has been placed in Truro—the stone with a tablet intended to identify the place where they found their first drinking water ashore. "Most distresed for wante of drinke," the Pilgrims at length "found water & refreshed them selves, being ye first New England water they drunke of, and was now in thir great thirste as pleasante unto them as wine or bear had been in for-times." This is just south of High Head, but it is not easy to find, and there are other reasons for not overworking one's historical zeal here.

The spring which bears the marker was "located" in 1920—three hundred years after the Pilgrims drank—and though shorelines, ponds, lakes and whole islands have come and gone on Cape Cod within even shorter periods, I would be the last to undo the well-meaning efforts of the Boston doctor who dug into the State archives, came down-Cape and wandered with eyes glued to the ground until he could cry "Eureka!" But if I go to High Head, I would refuse to let any foredoomed search for a 300-year-old spring keep my gaze from the distant dune-sculpture and the many-hued sweeps of sky and sea.

The long pond skirted by the highway at this point was formerly connected with the Bay, and it still is called East Harbor. My 1858 map shows the gap at the north end of it, with the bridge that was built in 1854. Before that, the down-Cape coach had to circle around the far side, and a ride had in it many fearsome possibilities. Instead of the coach getting the passengers to Provincetown, the order of service frequently had to be reversed. And sometimes the straining craft capsized, hurling passengers and crew into the briny deep.

East Harbor, since its closure from the Bay, has turned from salt water to fresh, and within recent years it has been popular with skaters and ice-boaters.

Truro and Provincetown have been afraid from their earliest days that the wind would blow them into the sea. Both towns have planted beach grass through the centuries to anchor the shifting dunes. The roots of this hardy growth go down twelve feet or more, and thus they are an effective mooring for the hills. In 1825 a State commission reported that the wind was folding the ocean side over, so that Provincetown was headed into its own harbor, and that unless measures were taken to check it, both town and harbor would be destroyed by the sand. Beach grass was recommended, and in the years since then there has been much planting of the grass and of pitchpines as well.

Meanwhile the towns have had to keep their other eye on the sea. In 1935 the State Senate was warned of the effects of erosion on the bluffs just south of North Truro.

"Erosive action here has threatened to let the sea into some of the deep parallel valleys which traverse the Cape from east to west, as far as Orleans," according to an expert. "Some of these, with their western terminals at Cape Cod Bay, are at their eastern ends separated from the Atlantic by only a few hundred feet, or even less, of bluff and dune. At Pamet River, where encroaching seas forced removal of the Coast Guard station to a safer location in 1933, the situation is threatening. The head of Pamet River, which empties into Cape Cod Bay, is separated from the Atlantic by a narrow barrier of sand. Once this is broken down, Truro Village, North Truro, and Provincetown might be left an island."

The sea has come through here before—once in 1896, when the Provincetown *Advocate* predicted that the lower end of Cape Cod would one day "be made an island.'" Again, in February, 1937, a ten-foot tide backed by heavy surf spread over the Pamet River Road and mingled with the source-waters of the Pamet River, 300 feet beyond. Parts of the bank were cut away, and seaweed was strewn over the road.

# CHAPTER XI

## PROVINCETOWN I

*On U. S. 6, end of Cape. Sixty-five miles from the Canal, 122 miles from Boston.*

Last time I took a pair of boots in to Joe Half-dollar, the old Portuguese fisherman who has gone into cobbling, I stopped to admire a new window display he had set out.

At the left side he had a big old shark-bitten seaboot, which he must have picked up off the beach, frayed and stringy around the top and showing a great gaping hole in the forepeak. Under this he had placed the legend, "BEFORE." At the right side, over a card printed "AFTER," a silver high-heeled dancing pump glittered in immaculate daintiness.

When I went in to congratulate old Joe on this achievement, he seemed shy. Then he gave me a wrinkly smile and explained—as he had heard so many others in Provincetown explain—it was just "his art."

Provincetown, whatever the summer may bring it, is a fishing town, and its people are fisherpeople. In July and August, when the population suddenly triples, there is some tendency to forget this. I have read wonderful descriptions of the town, from which one would gather that it is principally an art colony, festooned with nets and "picturesque" Portuguese fishermen who presumably have been planted for the convenience of the artists who paint them.

In the Cape-end eddies of summer traffic, which work into a dizzy whirlpool here, it is true that for two months of each year the town practically loses itself. One might add that it is beside itself. The tourists are now the most numerous, the artists and writers by long odds the most articulate. Hence it may come as a surprise to the visitor, when he is told that of the more than four thousand residents of the town—"year-round people"—three-fourths are Portuguese, seeking their livelihood in the fishery or indirectly from its earnings.

They are an engaging people. I do not see how Provincetown can be very life-like to writers who treat the Portuguese as incidental. Cape Cod, of course, has a rich historical interest without them, because the Cape's history goes back beyond their time; but the Cape today is very much with them, and has been so since the last quarter of the Nineteenth Century, when large numbers came to New England, attracted by success stories of pretty much the same stamp that all fish stories bear.

I find that to crowd Provincetown into one chapter would be like throwing all the exhibits of a menagerie into a single cage. Even if they don't start clawing at one another, such jamming together obstructs the view.

Before touring about the town for details, let us have a squint at it "with eyes half-closed," as the painters say, for a few broad effects. Let us meet these Portuguese, and listen to them talk of their fishing; let us wander through that scattered, elusive realm which the town calls its "art colony;"

and let us glance backward, through a couple of centuries, towards the hazy beginnings of the "Province Lands." Then we can tour the town in another chapter.

The large majority of the Portuguese have come from the Azores, or are descended of Azoreans; a small proportion are from Lisbon; and the remainder are descended of the *bravas,* a race brought into New England in whaling days from the Cape Verde Islands. The Cape Verdes, which belong to Portugal, are off the west coast of Africa, and the *bravas* are a mixture of Portuguese and native African, and are so called after the island of Brava.

Because of brutal treatment they met with aboard ship, the crews of the whalers often deserted. Many of these men had been "crimped" in the first place—lured by false promises or even drugged in the waterfront dives, to find themselves well out to sea when they regained consciousness. Desertion was therefore a matter of course, and whaling captains usually charted their voyages by way of the Cape Verdes, for there they could pick up crew replacements.

The *bravas* were good whalemen, and their descendants are good fishermen. They are thickest in New Bedford, though some were brought to Cape Cod and have made their homes here. The Azorean and Lisbon people agree that the *bravas* are their inferiors, but they disagree heartily as between themselves, which faction is the superior.

In introducing them, one must use their nicknames. For they have an odd custom of bestowing nicknames on one another—not in a spirit of levity, but in dead earnest. They practically forget their real names. Sometimes the sobriquets are not very delicate, but always they are highly descriptive; and once a man comes by his nickname, there is no escape. As it is always the surname that is replaced, whole families must abide by the practice. There is the "Rat family," for instance; there are the "Codfishes"—Manuel Codfish, Maria Codfish, and all the little Codfishes; there is the fisherman who lost both his legs—"Tom Low;" and there are Mike Molasses and Mrs. Jazzgarters. With good grace, the Rats, the Codfishes and all the rest accept what they cannot reject; cheerfully they answer to the names. Some have been in use so long that in the course of generations the real family names have become obscured, and legal problems have arisen.

There are a few of the old-time "fish stores" left in Provincetown—rough gray sheds on the harborfront where the men store their gear—and though these ramshackle warerooms are seldom noticed by the crowds that motor up and down Commercial Street, it is here that one must come, really to know the fishermen; here one must sit and listen to the talk, when the February sleet is falling, and the harbor is banging away at the bulkheads along-shore under a southeast blow.

Joe Flounder sits on a mackerel "kag" across from Tony Yellow and deals out the cards for a game of two-handed *bisqua*, while Tony leans over and pokes up the potbelly stove. There is fishing gear on the walls, in the corners, on the floor, everywhere—strings of netcorks, stacks of anchors, buoys, oars, and hangings of crackly yellow oilskins. The southeast breeze screams through the old timbers, and even Cap'n Two-time, the half-Siamese cat, edges a little closer.

Through the doorway you can see into the next room, where Big Billy is tarring nets. He looks like a god of darkness, hanging the room with shadows. In another corner old Pete Fayal is over-hauling his gear—a tub of trawl-line on which he is replacing the lost "gangin's"—and his huge fin-gers twist and tie with incredible speed as he makes the new strings fast and fixes a hook to each. But he pauses now and then to take a swig from the bottle of prune whiskey which is in easy reach, and when he has done this a sufficient number of times, Pete begins to spin a yarn for the boys.

"You fellers wouldn't remember old Cap'n John Santos—feller that had his leg et off by a shark on the Western Banks. But I can remember him, back when I was a boy, and how proud he was of the new jury-leg they rigged him up with. It was a sight, I tell you, to watch him dance a *chamarita* with that leg and not nick the floor once. Carried around furniture polish just like the doctor carries iodine, in case of a cut or scratch, and one time he copper-bottomed her to make sure the worms wouldn't get to him before his time.

"Well, you know once a man is chawed on by a shark, he's shark-jonahed for the rest of his life. Some day a shark's going to get the rest of that feller, if he keeps on going to sea. And Cap'n John kept on.

"The Cap'n's trawler, the *Hetty K,* was ten mile from the Race when the Portland Gale struck. That was November 27. On the 28th she come

crippling round the Point under bare poles with
two foot of harbor water over her lee rail. The
crew said Cap'n John was washed overboard,
along with two other men.

"The bodies of the other two drifted ashore; the
Cap'n wasn't never found. But a couple of days
after, Joe Barcia picked up the old man's wooden
leg off the beach. He took it home to Mary Santos,
the widow.

"Married thirty years, them two. When Joe
Barcia brought back the leg, Mary took it into the
house. She petted it and talked to it.

"Nothing more come of it till the night of November 26, a year later. That night, Mary said, she
set up in bed, and there, standing straight as two
yards of pump-water on his one leg, was old Cap'n
John. He hopped over alongside the bed and
canted over. Then he whispered to her.

" 'Barometer's falling, Mary,' he says, 'and the
wind's no'theast. We're in for thick weather, and
I'll want my store leg to keep me steady when she
strikes.' He pinched her cheek, and Mary let out a
yell. When she looked again, the Cap'n was gone.

"Next morning, Mary said, she had a little red
spot on her cheek. And before she turned in that
night, she took the skipper's leg out of the spice-
cupboard and left it laid out for him in a corner
near the fireplace.

"That night a breeze of wind come up, and in
a couple of hours it turned into a living gale—
from the no'theast. The willer tree outside howled
like the yo-ho bird of every dead sailor in hell
come there to roost. All of a sudden Mary hears a
thump-thump-thump across the floor, down below,
and then the door shut to. She stayed in bed.

"Next morning she went to look if the Cap'n's leg was still there. It was, but when she picked it up, it was wet.

"Well, it'd rained bad enough to come in by the chimney. But it gallied her so, the sight of that leg, with the water on it, that she got sick. She called in Doc Atwood. When he got through sounding, and didn't find nothing sprung, Doc said something was eating on her. Then she told him the whole story.

"When he'd went over the leg, he looked hard at the widow.

" 'You say you left it by the fireplace all night and rain come in on it?' he asks. Then he sets the leg down, comes over to the widow, and tells her straight out. 'Mrs. Santos,' he says, 'I'm going to ask you to have one of the men take this thing out to sea, and weight it with net-leads, and heave it overboard. I'm a doctor,' says he, 'and I don't listen to stories. But Mrs. Santos,' he says, 'I put my tongue to that wood. *It don't rain salt water!*' "

Provincetown fishermen go out mainly for mackerel, whiting, haddock, cod and flounder— very little for aesthetic atmosphere. If you have ever helped haul up the float-traps, or jumped aboard a seine-boat in a choppy sea, or tried to "haul back" trawl with them on the Banks, you will appreciate what a hardy, muscular set of decorations the town's art colony has.

They are grossly underpaid, always have been, and probably always will be. Fishing is definitely skilled labor. Its routine is exacting and irregular; large risks and constant exposure go with it. But fishermen have been, from the earliest times, vic-

tims of the "share" system, by which they have forever deluded themselves with the hope of a "big
stock." Occasionally they do come home with a
big "trip," and a good stock is divided among the
crew. These are the high spots, the trips that are
easy to remember, to hope for again. Lured by
such possibilities, it is the fisherman himself who
insists on the share system—and as a consequence
he averages so little over the long pull that his
labor, however skilled, has always been poor man's
work, and with a few exceptions those who make
up the crew of a fishing vessel are poor people.

I do not mean to say that the major spread goes
to the skipper. He, too, is a fisherman. To state
roughly what he is up against: when fish are
plentiful, fish are cheap. When fish are rare, the
price rises, but he has no fish to sell.

The "freezers"—fish packing houses—buy much
of the local fleet's catch whenever the price of
shipping it to better markets is prohibitive—
which is most of the time. The freezers also buy all
the catch of the float-traps and weirs in the harbor.
These companies hold ownership of the traps, and
the men do the labor of keeping them in repair,
putting down the weirpoles in the spring and pulling them up again in the fall—most of this on
their own time.

The Gloucestermen come in to tie up at Town
Wharf occasionally—seiners with their Italian
crews, trawlers with their Portuguese and Irish
and Nova Scotians.

One night not long ago twelve big Gloucester
mackerel seiners were tied up at the docks. One of
them, the *Frank Wilkinson,* had made the first

catch of the season—35,000 pounds—and the skippers of the others were wondering where she did it. But the *Wilkinson's* skipper was uncommonly shy and retiring.

The seiners watch from the masthead for the ripples that mean a school of mackerel, and when they raise one, they lay a "purse" of net under it and haul in the net with a winch until their big machine-driven "dipnets" can reach the fish caught in it. At night, the schools fleck the water with great phosphorescent patches—"fire the water," as the men say—and thus they can be spotted. You will find these schooners "laying over" in the harbor on nights of full moon. They can do no fishing then, for on bright nights the phosphorous doesn't show; and at such times the men play whist in the fo'cs'le and talk of the catches of other days. I heard one of them say he had helped haul in more than 100,000 pounds of mackerel in a single set.

"Sometimes they will school up so thick the vessel will run for ten minutes on top of the school."

The seiners are in Cape waters in the fall, when the schools of mackerel strike here on their way south. Where the fish winter nobody knows. Long arguments about this keep the fo'cs'les lively each November, and large companies have hired marine experts and spent thousands of dollars trying to solve the mystery. Some of the fishermen declare the mackerel burrows into the mud for the winter, and they point to his glazed eye and scrawny figure when he is hauled up in the spring. Others say they have seen schools in the Gulf Stream in those months.

The trawling schooners carry dories and go to the banks to set for groundfish—cod, haddock, sometimes halibut. They go over the side, two men to a dory, and each dory lays its long line on the bottom of the shoal water. The hooks are four to five feet apart and are baited with frozen herring, squid, sand-eels or whatever is plentiful. They let the trawl lie for half an hour or so, and when the schooner's horn gives them the signal, they "haul back." This is back-breaking business, at which even these men must take turns.

Sometimes they are rewarded with a doryful of haddock, sometimes with a dog-fish on every hook —"little sharks"—which have to be slapped off against the side of the dory. When you see a cloud of gulls around a dory in the distance, you know she is having poor luck. The gulls are there to snap up the wasted bait.

What the fisherman hates most is sharks; what he fears is fog. A doryman gone astray in the fog blows on his conch-shell, making a sound that rides down-wind for miles. His vessel either finds him by this clue, or hopes some other craft will pick him up. In several instances, dorymen have been rescued in mid-Atlantic, and among old fishing records I have seen sworn statements by men who went astray on the Banks, drifted out to sea, and— still in their open boats—reached Portugal, Spain or France.

Fog imperils the vessel as well as the dories. Most Provincetown trawl-fishermen can tell you the story of the black Newfoundland dog.

Old "Cheeny" Marshall, who was drowned on the banks when his dory capsized in April, 1937, told this story to me. Cheeny was just a boy, a "salt-passer" on one of the old hand-liners, when—so help him God!—it happened.

The vessel is well out to sea, off Newfoundland. She has not sighted a sail all day, when suddenly, out of a sea calm and smooth as an oil slick, up pops the great black dog. Cheeny lifts him over the rail and lets him lie, half dead, on the deck. The dog has webbed feet.

"Heave him overboard!" shouts one old-timer. "He's the divil!"

But the lad pleads for him, keeps him, takes care of him, puts him in his own bunk. And finally comes the day when the "soup" settles thick over the Devil's Graveyard, in the Bay of Fundy. The helmsman is steering blindly. The dog, standing in the bow, suddenly barks a warning. The helmsman —Cheeny Marshall himself—puts her hard over. And the vessel veers in time to clear by inches the massive bows of a steamer looming out of the mist! It happened, Cheeny Marshall assured me over and over—so help him God!

Fishermen "never get seasick." Of course not. But the candid ones will add that a northeast swell can make them "feel funny." A sou'west blow, no matter how brisk, has no effect; but sometimes, in no more than half a gale, they will admit being "bilgey in the stomach" if the wind is northeast. I have thought this curious, but I have had it demonstrated to my entire satisfaction. Hence even the fine points of weather forecasting are important in this business.

There are all sorts of ways to prophesy the weather when you go fishing. In Boston there was "Old Solitaire," a one-legged gull who frequented the wharves for years, and whose presence always meant a hard blow ahead. In Provincetown, when you see the gulls flying high over the harbor, be ready for a bad blow within a matter of hours. And if you look across the water, at the Truro shore, and the land looms high, you have another sure sign of heavy weather.

Your rheumatism should warn you of an easterly; but if it is hazy and a yeller-eyed sou'wester is in prospect, you may suffer no more than a wetting through the neck of your oil jacket.

There are ways, too, of looking still further ahead. When the oysters bed deep at Wellfleet, there will be a hard winter, and Provincetown Harbor will fill up with pack ice in February—floes so wide there won't be enough open water for a duck to light on, and so thick only the flatfish can navigate below. But if a chicken's gizzard comes away easily from the inner skin, look for an "open winter;" and if a school of herring is raised in January, stow your overcoat for another year—especially if the ducks start laying ahead of schedule and the willows on the swamp banks bud too soon.

The seiners may have the best weather eye, but the trawlers tell the weather with every bone in their bodies. For trawling is riskier. Any doryman knows that.

One of the riskiest things about it is the "night set," or what is known as "torch fishing." If the skipper's almanac shows slack tide in the middle of the night, out they go in the middle of the night —be it clear or black as a Frenchman's sail. They take along kerosene flares, one to a dory; and like a glowing string of beads hung out abaft the vessel, the line of dories stretches for miles across the water. If the swell is heavy, they are taking chances—two men in a tiny shell, out on the open ocean, getting miles away from the mother ship, and even out of sight of the nearest dory. But this is their job. The skipper who comes into Boston Fish Pier with a full hold, and sells his trip at the Fish Exchange for a good price, is called a "killer," and though he may drive his crew mercilessly, the "killer" never has any trouble getting new hands.

If you know how to "pass a curse," you can get as much free fish as you can eat. All you need do is go to the wharf in Provincetown and ask for it. If the men refuse you, you "pass the curse" on them. Then, the next time they go out, they will get no fish. But it's not quite as simple as it sounds; for you must know the ancient ways of passing curses—plain and fancy—and certainly no fisherman will teach you those.

Provincetown once had a hundred trawling schooners in her fleet. At this writing she has one such vessel left—the *Mary P. Goulart*. This schooner's masts were taller in the old days, carrying topsails; and where her mainsail once strained at the sheet, she now has a pilot-house, with the engine-room below. Like the Gloucestermen, she carries foresail and trysail, but only to steady her, not to give her headway.

In 1907, the schooner *Rose Dorothea* of the local fleet won the cup offered by the late Sir Thomas Lipton in a fisherman's race off Boston. Two weeks after the race, while Provincetown was

still so puffed with pride that her own beaches
could scarcely hold her, Theodore Roosevelt
visited the town, and spoke before the fishermen in
the Odd Fellows lodgeroom.

"I would like to go out on the Banks," the then
President said, "to have a chance to talk with you."

Three days after his return to Washington Mr.
Roosevelt received a letter from Captain Marion
A. Perry, of the *Rose Dorothea.*

"Speaking for myself and crew," he wrote, "we
shall be glad to have you with us; and we will do
our best to make your stay on board ship a profitable experience." But the President had a date to
bust a trust.

Competition has driven out Provincetown's
great Banks fleet. The fish have become harder to
find, partly because of the operation of the "beam-
trawlers"—great steam-driven vessels that go out
of Boston equipped to scrape everything from the
shoals with their huge mechanized dredges. They
drag up their fish by the ton, taking the baby cod
and haddock along with the big fellows, and pulling up the "shack" or bottom-stuff which provides
the groundfish with their food. They sort out the
catch, heave over what they don't want, and race
on to take another sounding, leaving tons of dead
small fry and tons of potential food, floating
worthlessly on the surface. The average haul of
these vessels is between 100,000 and 150,000
pounds, but hauls have been made up to 357,000
pounds.

For a few days every summer the tuna come to
Provincetown Harbor and whole boatloads of
them are sometimes brought in. Here they are

called the "horse-mackerel," and they are in fact a species of mackerel. They weigh from 100 to 1,000 pounds. A trip in the trapboats is exciting when the horse-mackerel are running. To watch one of the men "gaff" a five hundred pounder over the gun'ls, with a quick heave, is worth getting up at any time of night. The fishermen say if you get the blood of the horse-mackerel in a cut, it will poison you. I tried this, but perhaps my hands were too clean. They will tell you, too, of the trapman who saw his great horse-mackerel slipping away from him, stripped off his coat and jumped astraddle, riding the fish around Provincetown harbor until, like a bronco-buster, he had him tamed, then had a special saddle made for him and carried the mail 'cross-Bay to Boston.

When you buy a fish, look him in the eye. If his gaze is bright and unblurred, he has not been away from home long. If his gills are bright red, that is another sign he is fresh. But if his eye is dull and sunken, he probably has been witnessing the destruction of his race over a long spell in the hold of a beam-trawler. Professional fish buyers will also have a look at what they call the napes, but the eyes and gills will tell you the story.

Cod and haddock are "firm fish," which keep fresh longer than "soft fish," such as whiting or herring. America, great among nations, nevertheless has no sole. Boston calls flounder "lemon-sole," and a hotel calls almost anything "fillet of sole." Usually it is selling you flounder. Fishermen like "yellowtails" better than the more expensive kinds of flounder. They say it isn't so dry. "Black backs"

also are flounder, and halibut is one of the same
family's rich relatives. Fish dealers say the public
"won't take a mackerel west of Pittsburgh," but
whiting is popular in the west. Frozen whiting are
sent by carloads from Provincetown to St. Louis,
for the "fish sandwich" stands in that territory.
They used to call it "Jack salmon" out west, until
the law intervened in favor of just plain "whiting."

Our Congressmen know distressingly little about
fish, but they have learned one or two facts regarding whales. Recently Senator Norbeck had the job
wished on him of drafting a bill to ratify a treaty
for the protection of whales. Norbeck was from
South Dakota.

"Is a whale a fish?" asked one of the senators.

When he was informed that it was not, they proceeded to that part of the bill having to do with
"right whales." Congressman Tinkham of Massachusetts asked Senator Norbeck if he knew what
a right whale was.

"I suppose it is any whale that isn't wrong," the
puzzled sponsor of the bill answered.

They should have read Provincetown's own historian, one Herman A. Jennings, who was the town
auctioneer back in the nineties. Jennings gravely
penned a little book—now out of print—which can
still be obtained from the public library, and which
is really wonderful for the solemn, scientific essays
he included, embellished with the handsome idiom
of his time.

Some of the literary elegance he shed in his dis-
course on whales should be quoted if only for safekeeping:

"These whales [sperm] are not, as a general thing, much for fighting, seeking safety rather in flight, but occasionally a lone bull, that has been driven out of the herd, is fallen in with, and his ugly disposition, made more sour and morose by the want of companionship, makes him an ugly customer."

Yes, Jennings would have told Senator Norbeck that a right whale is the "largest specimen of known animal life," which swims "through the water with open mouth and takes in immense quantities of small shrimp and other animalculae called whale feed." The fins and tail are a "toothsome dish, and one not to be despised by epicures, the flavor resembling somewhat soused pigs' feet." He adds that the swordfish, "who is the John L. of the sea, delights in attacking the whale. . . . Why the swordfish should make this onslaught on the whale is a mystery, as the swordfish cannot eat any part of the whale, and it must be done purely out of spite."

In addition to writing his "history," which somehow gets the pirate Sam Bellamy aboard the British warship *Somerset* and does a number of other marvelous things, Jennings was an undertaker, wreck master, real estate dealer and auctioneer sans pareil. Once he made $10 with this speech:

"This, ladies and gentlemen, is what Cape Codders of another day used to prevent intrusion of members of different families upon each other when they spent the night in the same house and the number of trundle beds failed to come out even. You see, when more than one family had to use the same bed, they just took this board, made for the purpose and called a 'privacy plank,' set

it upright down the middle of the bed, and privacy
was insured."

He sold an ironing board.

Jennings was a contemporary in Provincetown
of David Stull, "the ambergris king," who bought
the precious substance from the returning whalers,
and was the world's leading dealer in it. Stull
shipped the ambergris to Paris, where he sold it to
the perfume manufacturers. During a fifty-year
period in the Nineteenth Century, a little more
than a ton of ambergris was brought into Atlantic
coast ports, and Stull bought most of it.

"A valuable secretion," Jennings writes, "is
found in this specie of whale [sperm] called Ambergris. This is found in hard bunches in the
whale's intestines; it is of a dark chocolate color,
and in most cases the specific gravity is greater than
water, though there are cases where it has been
known to float. It is one of the best known articles
as a base on which to fix perfumes, and is largely
used in France for that purpose. A good article is
worth more than its weight in gold, at present
prices [1890] about $200 a pound. It has a strong
pungent odor, but by no means unpleasant. Its formation is not fully known, but is supposed to be in
some way connected with the food this specie eats."

Specimens of ambergris are still owned in Provincetown. A collection was preserved by the
"ambergris king" and left to his daughter. Of the
town's whaling days, few other reminders are to be
found now—an occasional log or account book, a
chart or a harpoon, a trypot here and there, and a
scattering of whale vertebrae.

Whaling out of Provincetown was continued, however, long after Wellfleet and Truro had to give it up. The Revolutionary War killed it for the two neighbor towns, but Provincetown's whalemen resumed the chase, and again after the Civil War had interrupted it, the "fishery" persisted out of this port.

The last whaling skipper of Provincetown was Captain John Atkins Cook, who kept at it until 1916. Some of his voyages in the brigantine *Viola* actually paid better than those of the old days; a 25-month trip, ending in 1910, netted 2,200 barrels of sperm oil and 75 pounds of "first chop" ambergris—worth together $47,000. After he quit the sea, Captain Cook wrote a pretentious account of his voyages and had it published. But the story of Viola, his wife, will live long after the Captain and his book, his ambergris and his "ile," are all forgotten.

Viola went to sea with her husband. In 1893 he took her to the Arctic aboard his steam-bark *Navarch,* and returned to San Francisco in 1896. She spent the winter of 1900-01 aboard the *Bowhead* at Baillie Island, a hundred miles north of Herschel Island, where there was a 58-day spell of unbroken night, with the thermometer going to 57 degrees below zero. Boston and other New England newspapers were full of the story of the "courageous woman whose home was the frozen north." When she returned to Provincetown after her 1901 voyage, they quoted her as saying:

"Sewing helps to dispel the monotony that will manifest itself assertively at times."

On that voyage the Captain earned $115,000.

In the spring of 1903 he took her again. I have
an old manuscript account of the trip, written by
a relative and kept in a Provincetown home. It
says:

"Two years were spent in the land of everlasting
cold and desolation, only a few short weeks of summer whaling in partly open seas breaking the
monotony of the ten-months lockup periods. The
second summer in the ice was as fruitless as the
first. . . . The weather of the second winter was
unusually severe; the crew members were mutinous; scurvy and starvation were kept in abeyance
only by Eskimo hunters."

Upon the Captain's failure to turn back, as had
been expected of him, Viola, "inconsolable, hug-
ged the privacy of her cabin for weeks on end,
dwelling constantly upon her isolation. So great
was the shock of her disappointment, her reason
nearly fled, and for months following, Mrs. Cook
remained mentally ill."

The townspeople say she was "mentally ill" not
only for months, but until her death several years
later.

In the meantime, two Irishmen came down the
Cape. They were broke, and for several months
they lived in the hulk of an old wreck half buried
in the Truro beach. One of them, the elder, had
once worked in a shoe factory, had had a row with
his employer, and had made a solemn vow never to
work again. His companion had dabbled in prospecting for gold, in newspaper work, and in a
strange assortment of other professions.

Captain Cook had a housekeeper to take care of
his home on Commercial Street, a French woman,

who met these two wanderers, befriended them and told the younger man a strange story about a Provincetown sea captain, his wife, and a long and tragic imprisonment in the Arctic ice pack. On November 30, 1917, the Provincetown Players gave a performance in their Macdougal Street theater in Greenwich Village, New York. It was a new play, by a young writer who had been chopping away at the stilted theater in which Broadway was encrusted at the time. The play was built around a grim search for oil in Arctic waters; a long imprisonment in the ice; the suffering of the ship's people; and finally, the lapse of the captain's wife into insanity, coming after his refusal to turn back when he had the chance.

"I know you're foolin' me, Annie," says "Captain Keeney" in one of the closing speeches. "You ain't out of your mind. (Anxiously) Be you? I'll git the ile now right enough—jest a little while longer, Annie—then we'll turn home'ard. I can't turn back now, you see that, don't you? I've got to git the ile. (In sudden terror) Answer me! You ain't mad, be you?"

The title of the play was "Ile;" the author, Eugene O'Neill.

The Provincetown Players established themselves in 1915; the names that stand out from that group include, besides O'Neill, John Reed, George Cram Cook, Susan Glaspell, Mary Heaton Vorse, Max Eastman and Wilbur Daniel Steele. Since then a long list of nationally known writers have been in and out of the town—among them Sinclair Lewis—with a few perennials who have taken root and still pay property taxes. Outstanding among these is John Dos Passos.

At present, along with the fringe of dawdlers whose souls go sun-bathing in reflected glory and the hangers-on of the "old school," there are still "new writers" in Provincetown. In spite of the fact that the town really has no particular raison d'etre as a literary center, young people with some ability and no reputations do keep coming. Whether Provincetown will carry on its importance as a literary center through future years, I am not prepared to say, but as long as the "unknowns" continue to come here, I think it has a chance.

The art colony sails ahead under a healthier breeze than mere tradition. The dunelands and the harbor, the rooftops and the streets are tangible inducements to those who can paint, and there are established schools to attract those who want to learn. Architects say Provincetown has the greatest area of skylights in proportion to its rooftops of any city in the United States.

Evidence of a good sturdy condition, promising long life, is the fact that hostilities go on practically unabated between the "academic" and the "modern" factions. The moderns become the academics; then there are new moderns. It looks like perpetual warfare. And as long as there are reinforcements, the "colony" will breathe and good painting of all sorts will be done in Provincetown.

Heresy was already scandalizing the elders when the late Charles W. Hawthorne began to teach here. Hawthorne, equally famous as painter and teacher, ran a school that drew its students from all parts of the country, and his work outlives him not only in the canvases that hang in the Metropolitan and many other museums, but in the tradition which later schools have carried on, and in the work of men whom he taught, and who in turn have gained wide recognition. Hawthorne insisted upon strength and meaning in the pictures of his students, and he had a grand contempt for frills and fancywork. He was sharp-spoken in his criticisms, and he made it a practice to lash out mercilessly at his best pupils. Those who were obviously hopeless he passed with a vaguely encouraging word; but upon those who showed they "had the stuff in them," he came down with both feet, stamping and grinding until he drew sparks.

One day his most promising, and hence most browbeaten, student, made the mistake of stealing off to paint a "pretty" landscape featuring the High Land Light. It was no sin to paint the High Land Light, but a lighthouse does lend itself peculiarly to the sort of "pretty-pretty" sentiment that Hawthorne despised; and the well-meaning young man brought his finished product back, hope and pride welling within him as he placed it on the rack in front of the classroom, for the master's criticism.

The teacher was in a particularly sadistic mood that morning. From canvas to canvas he went, like a cyclone leaving the wreckage of fond hopes in its wake. Deliberately he saved the High Land Light for the last. When he came to that, he lowered his voice to a calm, ominous monotone.

"And now," he said, "we come to something I've had my eye on, trying to think of a title, so that when it is hung in the Metropolitan Museum, the name will do it justice. I think I've hit on it." With arm outstretched towards the "masterpiece," he declaimed:

"Papa Kiss Mama!"

Hawthorne died in 1930. Of his own pictures, the best are the portraits of the fishermen and their wives and children. Hawthorne knew them, was close to them. Like other men of his caliber who have lived in Provincetown, he was delighted with its people and disgusted with its politics.

The art colony carries on, and annually the editions of *Who's Who* and *Who's Who in American Art* show that whether or not the fire of inspiration flares, the smoke of reputation is still here in abundance. And now and then a really "great" painter still emerges from the mass.

# CHAPTER XII

## PROVINCETOWN II

The approach to Provincetown goes unchallenged, I believe, as the ugliest part of Cape Cod. I have not memorized the names that are flaunted from the nondescript string of summer cottages along this stretch of the highway, but they go something like

WEADOREIT

Or

COMEHERETOSITANDTHINK

And they are that kind of cottages. A painted board, a strip of tin—yet enough to mar what was once a stirring unearthliness in that bleak and barren duneland, where the world seemed eternally hung in a moment of indecision between land and sea.

But once beyond these smirking fly-by-nights, Provincetown makes it up to you. Her simple, white-clapboarded cottages, her four-square colonials, keep their faith with the ages. This town, in contrast to her neighbor villages, is compact and populous; yet her angular old rooftops, her lanes and gardens, remain true to the ancient tradition. Provincetown has not "gone off-Cape." She carries on a summer business comparable to that of the South Shore communities, yet she has not

lapsed into a summer resort. She is the Cape's only
touch of old-time urbanity. Her battered old soul
may have its scars, its dark spots along with its
highlights, but such as it is, she has withheld it
from the market.

Like a piece of silver that has just crossed the
palm of Cape Cod, Provincetown nestles within
the "closed fist" at the tip-end. The village is
nearly four miles long, and only "two streets wide."
Commercial Street, the main thoroughfare, is the
continuation of the down-Cape highway as it skirts
the harbor. Provincetowners call it "Front Street;"
and Bradford Street, the other long artery, paral-
leling it, is known as "Back Street."

The mere mention of almost anything in Provincetown carries with it the temptation to add,
"And thereby hangs a tale." Her thoroughfare, her
very soil, have their own stories. If you ask the
townsfolk what makes it possible for them to grow
so many kinds of flowers in the sandy yards along
Commercial Street, and what makes these flowers
bloom so violently, they will explain that the earth
for their gardens comes from all parts of the world
—brought in as ballast by returning ships in the
old days! And of the street itself, the historians
have given an account.

A century ago there was no street. The beach
was the thoroughfare, dories the vehicles; and the
houses faced the waterfront. Shebnah Rich mentions the Provincetown boy who, on seeing a carriage for the first time, "wondered how she could
steer so straight without a rudder." When the street
was proposed for Provincetown, it met bitter op-
position.

"The old were wed to old ways and content,"
Rich says. "Houses, stores, saltworks, fishflakes and
mills were to be removed, wells to be filled, and
rough places made smooth, before the road could
be laid out and sidewalks built." This was accomplished in 1838, but "the old people, particularly
the ladies, who had strenuously opposed the project, declared they would never walk on it, and
were as good as their word, walking slipshod
through the sand as long as they lived." And Provincetown itself still tells of these old ladies, and
how they hopped nimbly over the plank walk
whenever they had to get across it, or, failing that,
stayed at home—never once setting foot to it, to
their dying day.

A short distance beyond the town line, a sandy
trail meets the road at the right. It is called Snail
Road, and though you cannot drive over it as the
Coast Guard trucks do with their extra-wide tires,
it makes a pleasing walkway through the woods
and then across the "desert," fetching up on the
Back Shore. Along the way you get a cross-section
of the Lower Cape's flora, and on those miraculous
sand-surfaces, a written record of its fauna.
Blades of the beachgrass are little living compasses, starting their circles on the sand with a
southwest gust of wind and finishing them with a
northeaster. When you see full circles, you are
having fair weather and what the shiplog calls
"light baffling airs." And in and out among these
tufts, little tracks show that day and night the thin-
whiskered sandhills are teeming haunts for small
creatures.

Years ago, a local reporter, working at space rates, invented a wild story of other creatures haunting the dunes. A colony of nudists, he said—shameless night-revellers—were moonbathing on these puritan sands!

The story was taken up by the Boston newspapers. The town fathers, horrified, voted at once to send a purity-posse into the dunes by night and drag in the offenders.

Night after night the purity-posse lay in hiding, first in one hollow, then in another; and at last, showing the effects of their eager vigils, they gave it up and reported that the nudist colony had disappeared. One or two conscientious members of the posse went back for months afterwards.

The story dies hard and, even now, as new campers are led to a snipe-hunt, gullible visitors to Provincetown are sent on the long trek to the dunes in search of the nudist colony.

At the end of Snail Road is the Peaked Hill Bars Coast Guard Station, and beyond it, near the beach, the remains of "Eugene O'Neill's house."

The structure that stood on this brick foundation was an abandoned Coast Guard Station. Mabel Dodge and Maurice Sterne lived in it. Then she sold it to O'Neill, who did his writing in the boat-house beside it. He and Terry Carlin—the man who had made the vow never to take another job as long as he lived—would lock themselves up for hours at a stretch, doing their own cooking when they thought of it, but mainly talking out the problems that arose in O'Neill's plays. Carlin, brilliant in his own unproductive way, was something of a challenge and a stimulant to O'Neill They disagreed violently at times, and it is said that the shack rattled like a loose stove with the heat of their battles.

The house was toppled over by a wild storm in the winter of 1931, and hundreds of Provincetown citizens were on hand, not many hours later, carrying on the business which their forbears had followed so alertly. Furniture and other belongings of O'Neill were carted off to a hundred homes. Some of these "keepsakes" remain to this day—and are pointed to with pride.

But continuing "upstreet" in Provincetown, the Bissell house, number 621A on Commercial Street, at left, is where the Provincetown Players began, where they gave their first performance, and where O'Neill brought the manuscript of *Bound East for Cardiff* for them to read—while he sat shyly in the next room, hat in hand.

O'Neill lived at one time in the John Francis Apartment, the tall house at number 577, and other well known artists and writers have lived there.

Old John Francis was Portuguese. His father wore earrings, and went fishing, but John decided there was more money in running a store. People still remember John's store, a grand place where you could buy everything from a sailmaker's stitch-heaver to a brass-fitted pulpit. John prospered, bought property and rented it out to the artists. They loved him. Sometimes they even paid him. And O'Neill himself found a friend in John, whom he never forgot in the palmier days to come. There is a stack of letters written by O'Neill to John Francis.

In the same neighborhood are houses owned by
Susan Glaspell, John Dos Passos and Mary
Heaton Vorse, and down at the beach a few hundred feet west of the apartment house, a few old
piles are all that is left of the makeshift theater
where *Bound East for Cardiff* was produced—
the first first-night for the young man who, twenty-
one years later, was to be awarded the Nobel Prize.
The water lapped at the wharf-piles under the
stage that night, and as if provided especially in
answer to the stage directions, a doleful fog-bell
tolled across the harbor.

The little Church of St. Mary of the Harbor
(Episcopal) has been visited by thousands each
summer because the building incorporates the
work of several well known Provincetown crafts-
men, painters and sculptors.

The "Eastern Schoolhouse"—the large white
building on your right, at the beginning of the hill,
stands where the original Provincetown-Truro line
was drawn, in 1714. The "Committee for running
ye line between Truro and ye province lands at
Cape Codd" specified that this line should begin
"at the jawbone of a whale set in the ground by the
side of a red oak stump."

Next, on your right, is the "Figurehead House."

Schooner *A. L. Putnam,* Ben Handy, master,
was ten months out of Provincetown on a day in
April, 1867. The waters of the Indian Ocean lay
smooth and lazy under a blazing sun. From aloft,
suddenly, strange news was sung out:

"Woman all adrift! Two points off the weather
bow! Cable's length away!"

Orders came thick and fast.

"Stand by, there—stand by to lower away the larboard quarter boat! Jib sheets to wind'ard! Lower away!"

The second mate went out with the boat, made the "rescue," and then, as he was rowed back, stood in the sternsheets and grinned sheepishly up at the captain.

"We've got her, Cap'n. But you'd better pass me down a strap and tackle if you want to take her aboard."

Captain Ben took her aboard. And that night, he dusted off his dictionary, sat down and ground out this description of his find:

"A collossal full-length presentment of womankind, modeled with great beauty and vigor and measuring fully eight feet from the placid brow to the underside of the sandaled feet." She was a bit cumbersome, so the skipper ordered her sawn amidships, brought her home, and mounted his "collossal presentment of womankind" upon the house, whence she looks down contentedly today.

Number 473 Commercial, at left, is the home of Donald B. MacMillan, explorer and anthropologist, who was with Admiral Peary on his polar discovery expedition and who later led many scientific ventures into the arctic. MacMillan is not a "stunt explorer." His work has been in the interest of science, not for the advancement of newspaper headlines or radio melodrama.

In 1936, the explorer took to Hollywood a hundred thousand feet of motion picture film, the graphic narrative of nearly twenty-eight years in the far north. In these reels were scenes never before filmed, animals of the arctic, people, icescapes and all the phases of life in a country still little known to the rest of the world. But Hollywood failed to put them into commercial circulation. They wanted to add a love story—of Eskimo girls! Commander MacMillan made them send it all back.

Nearby, on the right, is the white square building of the Provincetown Art Association, housing galleries in which, for a part of each summer, the work of local artists is exhibited.

The Association has not been one happy family throughout its career. When some of the painters "went modern," a schism developed. Feeling ran so high that for a period of years to 1937 there had to be two exhibitions, one "modern," one "academic." Several times the hanging committees were all but hanged themselves. I may be drawn and quartered for saying so, but I think the dissent is wholesome. In 1936 it was decided that the Association would return to its old plan, and both factions would hang together. If the building can do likewise under the strain, I shall be surprised—and a little disappointed.

In clear weather you are likely to find art classes painting on the beach along here, as well as by the roadside. When Hawthorne took his pupils to the shore, he instructed them not to bother painting in the eyes of the subject, although they are, of course, the outstanding feature of a finished portrait. One of these students showed his work to a summer visitor, with the hope of making a sale. She came across a subject that pleased her, but the eyes were not completed. She said she'd take that one, and when the student suggested anxiously that perhaps she'd better let him finish it, she gave him a pat and shook her head. "Now, that's all right," she said sweetly, "I know you have your work to do. You just let me take it home. I'll put in the eyes."

At the left, as you approach the trading center, stands a store building with a little empty bell-tower atop. This was Provincetown's seagoing schoolhouse. It stood originally in a settlement across the harbor on Long Point, the narrow sand-spit which is the tip-end of Cape Cod. When it was built there in 1846, there were two hundred towns-people in the sea-lashed Long Point neighbor-hood.

It was an exciting neighborhood to live in. Children who might have been afraid of dogs else-where, here ran from the sharks. In time the question whether they were living on land or sea grew so perplexing to the Long Pointers, that shortly before the Civil War they launched out and moved 'cross-harbor—floating their homes on casks and scows. This schoolhouse was floated over with the rest of the village, and later became the postoffice. In 1871 a tidal wave rolled into the harbor. It drove the ship *Nina* ashore—and head-on through the postoffice wall. The skipper (perhaps with a thought for the yarn-spinners of posterity) jumped out and mailed some letters.

Town Wharf and Monument Dock serve now where a score of wharves once took care of the harbor traffic. The Boston excursion steamers tie up here. One of them, the *Romance,* collided with the coastwise liner *New York* in Boston Harbor on a foggy September evening in 1936, and it took only twenty minutes to send her plummeting to the bottom. She had more than two hundred persons aboard, who escaped with their lives in that short time through the coolheaded action of the seamen. The *Romance* was 38 years old.

The Town Crier makes his headquarters in the Board of Trade Building, which faces the approach to Town Wharf. Decked out in fancy Pilgrim rig, he marches "up and down-along," ringing his bell and pausing now and then for his say-so.

Time was, not so long ago, when the business of crying was dead serious. The crier wore no costume then; but now that the business has lapsed into a tradition, the frills go with it.

The town crier was retained in Provincetown long after he was dispensed with elsewhere because the town had no daily paper and it was not until 1873 that the railroad reached the Cape-end. Even then, the train was rather an uncertainty unless she had fair wind down the Cape. Later the service improved, but the custom of crying the news held on, mainly because the crier needed the job.

Walter Smith, who laid aside his bell in 1930, was the last of the non-theatrical criers. But the grandest of the lot was Smith's predecessor, little old George Washington Ready, the "Professor," who had been all over the world "and a good many other places besides." The newspapers said he was 88 when he died, in 1920, but that was gross libel; it was said over his dead body! He was 188 if he was a day. But it was always like that with George Washington; the whole world was given to understatement. One of his close friends was Jennings, the auctioneer-historian, and the Jennings-Ready combination startled the world one day in 1886, rushing a tremendous piece of news to Yarmouthport, where it appeared in the paper there and was picked up by the press throughout the nation.

In a chapter of his history, captioned "Sea Serpent of Provincetown," Jennings gives a detailed review of this astonishing adventure of his friend. He introduces his subject in a whirlwind of science:

"The recent earthquakes have so disturbed the bottom of the ocean, that many of the huge creatures which it is believed exist there have come to the surface. Sea serpents and other nondescript monsters, it is alleged, have been seen in various places besides Marblehead, the sea serpent's home. The latest and most collossal in dimensions has visited Provincetown."

It was at Herring Cove that Ready saw the monster rise out of the water, sending out jets of spray like steam, to a height of fifty feet. "The Professor" hid behind a clump of beach plum and watched the creature pass within thirty feet with "a slow and undulating motion" as it wagged its head, big as a two-hundred-gallon cask.

"It was about three hundred feet long, and . . . about twelve feet in diameter. The body was covered with scales as large as the head of a fish barrel, and were colored alternately green, red and blue. . . . The open mouth disclosed four rows of teeth, which glistened like polished ivory, and were at least two feet long, while on the extreme end of the head or nose, extended a tusk or horn at least eight feet in length.

"The creature had six eyes as large as good-sized dinnerplates," the history gravely continues, "and they were placed at the end of movable projections. . . . In the creature's moving along, these projections were continually on the move, so that the reptile could see before, behind and sideways." Three of the eyes were red, three were green. "A strong sulphurous odor accompanied him, and intense heat was emitted, so much that the bushes and grasses over which he moved have the appearance of being scorched with fire."

The creature moved to Pasture Pond. There he swam out, ducked his head, and slowly the long body went down after it.

"As the tail disappeared, the water commenced to recede from the shore till the pond was left completely dry, with a large hole in the center some twenty feet in diameter, perfectly circular, down which sounding leads have been lowered 250 fathoms and no bottom found. . . . Thousands are going to see and examine the track of the huge sea monster.

"For fear that this statement should be doubted," Jennings concludes, "I hereby append a copy of Mr. Ready's affidavit and signature:

> *"I, George Washington Ready, do testify that the foregoing statement is correct. It is a true description of the serpent as he appeared to me on that morning, and I was not unduly excited by liquor or otherwise.*
> *George W. Ready."*

The winter ocean breezes, Provincetown's frame houses and the eccentric oil stoves that warm them, together make a combination calling for a good, spry volunteer fire department. The villagers are uncommonly alert for a fire, and like all communities where the danger is accentuated, Province-town has its imaginary "firebug," a nimble phantom who has been operating through many generations. Four blasts on the packing-house whistles mean a fire, and three long blasts following mean the blaze is in the "east end," two in the "middle of town," and one in the "west end."

When the question of buying a steam fire engine came up in 1869, one voter gave a fine oration against such a purchase. He declared before the town meeting that "cold water would put out a fire as well as boiling water, and there would be no danger of scalding the spectators." The purchase was voted; but the old fire pumper which Provincetown used before that time is still kept in the basement of the Town Hall. It was made in 1836 especially for Provincetown, and it has extra-wide wheels for travel over the sand.

Also in the Town Hall are a large painting by Hawthorne and a mural by Ross Moffett, another widely known Provincetown artist; and the cup presented by Sir Thomas Lipton to the *Rose Dorothea*.

Among the town clerk's archives, the first birth record to be set down officially is dated April 28, 1698. A son Ezekiel was born on that day to Jeremiah and Hannah Cushing, and the page bearing this notation has been coated with transparent silk to preserve it.

But of the town's old records, the one I like best is the protest of a hardworking skipper who was driven ashore.

". . . then made the surf but being so near the Shore had not room to ware Ship So in an Instant was in the Breakers where we Struck and soon grounded Wherefore I do protest against the wind and weather and seas whereby said sloop & all concerned hath or may suffer any loss or damage this done & protested to at provincetown in the State of Massachusetts this 28th of Janury A. D. 1792 By Joshua Howard."

Caleb Howard, one of the crew, made another sort of protest, after the same wreck had taken place. His was not an infrequent complaint in Provincetown. He "made oath" that:

"He had his Chist broken open on Thursday morning, ye 26th of Janery, 1792 by person or persons unknown, but judge them to Be people which came on board the night before, Whilst he and others wass coming in from the Backside of the Cape in Search of houses."

In 1799 the town voted not to take care of Widow Hannah Rider because she was a Methodist, and immediately following, voted "to petion the Gineral Cort to let them know the Disturbance likely to arize concerning the support of the Methodis poor." Apparently the Methodists did cause quite a disturbance to "arize," for the next year it was voted "that Ebenezear Rider keep Hannah Rider for forty-five dolers this year, if the selectmen cannot get anybody to keep her for less."

The courthouse in Barnstable was burned in 1827, and the old town hall in Provincetown, which stood where the Pilgrim Monument is now, was similarly destroyed in 1877. In these two fires were lost all but a few local records. Consequently, the exact age of the old houses of Provincetown is unknown, or at any rate, claims made by their owners cannot be supported by official document. When "the oldest house in town" is pointed out to you—perhaps in half a dozen places—it will be well to bear this in mind.

Near Town Hall is a bronze bas-relief, depicting the signing of the Mayflower Compact, while the ship was at anchor in Provincetown Harbor in 1620. In the Town Hall yard, a tablet has been placed to commemorate the landing of the Pilgrims. The Pilgrim Monument itself, towering 252 feet from the hill behind Town Hall, was intended to commemorate both these events. The tablet and bas-relief are extra—placed, I suppose, to call your attention to these historical items in case the Monument fails to catch your eye.

The *Mayflower* dropped anchor in the harbor on November 11, 1620, Old Style.* That same day, "observing some not well affected to unity and concord," the men of the ship's company drew up and signed the Compact, by which they did "covenant and combine our selves togeather into a civill body politick, for our better ordering and preservation and furtherance of ye ends aforesaid; and by vertue hearof to enacte, constitute and frame such just and equall lawes, ordinances, acts, constitutions, and offices from time to time, as shall be thought most meete and convenient for ye generall good of ye Colonie, unto which we promise all due submission and obedience."

The Fourth of July orator likes to refer to this document as the "germ of our Declaration of Independence," the "foundation of our Constitution." and, in fact, as the origin of practically everything but our taxes.

*November 21, New Style.

The historian says it was no such thing, and that these flowery interpretations are "too sentimental." About the Compact, discerning students of early times in New England are generally in agreement that "there was nothing revolutionary or unprecedented."

The best explanation of the Compact, I should think, would be that offered by William Bradford, who was one of the signers. It was occasioned, he says frankly in his own history, "by ye discontented & mutinous speeches that some of the strangers amongst them had let fall from them in ye ship— That when they came a shore they would use their owne libertie."

However that may have been, the inscription on the monument, which was composed by the late Charles W. Eliot, reads in part:

"This body politic established and maintained on the bleak and barren edge of a vast wilderness a state without a king or a noble, a church without a bishop or a priest, a democratic commonwealth the members of which were 'straightly tied to all care of each other's good and of the whole by every one.' With long-suffering devotion and sober resolution they illustrated for the first time in history the principles of civil and religious liberty and the practices of a genuine democracy."

Twenty years after they did all this, Henry Coggin of Barnstable "rented" James Glass, his white servant, to a Plymouth man for fifty shillings and twenty bushels of corn.

The Pilgrim Monument, Provincetown's outstanding landmark for travelers by land, sea and air, is thoroughly American in its makeup. Although the Pilgrims had never been to Italy, the design is Italian; the plans were made by an army engineer of French and Swiss descent; it was built by the Irish and is taken care of by the Portuguese; and annually it is climbed by several thousand *Mayflower* descendants.

The tower stands 352 feet above the sea, being on a 100-foot hill. Built to "commemorate the arrival of the *Mayflower* and the signing of the Compact," it also serves as a landmark visible many miles at sea, as a vantage point offering a splendid view of the Cape, and as a floodlighted beacon for aircraft.

In addition, it serves to remind the nation that Plymouth was not the first place where the Pilgrim Fathers came, all poetry and all advertising based on such claim to the contrary notwithstanding. The Pilgrims spent five weeks here before they went to Plymouth; and wherever there is a fair opportunity, Provincetown has erected a marker to make this clear.

The cornerstone of the Monument was laid in 1907, and it was completed two years later, at a cost of $95,000, three-fourths of which was paid by State and Federal governments. On the south side is the doorstone of Governor Thomas Prence's home, brought from Eastham; and in the walls many commemorative stones are set.

Manuel Cook, custodian of the Monument, tells of a well dressed gentleman who once paid admission, sat down beside him and quietly asked, "Would you mind very much if I jumped off from the top?" Manuel looked the man in the eye, thought rapidly, then shook his head. "No, mister—*I* wouldn't mind!" The man went aloft, stayed more than an hour, and finally, to Manuel's great relief, came down again and went his way.

There are two "Pilgrim Monuments" on the shores of the Atlantic. At West Quay, Southampton, England, stands a fifty-foot stone tower, surmounted by a cupola on which is set a copper model of the *Mayflower*. From that point the vessel sailed.

The steel framework standing on the hill, near the Monument, is one of the storm-signal towers maintained by the United States Weather Bureau. Flags by day and lanterns by night warn mariners of "weather of marked violence."

The flags are red squares with black centers. One flag signifies a storm on the way, two a hurricane. If the storm is from the east, a red pennant goes up with the flag—above it for northeast, below for southeast; if the wind is from the west, a white pennant goes up with the flag—above it for northwest, below for southwest.

At night, two red lights with a white light between mean a hurricane; two red lights, a northeast wind; one red light, southeast; one white light above one red, northwest; and red above white, southwest.

On the Cape, the pronunciation is always "no'theast" (not "nor'east") ; "nor'west;" "southeast," and "sou'west." "North" is said "noathe," like "loathe." A wind blows from the "no'thard," the "s'uthard," from the "east'ard" or from the "west'ard."

In the old cemetery on Winthrop Street the dates go back to 1723. A tablet has been erected here to the memory of Governor William Bradford's wife, Dorothy, who was drowned while the *Mayflower* was in Provincetown Harbor, and to three others of the company who lost their lives at that time.

Southwest of this lot, on "Meeting House Plain," stood the Old White Oak meeting-house, which closed in 1830 when the only way to silence a too-zealous minister was to bring the church down around his ears.

On January 12, 1789, the town elected "John Conant keeper of the meeting-house, and to swepe it every four weeks and shet and open the winder shetters all the year round for which serves he is to receave two dolers."

It was here, too, that "Mr. Lyman, teacher of writing," held his classes in the vestry. When a new pupil came to him, the first thing he had to do was to set down for the record:

> *"This is a specimen of my handwriting before taking lessons of Mr. Lyman."*

And upon graduation, the pupil was asked to put down:

> *"This is a specimen of my handwriting after taking lessons of Mr. Lyman."*

Some of the double specimens Mr. Lyman placed on exhibit. Others he whisked into the fireplace.

Continuing westward now on Commercial ("Front Street") from Town Hall, you reach the Historical Museum. On display here are a whaler's log, a collection of Sandwich glass, a fine

*Provincetown, Summer 1937.* Trap fishermen return home from a day's work at eight or nine in the morning. The trap fishing industry ended in 1975, after draggers had destroyed the bottom of the fishing grounds. Photograph by Edwin Rosskam, U.S. Dept. of Agriculture, Farm Security Administration, courtesy of the Library of Congress.

*Chatham Windmill, Chatham, April 1934.* Photograph by Arthur C. Haskell, for the Historic American Buildings Survey, courtesy of the Library of Congress.

group of ancient dolls, a ship's Bible that was pil-
fered from the *Somerset,* a roomful of old documents, another of dresses, and a floor of arctic
exhibits lent by Commander MacMillan.

In the museum's picture collection is a rare photograph taken in 1861 of the old lighthouse on
Long Point, which guided mariners from 1826 until a later structure replaced it.

The Point is building out now. If you look
across the harbor, you can see how much has been
added on. Soundings taken near the present tip,
however, show an abrupt falling-off of the shelf.
I would hesitate about going into any real estate
speculation based on the chance of that sandbar
building out much farther.

At a traffic dummy in the west end of town, the
Front Street bends left. Straight ahead is Tremont
Street, and where Tremont intersects with Cottage
Street is located the so-called "Norse Wall Cot-
tage," on Chip Hill.

In 1805 Chip Hill was graded down 25 feet and
a salt works built there. When the works was abandoned, about 1850, this house was built on part of
the site. Workmen, excavating for the cellar, struck
a stone wall. The wall was a mystery then, and
remains so today; for stones of the size that went
into it are not to be found on the Lower Cape.

The practice of the Norsemen of ballasting their
vessels with stone is cited by those who believe, or
want to believe, that the wall is really a Norse
relic, and the depth to which it had been buried
under Chip Hill—about thirty feet—does suggest
antiquity.

The theory that the Norsemen came to Cape

Cod antedates the discovery of Provincetown's "Norse Wall" by many years, but the find is now offered as evidence to support it, and indeed is the only tangible evidence the Cape has. On this speculation Thoreau says, "But as Biarne, and Thorwald, and Thorfinn have not mentioned the latitude and longitude distinctly enough, though we have great respect for them as skillful and adventurous navigators, we must for the present remain in doubt as to what capes they did see. We think they were considerably further north." Thoreau began writing his book in 1855—two years after the wall at Provincetown had been unearthed.

The wall has never been scientifically examined by archaeologists, and whether any of its stones bear inscriptions is not known. Harvard representatives did approach the owner during the 1890's. They were told that if they promised to put everything back shipshape, they could go ahead and dig. For some reason which escapes the present version of the story, they evidently couldn't promise that. And so, the "Norse Wall" makes up in mystery what it may lack in authenticity.

In the winter of 1936-37, archaeologists of Dartmouth College let it be known that they were planning an expedition to Hampton, New Hampshire, "in search of the bones of Thorvald." In that place, according to the announcement, "a large stone, with curious marking, as yet uninterpreted, discovered in a windswept field close to the ocean, is believed to be the grave of Thorvald. Crosses, chiseled into the hard surface of the granite stone, could not have been made by glacial ice." It was added that Norwegian and United States government officials had interested themselves in the

story, and if the legend were borne out, "leaders
in the town were planning to make the spot a national shrine." With town leaders everywhere
keenly aware of the commercial possibilities, we
may have within a few years an imposing array
of Thorvalds all down the Atlantic Coast, and the
tourist may take his choice.

Around the bend, Commercial Street leads past
a summer theater, and up to another tablet, on the
right side of the road at the extreme west end of
town. This one marks the "Place of the First Landing of the Pilgrims."

The stone breakwater extending from this point
to the sandbar at Wood End Light was built by
the Federal Government in 1911, when it was believed the tidewaters were threatening to cut away
the slender strip of beachland and inundate part of
the town.

Provincetown has always had the problem of
keeping the whale from the door. Every few years
some engineer's report warns of a new encroach-
ment of the sea upon this beleaguered townsite. In
1936 an engineer stated:

"The shore line along the thickly settled portion
of Provincetown is constantly in need of protection, with new sea walls and repairs to bulkheads.
In many places the shore line at high tides is within
100 feet of the main street. . . . The tide ebbs and
flows under several buildings in this area and in
cases of flood tides coupled with strong winds,
much damage is done."

Viewed from the breakwater, both the village
and the harbor take on loveliness anew. Perched
out at land's end—the tip of Cape Cod—is Long

Point Light, by which all homecoming fishermen steer. To the right, the odd, hump-like formation was once a fort, thrown up there during the Civil War but never used; and ahead, at the end of the breakwater itself are Wood End Light and Wood End Coast Guard Station.

Off Wood End the submarine *S-4* was rammed and sunk on the afternoon of December 17, 1927, taking the lives of forty men.

Provincetown, long hardened to wrecks, now witnessed horror such as she had never known before. Slow suffocation within steel walls, 110 feet below the surface, went on for four days, while divers struggled to save the men with whom they could exchange messages by tapping in international code.

On the day of the accident, the Coast Guard destroyer *Paulding* had come across-Bay from Boston to comb the vicinity for rum runners. Through lack of coordination between the two branches of service, she was unaware that the submarine was at that time undergoing submerged trials in the deepwater course outside Provincetown Harbor. At the same time, storm warnings were flying, the wind was northwest—the worst possible weather for that particular stretch—and white water was already making over the submarine's projected course.

The *Paulding,* finding no rum-running craft in the outside waters, rounded Race Point and headed for the harbor, steaming straight into the submarine's testing-ground. Meanwhile the *S-4* had been put through several dives, and at the moment was proceeding with only a few feet of her periscopes

showing. A heavy sea was running, but the periscopes would have been clearly visible to any alert
observer aboard the destroyer. They had been seen
and recognized from ashore by Lookout Frank
Simonds of the Wood End Coast Guard Station.
Boatswain Gracie, coming up to the observation
room, asked Simonds what he had seen offshore.
The lookout said, "Not much. But there was a submarine on the test run not long ago." Gracie anxiously took the telescope. Near the end of the measured mile he caught the little foaming wake of
periscopes. "Good God, there's going to be a collision!" And he ran down to get his lifeboat ready
for launching.

The *S-4* was just slanting to emerge, and her conning tower was half out of water when the speed-
ing destroyer struck. She smashed her stem into
the battery room of the submarine, just forward of
the conning tower, on the starboard side. The hole
was only about a foot across, but the impact and
the leak it caused were enough to send the steel
shell reeling to the bottom.

That the *Paulding* had been unaware of the
*S-4's* presence in those waters is clear from the
radio message she sent out:

RAMMED AND SUNK UNKNOWN SUBMA-
RINE OFF WOOD END PROVINCETOWN

From New London sailed the *Falcon,* the
Navy's only salvage ship in the Atlantic, and from
Newport came Divers Eadie, Carr and Michels.
From Portsmouth came the mother-ship, *Bush-
nell.* From New York were sent pontoons—in tow
of hopelessly slow tugs.

The collision occurred at 3:37 o'clock on a Saturday afternoon. The *Falcon* did not arrive on the scene until 7 the next morning. Meanwhile Boatswain Gracie of the Wood End Coast Guard Station, venturing out in his surfboat, spent twelve harrowing hours in a big sea, whipped by the icy nor'wester. He had found the submarine with his grapnel—and lost her again—before the *Falcon* arrived! Trying it once more, he struck at 10:45 o'clock Sunday morning, and about three hours later Diver Tom Eadie went down the grappling line.

Coming down with lead shoes on the steel hull, Eadie caught an answering signal from within. Forward, from the torpedo room, it came to him unmistakably—six taps—six men still alive! Aft, there came no answer.

The *S-4's* conning tower was equipped with two emergency connections to the outside, one for an air line reaching crew compartments, the other for a line to the ballast tanks. It was now up to the rescue operators to decide which of these connections to make, for the divers could only take one line down at a time.

When Eadie came up, Diver Carr went down with an air line. He did as he had been instructed: instead of coupling it to the *S-4's* crew compartment connection, which would have enabled the surviving men to breathe, he attached it to a connection designed to blow ballasts, with the object of raising the submarine herself. But two compartments were flooded and the ballast system was broken; and the result was that instead of lifting the *S-4,* the pumps at the surface were merely blowing air into the Atlantic Ocean through her punctured lungs.

Upon discovering that they had guessed wrong, the officers ordered Diver Michels down, to make the other connection. But now the sea was so great that diving itself looked like suicide. Michels went anyhow, became fouled in some wreckage, had to be rescued by Eadie, and was brought up three hours later in a serious condition. At this stage all vessels but the *Falcon* ran into Provincetown Harbor for shelter from the gale.

The prostrated diver was kept in the *Falcon's* recompression tank. Monday morning the *Falcon* left the scene, going all the way to Boston to put Michels in a hospital. It was explained by those in charge that further diving would be impossible until the storm abated. When the salvage ship returned, diving was still out of the question.

Meanwhile communication with the imprisoned men had been continued by Morse signals sent on an oscillator. On Sunday evening the *Falcon* sent down the query:

"How many are there?"

"There are six." And the taps from below added, "Please hurry."

The next night the *Falcon* relayed a message to Lieutenant Fitch, in the submarine:

"Your wife and mother constantly praying for you."

No answer came, and through the night the message was repeated. Still there was no answer. Then, on Tuesday morning, from the sunken ship at last came a message:

"We understand."

After that, the six suffocating men sent no more messages.

On Wednesday morning, when the storm had

abated and diving was possible again, the *Falcon* discovered that her single manila buoyline had parted. The submarine was lost again! Another grapnel was put down for her. While it was being dragged back and forth, the fishermen offered to help. They said they could line up their flounder draggers, moving abreast with their wide dredges dragging astern, and save time locating the wreck. The suggestion, though seemingly practical, was refused. And those last precious hours, when there might still have been some slight chance for the men below, were lost while the single grappling-iron went back and forth, back and forth, groping for the *S-4*.

That afternoon a line finally was made fast, divers went down, and the air line was attached to the crew compartment connection.

Then fresh air was pumped into the forward compartment—where lay six lifeless bodies.

When the Navy Department was informed that all on the *S-4* were dead, it decided to leave the submarine on the bottom until the spring. But "public opinion demanded a continuance of the salvage efforts," and so, work was resumed. The bodies were taken out, and three months later the ship was raised and towed to Charlestown Navy Yard.

The court of inquiry placed the blame on commanders of both the colliding craft, and also on Rear Admiral Frank H. Brumby, in charge of the "rescue" operations. Secretary of the Navy Wilbur overrode the decision of the court as it applied to Brumby and to Lieutenant Commander John S. Baylis, captain of the *Paulding*. Thus upon the dead commander of the *S-4* officially rests the full responsibility.

Since the tragedy, the Navy, according to newspaper accounts, has perfected "many escape devices to insure against a repetition of such losses." When the *S-51* went down off Block Island in 1925, snuffing out 33 lives, much the same sort of thing was said. Two years later the horror was repeated. From 1927, the record is clear.

The continuation of Commercial Street beyond the end of town is the "New State Highway," which passes "New Beach." On a clear day the Plymouth shore is visible from here.

The way lies through the Province Lands, from which the town gets her name. Some odd tangles of land ownership have arisen from the unique status of this township.

In 1691 the Commonwealth was named owner of the Province Lands, which then included the whole town. The rugged little settlement of fishermen, freebooters and beachcombers along the harbor was made a precinct of Truro—an unruly precinct, the "poker flats" of Cape Cod, which pious Truro decided to get rid of as soon as possible—and in 1727, when the precinct was granted incorporation as a town and was named Provincetown, the title to all lands still rested in the Commonwealth.

But Provincetown bought and sold the lots in the village, and became very much aware of the right of private property—save at such times as a ship ran aground on the back shore with full cargo. Many of the old deeds read, "from sea to sea," as if the State's title did not exist. And anyone "trespassing" against such rights was apprised of his mistake quickly enough.

But there was widespread agitation. The thing was fought out in the State capitol, one member of the assembly demanding:

"Where do the people of Provincetown get their authority to appropriate two miles of valuable shore front to private ownership and use, when the act of incorporation distinctly says it is public property and is to be used in common? Where do the selectmen get their authority to concede the right of outside speculators, non-residents, to take up these public lands, held for the use of the fishermen, and compel these same fishermen to buy what in law and equity is already theirs?"

And so, shortly afterwards, in 1893, the State voted to surrender its ownership of land occupied by the village proper, retaining only the Province Lands. The politicians of Provincetown, who have seldom lost weight through worry over the welfare of fishermen, were satisfied. "Outside speculators" could now deal in the two miles of shore front without hindrance; the duneland which the State retained was worthless commercially, and in "owning" it, the State was obliged to spend many thousands of dollars to anchor the blowing sandhills.

But, within recent years, summer people have been building houses farther and farther back on the Province Lands; some doubt has been raised about the worthlessness of the dunes; and so, early in 1937, Provincetowners petitioned for a set of definite boundaries on the Province Lands. "Outside speculators" are at it again.

At the next intersection of roads, take the left turn and drive past the airport to Race Point. "The Race" is the end of Cape Cod's dreaded Back

Shore. Once a mariner has rounded it in a north-east blow, he is in more merciful waters. Fishing vessels are often in distress, however, before they can slip out of the clutches of these gales, and the Race Point Coast Guard Station answers many calls. Further to the southwest is Race Point Light, but the road ends here. If you drive out on a summer evening, you will find the big parking place crowded with other cars on the same mission. Sunset on the Race is an unfailing spectacle—but it has to be witnessed, usually, to the accompaniment of a dozen shrieking crooners from automobile radios going full blast.

Down at the beach, below the parking place, a weathering hulk lists in the sand—and brings you face to face with shipwreck. She is the *Spindler,* and if her old bones had speech, I would willingly leave the tale for them to tell.

A "rummy" she was, in the prohibition era. She had cleared Yarmouth, Nova Scotia, with a full hold—several thousand cases of "high grade"—and she had her papers in perfect order, made out for a voyage to the West Indies. It was common practice of vessels bound for our shores with "hot cargo" to have their papers made out for the Indies. The *Spindler's* real destination was a spot on the Plymouth shore, where by prearrangement assistance was waiting.

Her skipper was a short, stocky French Canadian, with all the grit required for the assignment. She had been jogging along merrily and was half way across Massachusetts Bay when she was overtaken by a "gutterin' no'theaster." On she scudded, under bare poles, but the storm grew steadily fiercer. Off the Race, the skipper tried to square away for the Plymouth shore, but the vessel was batted back like a shuttlecock. Then she struck. She went wildly bouncing over the sand, and at last—on the fourth bounce—landed high and dry.

There sat the *Spindler* with her "hot cargo," neatly delivered at the Coast Guards' front door. Yet everything was still quite legal. The skipper showed his papers and pleaded "stress of weather." He had been beyond the twelve-mile limit, bound for the West Indies, was driven helplessly off his course, and hence his appearance, not only in American waters, but on American soil.

Meanwhile half of Provincetown had got wind of the wreck and had rushed out to the Race for pickings. The citizens "salvaged" what they could find on the beach, and a couple of the more venturesome boarded the vessel. The skipper, who was still in the Coast Guard station, explaining his presence, rushed out, picked up the raiders bodily and threw them overboard—onto the sand.

For safekeeping, the Coast Guardsmen broke open the hold and took the entire cargo into the basement of the station. There it was withheld from Provincetown's army of volunteer "rescue workers" while the skipper got in touch with his owners. A few days later another vessel was sent to Provincetown from Nova Scotia. She tied up at Railroad Wharf, and the obliging authorities of the Coast Guard provided trucks and took enough men off rum patrol duty to transport the *Spindler's* cargo from Race Point to the wharf. There it was loaded on the second vessel, which also had papers made out for the West Indies.

That night the liquor was taken across-Bay and unloaded at Plymouth.

There was smuggling on Cape Cod long before 1800; there was smuggling during the prohibition era, when the "rummies" bestowed on the Coast Guard the nickname of "Hooligan Navy;" and as this book is being written, there is still smuggling here.

Here is Cape Cod, 1705:

> *Squier Dudley:*
> *... Very often hear is opportunity to seas vessels, and goods which are upon a smoglen acompt. i believe had i a comishon so to do i could have seased a catch this last weak ... your homble and unworthy sarvont*
>
>                            *Wm. Clap.*

And here is Cape Cod, 1937:

> *A government ambush that barely failed to trap a band of liquor smugglers and ended in gunfire on the Brewster Beach early yesterday, drew the curtain of secrecy from the determined effort of Coast Guards and law enforcement agencies to stamp out the smuggling of liquor, cologne and narcotics in the Cape Cod area. The incident marked the second time within two weeks that Coast Guards and customs inspectors have blocked attempts of smugglers to land a cargo on Cape shores. At Cotuit two weeks ago tonight, law enforcement officers ashore, aided by Coast Guards offshore, cooperated to prevent a landing.*

Throughout the years of prohibition there was gossip—and frequently something more than gossip—in Provincetown. One night a fishing vessel made in from the "mother ship" off the Back Side, so heavily loaded that the water was running both ways through her scuppers. A spot was picked in

Dennis for the unloading, behind an abandoned hotel on the Bay Shore, but the Bay waters grew so rough the skipper couldn't chance the run across. He headed around the Point and dropped anchor in Provincetown Harbor, a few hundred yards offshore at the East End.

There the vessel lay, until the Coast Guard cutter, anchored near the Point, began playing her searchlight over the harbor. The skipper knew, once he was spotted riding so low in the water, he would be boarded and searched. No trip of mackerel could have brought her that far down. So he resorted to the usual device in an emergency— heaving overboard the burlap sacks in which the bottled liquor was tied, with the intention of coming back to grapple it up at a later opportunity. The men dropped eight hundred "cases," in water that covered it by only two feet at low tide.

The next night, with a truck ready ashore, they rowed out in dories to begin the work of recovering. They loaded 160 cases on the truck that night and sent it on its way up-Cape.

But the following night a full moon was out. The work was ticklish. Meanwhile, a gang of high school boys, celebrating a football victory, was cruising up and down the Front Street in cars, giving their yells. A couple of the lads saw a large truck, half loaded with liquor. They stopped their car and boarded it. The truck driver, coming back from the beach, seeing the boys in his cab and thinking they were revenue men, ran for dear life. And the youths hilariously drove up Commercial Street with several hundred dollars' worth of fine whiskey. Eventually the Coast Guard got word of

the cache, rowed out in their own dories, and con-
fiscated what was left.

Returning to town, go straight ahead on the
"Old State Highway," through the Province
Lands, and so into Bradford Street, which, if you
must go, will put you back on the highway up-
Cape.

I have called out the "sights" of Provincetown
to you, but in my space allotment I cannot call out
the life of the town. There are more facets than I
can hold to the light; the water is bluer than any
man can paint it.

# CHAPTER XIII

## CHATHAM

*Return on U. S. 6 to Orleans. Left from U. S. 6 on State 28.*
*Five miles to Chatham village.*

"I don't care who put her there, she ain't set right! If that's magnetic north, I'll eat a sunsquall!"

Captain Noadiah Bearse called to him the eight other retired sea captains of Chatham who had been invited as dinner guests at the "launching" of the town's swankiest hotel. The nine old shipmasters had approved of everything, until Captain Noadiah discovered the compass set out front as a decoration. Gathering around it now, the others agreed she was out of line; the whole hotel was off her course; no good could come of it.

Captain Ezra Nickerson peered at it, snorted, turned away. "Mph! Wouldn't lay me a run for Vineyard Sound with that thing—for fear of hitting the Old Gray Lady!" The "Old Gray Lady," in case you haven't met her, is the island of Nantucket. "Why, anybody'd know magnetic north lays along here—a line with the peak of that shingled house!"

"What?" Captain Noadiah demanded. "Along there! Ezra, it's been a long time, all right, since you've navigated anything bigger than a cane-seat rocker, I can see that! Magnetic north lays directly by the sternsheets of the pungo alongside the house."

Seven other deepwater men raised an outraged chorus. They not only disagreed with Noadiah; Ezra was wrong too. And then as each pointed out magnetic north—somewhere between the pungo and the house—the others declared he'd lost his wits.

"Well, I've still got my compass," Captain Noadiah said. "She's pointed me to China six times. I'll just fetch her over tomorrow morning and prove I'm right." He looked about him contemptuously and added, "Just for myself. I may be old, but I hope to show I haven't gone clean adrift into second childhood yet!"

Next morning nine sea captains, bearing nine ancient compasses, appeared in front of the hotel. Each took his bearings, each gave a nod of satisfaction and tenderly closed the worn cover on the instrument, then turned and trudged home without a word to the others.

Nine old souls with nine battered, beloved relics of their seafaring days, had set the world to rights. And who are we, who have never trodden the quarterdeck of a square-rigger, to deny that from the Chatham Bars Inn magnetic north may lie on nine points of the compass?

At this late stage it would be an unsafe policy to include within the covers of a guidebook the names and addresses of the sea captains still living in the various towns on the Cape. Since 1920 I have been reading that "they are all gone," a statement many of them have denied; but the dissenting voices are growing few and faint. Two well-known Chatham skippers, Captain Elmer Mayo and Captain Seth Ellis, who moved to Harwichport, died in 1936.

Both these men were voted Congressional medals for life-saving. Two others, Zenas Hawes and Captain George Bloomer — also decorated by Congress—were still living in Chatham in that year. And from Chatham up the Cape and down, the ranks of the men who were "all gone by 1920" might have surprised the visitor of 1930 who knew nothing of Cape Cod longevity.

As I have been at some pains to point out, these sea captains were not all heroes, and in many cases those who write sentimentally have sometimes given the skipper credit for what the crew has done. But the four men of Chatham I have named —and many others I have not—rightly belong among the great men of the sea; some have earned a place in this long roll of honor for saving life in the face of threatened disaster; others for the less spectacular heroism of sailing a ship decently— with human decency—against great odds.

Seth Ellis went to sea at nine with his father, skipper of an Indies trading schooner. At eighteen he had his own fishing vessel, and later was master of the *Novelty,* a Boston steamer. In 1895 he enlisted in the life-saving service.

On March 17, 1902, the Monomoy station discovered a barge, the *Wadena,* in distress off the Point. A northeast gale had whipped up breakers which looked as if they could swallow a surfboat head-on, yet Ellis and seven others manned the boat and reached the barge. All five men were taken off, and the boat headed shoreward, when the seas she was shipping alarmed the bargemen, and in their fright they forgot to obey the order to sit perfectly still. The boat was tossed broadside to the sea, capsized and lay bottom up, with the men clinging to her. One by one they dropped off as their strength gave out.

Captain Mayo, who was aboard the barge *Fitzpatrick,* anchored hard by, could see the overturned surfboat clearly. He got ready a tiny dory and, having no oars, improvised a pair. Others aboard the barge told him it was suicide to go out. Mayo answered he had had enough of watching men drown before his eyes. Out he went, and he reached the overturned lifeboat. But by that time only Seth Ellis was holding on. Mayo got him aboard and rowed him back to the *Fitzpatrick.* The sea had taken twelve lives. Elmer Mayo had cheated it of one.

In a cold southeaster the Maine schooner *Grecian* was sighted at daybreak, grounded on the outer bar at Chatham. She was about 750 yards offshore, and about opposite where the Chatham Coast Guard Station is now. The crew had taken to the rigging, where they would freeze to death or be spilled into the sea, unless—by a long chance—they were somehow taken off and brought ashore. Two boats were manned with volunteer crews at the life-saving station. Captain Bloomer was in one boat, with four other men; Zenas Hawes and six companions were in the other.

With a full gale from the southeast, they could not approach the schooner except from the windward. To do that, they had to row several hundred yards beyond her, swing about, and let the great seas carry them back. With the current that was running, they couldn't stop when they reached the *Grecian,* but the men on board knew they were expected to jump for it as the boats sped by. Several times they could not steer near enough, and they had to try again, but at last all five of the schooner's men were taken off safely and brought ashore. The *Grecian* was beached soon afterwards, and lay for years in the sand. Her timbers were unusually heavy, but the breakers finally smashed her to pieces.

George Bloomer and Zenas Hawes were young men at the time of the wreck. Their medals read: "In testimony of heroic deeds in saving life from the perils of the sea. To (name) for brave assistance in rescuing five persons from the wreck of the schooner *Grecian* December 6, 1885."

Significantly, in its 1937 town meeting, Chatham voted to change the name of "Captains' Row" to "Cross Street."

Yet this town, with four square miles of land and 48 miles of waterfront, is still very much in the embrace of the sea, and so is its business. The trapmen, scallopers and eelmen keep at it, and the Provincetown fleet comes here to fish.

Now and then Father Neptune flips the town into the front page news. Recently a 5,000-ton freighter, the *Minnesotan,* buried her nose in the sand at Shovelful Shoal, the same treacherous shelf where the *Wadena* disaster took place, and narrowly missed destruction; in the same spot, the liner *President Hayes* ran aground in 1931, and off North Chatham, in 1907, the big Clyde liner *Onondaga* met the same fate.

On a recent winter morning, the Coast Guard craft *Argo* heard a call that gave her skipper quite a start: "Mutiny. I need assistance." It came from

the four-master *Alvena,* which was in a dangerous
position south of Pollock Rip channel. It turned
out that four of her crew had refused to hoist a
sail. The difference was ironed out in time to clear
the vessel from a rather tight spot.

To see the town of Chatham, we shall have to
commit a trespass, but the law is on our side.
Father William Nickerson has lain in his grave
these 250 years; and still, you can never be certain, as you drive through Chathamport, that you
will not one day see a shadowy ancient "proprietor"
rise out of the ground, point a finger at you and
cry, "Get thee off my acres! For I, and I alone,
am The Proprietor."

William Nickerson, who came in 1656 from
Yarmouth, and hence was not without some polish
in the art of flimflamming the Indians, offered the
Sachem of the Monomoyicks a boat, a few clothes
and a heap of the usual trash that the white man
held out as bait. It was a handsome tract that
William was after here at the elbow of the Cape—
four thousand acres—and he felt pretty much as
a picker-up of first folios feels in the attic of some
unwitting book owner. William held his breath.
The Sachem smiled, nodded, and made it a deal.
Both parties were simply delighted. Sachem Mat-
taquason shook hands and, still smiling, climbed
into his strange, wonderful new boat, nearly cap-
sizing her in his excitement, but finally getting
under way.

The historians tell us that while it is true Manhattan Island was "sold" for $24 worth of trinkets,
the Dutch who bought it were cheated, for it had
already been sold once by the Indians; the Dutch

had to buy it again before it became theirs. And apparently the Sachem of the Monomoyicks had heard of this kind of deal from his New York cousins. Poor William Nickerson learned, not only that his magnificent tract had already been purchased—and for less, which must have hurt him terribly—but also that the court at Plymouth was fining him for giving the Indians a boat!

For sixteen years Nickerson fought the case out with the Plymouth crowd, who had the advantage of being headed by Thomas Hinckley, the Governor's own assistant. Finally William bought them off for ninety pounds—many times the value of his price to the Sachem—and gained possession of the land. It was a hard fight, but when Chatham became a town in 1712, the Nickersons owned it. Occasionally the Indians made nuisances of themselves.

Route 28, which I shall call "the highway" from here on, passes the big station of the Radio Corporation, which handles ship-to-shore communication, and which sometimes relays messages of life-and-death importance for vessels in distress. It has also served in thousands of cases of sickness aboard small craft which have no doctors, relaying the medical advice from Boston. But its principal routine business is in private messages and in supplying the news bulletins to the little papers that ocean liners print for their passengers. Some day it may have to serve transatlantic air travel.

If your time in Chatham is limited, and you want a continuous circle of the town, instead of turning with the highway at the crossroads beyond the laundry, keep straight ahead, towards the

shore. (I confess that I would rather not route you
around like this; if you are to see these old towns
as they should be seen, your way must be leisurely.
On the other hand, some sort of itinerary does prevent a "guide" book from taking your time and
your energy tracking down the things mentioned
in it.)

Driving along the crest of the bluff now, you
can look down at the wharves used by the fishermen who go out for cod and haddock in their gasoline dories and other small craft. A large part of
the Provincetown fleet frequents these waters in
the winter, though they are hampered by the
shoals. It is an uncomfortable stretch to be caught
on, even in half a gale, and coming through the
bars is ticklish business in any sort of weather.

Passing the summer home of Joseph Lincoln—
the house at the left just beyond the Hawthorne
Inn—the shore road fetches up at Chatham Light.

A lighthouse is something more than a decoration for these waters, and there have been lights
on the bluff since 1808; but the sea has come in
after them, bringing one down every few decades.

Some day, Lightkeeper Woodman has told me,
the sea will get his tower too.

Nowhere on the Cape's shorelines has the sea
kept busier at her handiwork than here among
these storm-bitten sands. Directly to the south of
the bluff, Monomoy lies beckoning like the bony
finger of death which it has been to countless ships.

I cannot tell you when Monomoy rose out of
the sea; but my large detailed map of 1858, for
which the coastline work was supplied by the U. S.
Coast Survey, shows it as an island, about seven

miles long, and cut off from the southeast corner of the Cape by two miles of ocean—"breakers" it is marked here. Today, a bus will take you down the length of Monomoy on dry beach. For want of the same, more than one wrecked mariner has perished where your bus wheels are leaving their imprint in the sand less than a century later.

It was in the waters off this part of the Cape that the *Mayflower,* southbound, "fell amongst deangerous shoulds and roring breakers," and turned back to make a run for Provincetown Harbor, "hapy to gett out of those dangers before night overtooke them."

Another ship, on October 4, 1729, lay in distress off Sandy (Monomoy) Point, bringing to a close a tale of horror and almost incredible cruelty.

Charles Clinton, of Longford, Ireland, was fired by tales of the New World. He induced a number of his friends to join him in the venture and in May, 1729, the *George and Ann* set sail from Dublin for Philadelphia.

These people were burning their bridges behind them. The women talked of their homes in the new world; the children waved a last farewell to Ireland; the men, who had converted their estates, felt the gold in their belts. In all, there were 190 passengers, 30 of them children.

The master of the *George and Ann* was a Captain Rymer, "a cold-blooded tyrant," says Amos Otis, "of whom his sailors were in constant fear." Knowing that these Irish families, many of them of large estate, had brought gold representing all they owned, Captain Rymer conceived the idea of stretching out the voyage until all the passengers had starved to death!

The voyage lagged; the passengers were placed on short rations; some had already died. But two men had a smattering of navigation, and one night they discovered the ship was tacking against the wind on a course due east. They asked the helmsman about it. All he would say was that he was carrying out the captain's order. The two men called together their emaciated fellow-passengers. They were an innocent lot. Some wouldn't believe what they heard; and those who did suspect the captain were too weak to cope with him. One possessed a brace of pistols. He gave them to the men who had queried the helmsman. Then they marched into the captain's cabin, and accused him of delaying the voyage. Captain Rymer denied everything and "made fair promises."

At last they raised the Capes of Virginia, but the captain's "luck" held, and he had to stand off in a gale. Then, according to the captain's later testimony, the vessel was driven all the way to Cape Cod without a chance to make any of the intermediate ports.

The arrival of the *George and Ann* off Chatham is described in the New England *Weekly Journal,* November 10, 1729:

We hear from Martha's Vineyard that some time last month Capt. Lothrop, in his passage from this place [Boston] to that island, off of Monomoy espied a vessel which put out a signal of distress to them. He making up to her went aboard; found her to be a vessel from Ireland, bound for Philadelphia, (as they said) who had been from thence 20 weeks and brought out 190 passengers, 30 of whom were children, being destitute of provision, (having then but 15 biscuit on board) 100 of them were starved to death, among which were all the children except one, and the remainder of the passengers looked very ghastfully.

They craved hard for water, of which one drank to that degree that he soon after died; and two more died while Capt. Lothrop was aboard. Only three of the sailors were alive (besides the master and mate) and they sick.

Captain Lothrop brought the surviving passengers ashore a little further down-Cape, and Captain Rymer proceeded to Philadelphia in the *George and Ann*. There the three sailors brought charges against him. He was arrested, sent in irons to England, and there hanged. Charles Clinton and his wife, who were among those surviving, went with the others to Ulster County, New York. There have been several famous Clintons of Ulster County, among them George and DeWitt Clinton, both governors of the State.

In the eerie annals of Monomoy there is one blank page—blank save for certain bloodstains which, in 1772, Ansell Nickerson tried to explain to the magistrates in Boston.

When Captain Joseph Doane boarded the Chatham schooner *Abigail* in answer to a distress signal, he found her decks running red, and of her crew of five, only Ansell Nickerson remained. The lone sailor told a story of pirates, men from a mysterious topsail schooner, who had boarded the *Abigail,* murdered three men and the ship's boy, and then, breaking out a barrel of Jamaica rum, drank with gory hands to the success of their pointless raid. He himself had escaped, Ansell said, by hanging unseen to the taffrail.

The dread cry of "Pirates!" ran like wildfire up the Bay Shore, and on to Boston, where Ansell was taken to tell his story again. A frigate went out at once to comb Bay and Ocean. She was joined by others from Rhode Island. But when no pirates were found, the burden of proof fell back on Ansell Nickerson. He was committed to Boston gaol, on a charge of murder. During the eight months he was kept there, the search went on, and his guilt or innocence was the talk of every wayside tavern. The murdered men were Nickerson's own kinsmen, his defenders pointed out. There were character witnesses by the score. And Ansell was the only eyewitness the court had.

He was found not guilty—though the judges were divided four and four on their verdict. "The Court," they told him, "do not think that the Evidence offered . . . is sufficient to support the Charge alledged against you." John Adams, Ansell's attorney, later wrote in his diary, "I know not to this day what judgement to form of his Guilt or innocence."

On November 22, 1936, Wesley Eldredge, Chatham fisherman, picked up a tattered boot that lay on the beach at Monomoy, half a mile below the Coast Guard station. The Coast Guard patrols made a careful search of the beach, but saw nothing more. The boot had a human leg-bone in it.

"Mooncussers," if you have an ear for the old-time talk, did a tidy business alongshore in the days before Chatham's old "twin lights" flung their first bright beams oceanward. Certainly in no other spot on the entire coast had Mother Nature played into the Devil's hands as recklessly as on Monomoy shoals. The setting was perfect, and the legend of the swinging light to lure unwary mariners onto the bars has hovered over this place through the centuries.

Old Nick picked up a belaying pin, drew a line in the sand of Monomoy, and said to Granny Howland, "I'll lag ye for the next one, best one out of three, and no crow-hopping, ye groggy-billed old shrew!" Granny Howland stooped over the line to see that he'd drawn it true, and slyly slipped a razorfish into the sand while Nick was buttoning a scarletcloth greatcoat close around his neck to keep out the wild no'theaster the pair of them had set ablowing.

"Done, Nicholas!" she cried. "Best out of three, from twenty fathom."

Together they paced it off down the beach, and at the agreed distance, Nick pulled a grinning sailorman's skull from his dittybag. Thumb in eyesocket, he held it aloft, struck a pose, swung his arm a couple of times for practice, and then let fly. Bumpity-bump, down the beach rolled the death's head, but a chip that had broken out of one side threw it off course. Nick swore.

"Batterbrained dog! If 'twarn't for the hole there, Granny, where that lime-juicer's third mate bashed it with a marlinspike, I'd have sent it straight to the line! Well, I ain't forgotten the mate's name, nor his vessel neither." And Nick took out his second sailorman's skull, and repeated the operation. This time he struck a stick of driftwood. Granny Howland sniggered.

"You're losing your eye, Nick," she said, hoping this would rattle him. But now Nick turned cautious. He sighted for the line and he took his last heave. This time he smiled. The skull had stopped a wind'ard spit from the line.

Up stepped Granny, squinting her good eye and clutching her death's head by the main-hatch. She

aimed for the razorfish, and whish!—along the
sand the skull rolled merrily, up to that point on
the line, where it stopped with a click.

"Ah! That's Cap'n Simmons for you!" Granny
chuckled. "A born navigator, Nick, keeping a
straight course to the last!"

She lit her bullseye lanthorn, tied it to the end of
a long lily-iron, and then, holding the light aloft
with one hand, swung herself nimbly aboard a
lean white horse. And down the beach she went,
towards Monomoy Point, waving the lanthorn in
wide arcs from side to side.

So the tales go. Whether there was "mooncussing" by the use of false lights, I am not prepared
to say. And except to the poor ghosts of unavenged
mariners, I don't think it matters now. Those who
would ram a clean bill of health for Cape Cod
down history's throat declare there never was such
a crime on the Cape because there is no record of
it. That is to say there never was a case of mooncussing because no mooncusser ever was caught.

"Mooncussing" has come to mean beach-comb-
ing of any kind. And some of the historians excuse even this. One writer, for example, attri-
butes the acknowledged thievery of the "wreckers"
to the mystic influence of the beach; the people were honest enough—when they were not
on the beach; and he goes on to prove this
with the remarkable example of a wrecker who
had a fine opportunity to make off with a flail and
a grindstone from an inland farmhouse, but who
manfully turned his eyes away from the tempting
objects! Fortunately, the wreckers did not spend

all their time inland. For if they had, they might
have starved to death.

On the bluff at Chatham, next to the light, you
will find the Mack Monument, erected in memory
of the owner of the barge *Wadena,* who perished
in the disaster that I have described.
Behind the monument, in a little federal
cemetery for lost sailors, there is only one small
stone. One hundred six other sailors who were
brought ashore by the tides at Chatham were never
identified.

Continuing past the lighthouse lot, bear right
on Bridge Street. Half a mile beyond, at some unmarked spot on the seaward side, lies buried
Squanto of the Monomoyicks. The history teacher
who darted names and dates at me with the zeal
of a picador never annoyed me with Squanto;
probably she had never heard of him. Yet to this
Indian, America owes her salvation from a very
tight spot.
When Thomas Hunt, an early adventurer, kid-
napped his cargo of Monomoy Indians to sell them
as slaves, Squanto was among the victims. But
in Malaga, Squanto "got away for England, and
was entertained by a marchante in London, &
imployed to New-found-land & other parts," and
after these wanderings, he at last returned to his
homeland. There he met the Pilgrims, befriended
them, and being able to speak their tongue, acted
as guide and interpreter. In the spring of 1621,
when they were planting the precious corn on
which their lives depended, Squanto "stood them
in great stead, showing them both ye maner how

to set it, and after how to dress & tend it. Also he tould them excepte they gott fish & set with it (in these old grounds) it would come to nothing."

The following year, while he was acting as guide for Governor Bradford, Squanto "fell sick of an Indean feavor, bleeding much at ye nose (which ye Indeans take for a simptome of death) and within a few days dyed ther; desiring ye Govr to pray for him, that he might goe to ye Englishmens God in heaven, and bequeathed sundrie of his things to sundry of his English friends, as remembrances of his love; of whom they had a great loss."

Where your road forks, across from the mill on the hill, turn left. A tablet at the left side of the road, beyond this turn, marks approximately the landing place of Samuel de Champlain, who came in 1606 with hopes of founding a new nation. Champlain's vessel had split her rudder, and when the men came ashore they built a forge for the task of mending it. The ship's cook came with them, bringing the makings for a two-weeks supply of bread; while the forge was red, he did his baking.

Champlain's sailing master, the pompous Sieur de Poutrincourt, also came ashore, mainly for the purpose of showing off before the natives. While the explorer was busy making maps, the Sieur strutted among the braves and now and then demonstrated the superiority of his gun over their arrows. The temptation to show what a musket could do to a live Indian became more than he could bear. Hostilities broke out on the tenth day of the white men's stay, and before they were over, three Frenchmen and seven Indians lay buried at "Port Fortune" (Stage Harbor, which is just beyond the tablet) and Champlain's hopes of founding a new state went up in musket smoke.

De Poutrincourt's excuse for starting the war was that he had caught one of the Indians stealing a hatchet. Where Samuel de Champlain's proud air-castles, peopled with his own countrymen, reared imaginary towers at Stage Harbor, the shacks of Yankee and Portuguese scallopers and weir-fishermen now squat along the waterfront; near the place where he mended the rudder of his bark, a Yankee boatyard carries on.

On Oyster River, above Stage Harbor, is the summer home of Supreme Court Justice Louis D. Brandeis, who has been a Chathamite for more than a score of years.

Across the inlet, you can see one of the many lighthouses on the Cape that have outlived their usefulness. This one, Harding's Beach Light, was auctioned off in 1935, and is now privately owned. Another, old Monomoy Light, which is located about two miles from the tip of the point, was disposed of in the same way, after it had served the government 100 years. It was built originally to cover Pollock Rip and Bearse's Shoal. The old-time mariner, traversing the Back-Side, saw Monomoy marked by one light, Chatham's bluff by two, and Nauset by three.

Pollock Rip Channel has been dredged since then, and Pollock Rip Lightship, which is visible from Chatham Light, serves where a whistling buoy was anchored formerly. A Chatham man bought the Monomoy light, and decided to restore it as an authentic example of the old type of beacon used on the Cape.

From Stage Harbor, your road continues past
the pine woods to a juncture with three other
roads. The last house on your right before you
reach this juncture is the home of Elizabeth Reynard, whose book of Cape Cod lore, *The Narrow
Land,* stands as one of the few lasting contribu-
tions made to the literature of the Cape in modern times.

The Atwood House, set back on your left, is
called the "oldest house in town." Whether any
other is older or not—a question that matters not
at all—this is a fine old place indeed, offering, inside and out, one of the best exhibits of its kind on
the Cape. And since it was made into a museum,
it has been open to the public.

Captain Joseph Atwood was an Eastham man,
a "navigator of unfrequented parts," according to
the family record. When he was skippering the
snow, *Judith,* in 1749, with a mate and three sailors
for his crew, his Boston owners told him to watch
out for the Spanish in Honduras, where he was to
take on a cargo. In case their warships should
swoop down upon his tiny craft there and demand
his cargo, he was expected, they solemnly said, "to
put up a manly defense."

With a set of landsharks like these to give him
instructions, it is little wonder that the skipper
went home to find a "snug harbor" as soon as he
could scrape up the price. He went back to Colonel Doane, who owned everything for miles
around, and bought thirty acres in Monomoy. In
1752, he came here and built his "Mansion House,"
as the little cottage was referred to in his will.

The Atwood tribe increased apace, and the
"Mansion House" was always left to the eldest

son. One of the heirs, Sears Atwood, had many children, who grew up and owned homes in the neighborhood. It was this old patriarch's boast that he could stand in his own doorway and call all his children to him. And members of his patient family have remarked that it became quite a habit.

When it was young John Atwood's turn to inherit the cottage, he told Marjorie Smith, of Chathamport, what a grand place the "Mansion House" was. In 1832, Marjorie married John; and when he brought her here, she looked across at the cottage and timidly asked about the "mansion." John told her this was "it," and added, "Mebbe I did make it out a mite handsomer than 'tis—but Margy, that was only courtin' talk!" And so, either to quiet his conscience or his wife, he built on the ell—without even waiting for the first baby!

I shall let the exhibits kept here speak for themselves, only suggesting that you be sure to see the model of the saltworks, in the little room off the kitchen—and offering a word of caution, too, against missing the house for the "treasures" within. Its nails, latches and hinges are handwrought, and its shingles handshaved.

There are other houses in Chatham which are crammed with treasures or with history; there is the home, now owned by Harold Brett, the artist, which was dismantled down in Maine, successfully run through the British blockade during the War of 1812, and set up again in North Chatham; there is the Crowell homestead in Chathamport, with its fourteen doors to a room; and the Rogers home in the village, with hand-hewn timbers and ancient

furniture from cellar to attic. There are scores of
these places on the Cape, but few are open to the
public; and in those that are, I would not want to
spend all my time on "museum pieces"—these
everlasting souvenirs, like the "key to the front
door of the White House on Pumunky River"
which some Cape Codder brought back to the Atwood House, where it won't open so much as a
spice cupboard.

The "Church of the Murals," as it has come to
be known, is one of the town's showplaces. Your
return to Route 28 brings you to the Chatham
Congregational Church, where the paintings of
Alice Stallknecht Wight adorn the house of God
with the image of man.

In 1932 Mrs. Wight painted a large mural,
which she called "Christ Preaching to the Multitude." Christ was represented by a fisherman,
preaching from a boat; and for her multitude,
Mrs. Wight put in the figures and faces of several
of her Cape Cod neighbors, members of the
parish.

The painting was spread upon the church wall,
and the town of Chatham came and looked.
Promptly it was set abuzz. Folks didn't quite know
what to make of it. There was old Sam Harding,
all right—big as life!—and Mrs. Atwood and Mrs.
Eldredge and the rest of 'em. But—well, what
about it, putting these folks up on the meetin'-
house wall? They were good folks, of course! But
they were neighbors—*right here in Chatham*—
and this was supposed to be a piece out of the
Bible! Why, Nathan Buck, up there—he didn't
live more than a mile from this very spot!

But among the off-Capers, the painting was a sensation. Reporters came, newspapers in New York and other cities reproduced the picture and printed long stories about it. And tourists began flocking to the Congregational Church.

Three years later, Mrs. Wight finished "The Last Supper," and it, too, was placed in the church. This is a regular New England Saturday night supper of baked beans and brown bread, and instead of the disciples there are Coast Guards, a couple of sea captains, and other townsfolk. It was a scene even homier than the first. But the townsfolk were getting used to it now. They could look at the second picture without a single gasp.

As I see it, a courageous minister has given space on his church walls to the likenesses of those who come to worship; and anyone who has followed clerical history in Barnstable County will be inclined to give as much credit for this unique piece of work to the pastor as to the painter. Whether the future shepherds of this flock in Chatham will always take as tolerant a view of the murals, I have no way of predicting; I do know what would have happened to such pictures had they been offered a few generations ago.

In 1887 the steeple of this church was struck by lightning; and in the same storm, the bark *R. A. Allen* came ashore and was wrecked off Monomoy. The carpenter who was hired to repair the steeple found "her tiptop ornament" had been splintered. For a moment he thought hard. And the result which is up there today, is a "tiptop" for the steeple made from the maintruck of the *R. A. Allen.*

There are those who say that when the ghosts
of wrecked mariners—on some dark night of judgment—rise out of the waters to claim their own,
half of Chatham will be missing in the morning.
The yard of John C. Anthony will be minus its
flagstaff, which was the foremast of the wrecked
schooner *Little Jenny*; the master of the steamer
*Portland* would have several calls to make here
on his farflung collection rounds; and the town
would be crowded with skippers of all the ages
looking for their ships' quarterboards. The master
of the *Martha A. Berry* would find his on one
Chatham shed, and the *William F. Garrison's*
would be recovered from another. "It is an ancient
custom on Cape Cod," writes an innocent lady
observer, "to place the name of an old boat on the
front of a barn."

Half a mile beyond the Congregational Church
a dirt road branches off the highway to the right.
At the end of it, on a hill, are two old cemeteries,
where the graves date back to 1718. Here, at a
meeting of the villagers in 1700, they voted to
"bild a meten house of 20 and 2 foot floor and 13
foot in the wale." What were doubtless some of the
most interesting records of old Cape Cod days—
the chronicles of this pious little parish of the
marauding beachcombers of "Scrabbletown"—
were lost forever when a fire destroyed them in
1861.

# CHAPTER XIV

## HARWICH

*On State 28, between Chatham and South Dennis. Five miles between Harwich town lines.*

"Harrich? Never heard of it. What's that ye say? Oh! Har-wich! Ye'd like to know the turn to take for Har-wich, eh? Well, now, let me study a mite. 'Pears to me, ma'am, ye take the starboard tack, along that one there, about two miles to fetch ye into Harwich Center—that is, if I ain't picking the wrong one of the two. How's that? Well, no, I can't say as I'm sartin sure of it. Oh, yes, I'm a native. Been living here to home ever since I quit going to sea, and that was back in '98. What say? *Why* ain't I sure of the road? Well, ma'am, I've been around the world eight times in my day, but I ain't never had no business over to Harwich."

One version of this was given in the old Cape Cod Magazine; but with variations, and always with a touch of local pride, the same tale is told in every town on the Cape. I suspect it really belongs to Harwich. For the old mariner may well have been a citizen of the neighboring town of Brewster, where, in his boyhood, he had been taught that all Harwich children were born with four thumbs and a tail. Or he might have been a wrecker of adjacent Chatham, where feeling for "the hairleggers of Harwich" was equally cool.

Harwich was loudest of all the righteous towns that cried out against the "dirty doings" on the beaches of Chatham; for Harwich, so close to the

310

scene at Monomoy and the other ships' graveyards, was on the lee side, and her own beaches were therefore innocent of worthwhile wrecks. It was not only disgraceful, this mooncussing that went on in Chatham—it was heartbreaking.

I have tried to track down something specific in the town's history and legend to account for the epithet "Harwich Hairlegger," but aside from the sincere belief of neighboring villagers that the people of Harwich were simioid, and that if they didn't live in the trees they should have, my researches have gone for nothing. The growing of cranberries, which is now the town's main industry, could not have accounted for it, for by the time a man "picks his row" in the bogs he has less hair on his legs than when he started. Like the strange traditional greeting of Marblehead fishermen, it has become a figure with a lost origin. When two Marbleheaders meet, they say to each other, "Down bucket!" or else they say, "To hell I pitch it!" Why they say it, or how they began, the Marbleheaders themselves can't tell you.

Before the cranberry, Harwich disputed religion six days of the week; on the seventh, the villagers went their separate ways to the churches of fifteen denominations, all within town borders.

Some idea of the relative importance of the church is given in the vote of annual salaries in a 1739 town meeting—Reverend Stone, the Congregational minister, £150; Mr. Philip Selew, the schoolmaster, £86. When Mr. Selew's salary was raised three years later to £100, Mr. Stone's went to £200. Such encouragement to the minister was not enough, however, to keep the wayward flock together. In 1743 came the "Great Awakening," and with it the rise of the "New Lights," a strange and troublesome sect who "made the Pine woods of Harwich ring with Hallelujahs and hosannas, even from babes!" The evangelist who came to town not only set the babies howling, but when he "rose up and persuaded the multitude," the grownups joined in with "a screeching and groaning all over, and it hath been very powerful ever since."

These people not only carried on in a manner to bewilder and distress Reverend Stone and his faithful; they sneaked into meeting, and in the midst of the services stood up and shouted and sang songs of heresy. Some called themselves "New Lights" and some "Come-Outers." Kittredge, in his history, relates that "when under the spell of their mania, they walked along the tops of fences instead of on the sidewalks; affected a strange, springing gait, and conversed by singing instead of by ordinary speech, in the distressing manner of characters in light opera." A favorite tune for this purpose, he adds, was "Old Dan Tucker."

I do not blame Ammiel Weekes, who was chosen constable at a town meeting in 1749, and who made another meeting necessary two weeks later to choose a man to take his place in that job, "he having hidden himself so that he could not be warned."

The Harwich branch of the Nickersons went in heavily for the New Lights; but the Chases, a family from sedate Barnstable, had their own faction of "separatists" and formed a Baptist Church.

The Baptists stood for no nonsense. In 1757 four men were assigned to "take care of the Boys on

Lord's Day and whip them if found playing." In
1787, the Reverend Richard Chase, their first minister, was deposed for intemperance.

Despite her stingy beach and shallow harbors,
Harwich has had her fat fishing years, her "Corn-
crackers"—in coastwise trade—and her deepwater sailors.

Captain John Kenrick—the Orleans skipper
who, you may recall, didn't circumnavigate the
globe—was more properly a Harwich man; he did
not move away, but the town did, shifting its
boundary so that the cottage he built in this town
changed addresses to Orleans in its later days.

Another Harwich skipper, Jonathan Walker,
has something better than a historical error at the
base of his fame. He sailed away from Pensacola
in 1844 with seven runaway slaves aboard, was
caught, brought back to Florida and imprisoned.
Eleven months later he was freed and came back
to Boston; but before they let him go, the forces
of law and order in Florida had caused him to be
branded with the letters "SS" (Slave Stealer) in
the palm of his hand. Captain Walker advanced
the Anti-Slavery cause by going on an illustrated
lecture tour—the illustration being in the palm
of his hand. The sentiment in which this exhibit
was held at the time lives in the poem Whittier
wrote about Jonathan Walker—"The Branded
Hand."

The cranberry came into its own as a commercial crop in the middle of the last century, and to
Harwich, still a leader in the business, belongs the
credit for developing it.

As for the man who made the discovery that cranberries are good to eat, so many local claimants have jerked the laurels for this out of the feeble grasp of History, that now she stares bewildered and knows not who it was that fathered the industry. Almost anyone in Harwich can tell you it was great-uncle Emulous, or great-great-grandfather John.

But "cranberry consarve" goes back to Old Colony days, and probably everyone had a hand in shaping the belated career of this noble fruit. In one local history I see that Captain Abiathar Doane began to lay out his bog in 1847 with the vines set close together, a new-fangled method that made the neighbors laugh at him; but the historian adds a eulogy for Captain Abiathar, giving him the place of honor as cranberry pioneer and declaring, "He has through life carried just enough sail to produce satisfactory results."

The Cape Cod area has been producing, in recent years, roughly half of the nation's cranberries. New Jersey, Wisconsin, Oregon and Washington account for the rest. The business brings between three and five million dollars to the Cape each year; since canning methods have been improved, the demand for the sauce has grown into more than a seasonal novelty. Experts have recently warned Cape growers, however, that unless they "renovate" their bogs, the whole industry faces loss through what is known as "false blossom disease."

The cranberry harvest has always been a colorful bit of the autumn on Cape Cod. Joseph Lincoln's *Cape Cod Yesterdays* gives a nice picture of those old Octobers—a picture which pleases me

because, beneath the glamour, it accurately represents the work as hard and the pay as anything
but bounteous. Other writers have repeated the old
Cape saying that "Cranberry money went farther
than any other kind." But here is what the Provincetown schoolmaster had to say in 1870, in his
report printed in the "town book" for that year:

"Thirty-five permits were granted to absentees,
a very large proportion of whom were cranberry
pickers. There may be, and undoubtedly are, some
families where the parents feel the need of all the
assistance their children are able to afford, to aid
in the support of the family; but in several cases,
concerning which special inquiries have been
made, the amount earned has been so trifling a
sum that it would scarcely meet the extra expense
caused by necessary destruction of clothing while
engaged in the picking. One was out of school a
week and earned seventy cents; another three days
and earned fifty cents. . . . The injury done the
children, the mortification they suffer, caused by
losing their position in the classes, is of tenfold
greater hindrance and loss than the benefits derived
from the money earned."

A good view of the "South Sea" is to be had
from the town landing, reached by the road
marked "Wychmere Pines." The windmill on this
shore is one of the few remaining on the Cape
with works intact. Wealthy summer residents began to buy the old mills as adornments for their
estates, and many of them had the machinery removed and junked, using the empty tower for
storage of lawnmowers, bridge tables, children and
other impedimenta; so that now, with a large pre-

mium attaching to any mill that works, many an owner can stand in the hollow tower and regret the day he stripped her of her drive-shaft, her wheels and spindle, and followed the fashion of setting the millstone down for his doorstep. Before the market for windmills was bid up, this old Harwich relic was weathering neglected on the town poor farm. She would doubtless command several thousand dollars now, if she could be bought at all.

The old "Coast Pilot," Bible of the skipper of sail, recommended no harbor on this stretch of shore-line from Chatham to Hyannis for any but the smallest craft, with "local knowledge." The fishermen have always complained of the difficulty of finding channels, and even the yacht owners have had to race their craft elsewhere. But possibly by the time you arrive here, work will have been started on the projected "Harwich Outer Harbor."

The government project to improve the harbor facilities here included widening and deepening the channel, enlarging the town landing, and extending the jetty a quarter-mile into the Sound, so that a yacht basin with facilities to compare with Nantucket would result. The principal users of the harbor are now "summer people" and in their appeal for government aid, the town's representatives pointed out that Harwich was "dependent on the summer residents for seventy-five per cent of its income."

Originally the harbor was a little "salt pond." When the houses along shore began to fill up with

retired skippers, these old men built a racetrack
around the pond and set out after each other in
their sulkies as they once had done aboard their
vessels.

The races rang with excited commands such as
no inland horse could have made head or tail of,
but they were innocent of high stakes. Nevertheless it was horse-racing—and this was Harwich.
So a channel was made through to the sea, and the
pond was turned into a half-pint harbor for yachts
and such fishing craft as could squeeze into it. A
score of shore-bound old sea captains saw their
racetrack cut away from under them by the sharp
edge of New England conscience.

At the traffic light on Route 28, turn right for
Harwich Center. In the Center, the church across
the street from the town hall stands on the site
of the old "meeting-house of the South Parish,"
which was built in 1747 as an offshoot of the
Brewster church. The lines of the present building,
erected in 1834, are said by experts on such matters
to be unusually fine, and many etchers and photog-
raphers have used it as a subject characteristic of
New England.

A collection of forty-seven original statuettes by
John Rogers, a leading sculptor of his time (1829-
1904) rather unexpectedly pops up in Harwich
Center, where they have been hiding for forty
years or more despite several handsome offers by
collectors and city museums. They were given to
the town by one of the Nickersons, and placed on
exhibit in the Brooks Library. And as the library

is open only on Saturdays, the public enjoyment of the display is held in very proper restraint.

In the yard of the Brooks homestead, next to the library block, there is a tiny shed with the inscription, "Old Powder House. Used by the town of Harwich 1770-1864." From its size I gather that the community during those years was fairly peaceful.

Among the byways of Harwich is the cross-Cape route to Brewster, which passes Pleasant Lake and takes you through the best of the cranberry country. Of the magical color and sheen of this pond I can say no more than the Cape Codder who paused with me one day, stood and looked across it for fully five minutes, and then reluctantly muttered, "Perty, ain't it?"

A shorter departure from Route 28 on the Lower County Road brings you to Allen's Harbor, where Captain Abiathar Doane "put away his chart and glass and took to raising cranberry sass." A few years ago, this tiny salt pond produced a mystery that turned the "stove-argyfyers" from here to Hyannis away from town politics. A dredge was scooping out the bottom of Allen's Harbor when the bucket came up with a strange cargo. Old Cap'n Hall swore it was the jonah-bone of a whale.

"A whale couldn't no more make in to Allen's Harbor than I can shake hands with a beach-gnat!" objected Cap'n Baker that night in the general store where "the boys" gathered. "Don't see how it could have been a whale."

"Don't, eh?" said Cap'n Hall, rising. "Well, let me tell you, Zenas, when I see a whale's jonah-bone, I know it from a marlinspike. And I saw that bone! I don't care how he got there, he was a whale, if he had to fly it!"

Night after night the debate went on, in general store, depot and postoffice. The "Jonah-boners" held out staunchly for the whale, though they could not explain how he got there; their opponents were as steadfast in declaring it was not a whale, though they could show no agreement on a substitute. At last, facing demoralization, the town called in experts from the Natural History Museum in Boston. They pronounced it the flipper bone of a finback whale. And Cap'n Hall said that was exactly what he meant when he called it the jonah-bone.

# CHAPTER XV

## DENNIS & YARMOUTH—SOUTH SHORE

*On State 28, Harwich to Barnstable, including Dennisport,
W. Dennis, S. Yarmouth and W. Yarmouth, eight miles.*

In 1664 Goodman Annable of Barnstable was
presented at Plymouth Court for "removing a landmark" on Cape Cod. It was a serious charge. Only
after many hours of debate was he cleared, on a
plea that he didn't know any better.

In 1935 Henry Ford of Dearborn removed a
windmill from Cape Cod—one of the oldest windmills in America and certainly one of the finest
landmarks on the Massachusetts coast. A group of
dealers was delegated to buy it for his "Early
America Museum." This was the handsome old
gray tower at West Yarmouth, which had been a
delight to thousands of visitors each summer, giving them a more vivid bit of Old Colony days than
they could get from all the histories ever written.

The West Yarmouth mill was duly bought and
paid for. The automobile magnate had nothing to
fear from the legal bogeymen who had pounced
upon poor Goodman Annable. Nevertheless, the
sale of the old mill brought a storm of protest from
all parts of the country. "Windmills all at once
began to turn picturesque and archaic arms in the
landscape of American public consciousness recently when Cape Cod's collective voice was heard
throughout the land," observed the New York
Times.

Native Cape Codders, when they heard of the deal, seemed to be taken by surprise. They wrote letters to Mr. Ford, called the deal a "historical crime" and quickly organized protective associations. Indignant letters came from many prominent summer residents who, at that time of year (November) were not on the Cape. The papers had been signed, but the question was raised whether it was good taste, however legal, to tear down such a beautiful and utterly irreplaceable landmark, cart it from the one section of the country where it belonged, and set it up in a museum a thousand miles away.

The protests, appeals and arguments received a curt answer: a few weeks later the mill was dismantled and trucked away.

The Boston doctor who sold the mill declared that he had tried to get the town of Yarmouth to take it as a gift, making the land around it a town park; but the selectmen had refused the offer because of the taxes the mill was bringing in as private property!

Ford had been angling for a Cape Cod mill for years. He had already taken away the last of the old Humane Society's life-saving stations from Nantucket, completely equipped with long boat and gear. He had got his hands on the ancient fire pumper of Sandwich, handbuilt by Blacksmith Ellis and Wheelwright Nye of that town; and in 1926—nine years before he got the windmill—the Cape Cod Magazine printed a note assuring the Cape that its windmills "are safe at last, for Henry Ford has found one nearer home for his Wayside Inn estate. This mill, in Haverhill, is one of the oldest in New England."

One good comes of it all. Following the removal of the mill, the newspapers carried such headlines as: "SEES NEED TO GUARD RELICS" and "CAPE SEEKS TO SAVE ANTIQUES." As in the days of ships and wreckers, they need to be saved, not so much from the storms that beset them as from the acquisitive souls who go by the law of buyers-keepers. Mooncussers on the beach of history will find it harder from now on.

"Antiques" in this sense, of course, are not the articles on display in the South Shore shops; you may enter them with a clear conscience as to carrying away anything irreplaceable.

The "antique belt" extends from Chatham to Hyannis, with many other shops dotting the Cape. Most of them do a legitimate business, and with a wise choice you can get your money's worth. The only thing to bear in mind is that Lloyds of London has the measurements of the *Mayflower* on record as 90 feet from stem to stern and 20 feet in the beam, with a depth of hold of 11 to 14 feet, and that enough objects have already been established in this country as genuine *Mayflower* cargo to fill a warehouse of a hundred times this cubic area. I doubt if anyone will offer you a piece of the *Mayflower* herself, though I have heard of such sales in years past. Rollins College, in Winter Park, Florida, has a building called Mayflower Hall, and "a timber from the *Mayflower*" is offered as an exhibit there; in the international bridge between the United States and Canada is another; but how these treasures were authenticated when the best informed historians declare they do not know what

ultimately became of the *Mayflower,* I am at a loss
to explain.

On your way to South Yarmouth you pass
through Dennisport, once an active fishing town,
and West Dennis, where the keel was laid for
many a small coasting schooner. Both villages have
long ago given up their seafaring. At the end of
Sea Street, in Dennisport, there is bare beach
where once stood sail-loft, fish-flakes, a wharf and
stores, and offshore a score of sails.

There is an amusing picture of this scene in
1860, in the home of Captain John Wixon, on
Depot Road. It shows the wharf, and the girls
who used to "set" the fish-flakes, and the packing
house of Captain Joseph K. Baker, who operated
a fleet of thirty vessels out of "the Port." His son,
Joseph Lincoln Baker, went west and became several times a millionaire, largely through control
of two mountains of gypsum and the formula for
making a well known scouring powder. The Baker
home is next the Dennisport Post Office—the house
set back from the road and shaded by large trees.

Once the streets of South Yarmouth were lined
with majestic "silver poplars" that rivalled the
elms arching the King's Highway, 'cross-Cape.
When snow tidied up the village with a clean white
tarpaulin, the old men would gather in "Russell's
Store"—that grand "emporium and winter ly-
ceum." Captain Baxter, in the thick of his analysis
of the wreck of Otis White's clipper, the *Ring-
leader,* at Formosa, would suddenly pause and
rush to the window. The others would join him—
a line of graybeards pressed against the window-

pane—while through the streets dashed the sleigh-racers of South Yarmouth, the young folks with their jingling rig, their peals of laughter.

"Go it there, Isy!" Captain Baxter would call to his son. "Jibe, you fool, jibe!" And when they were gone, the old men would crowd back around the stove, and the analysis of the wreck in Formosa would be gravely resumed.

Miss Catherine Aiken, who lived on the corner of Bridge and Main Streets, was the principal of "a select seminary and finishing school for a few refined young ladies" in Connecticut. In the summer of 1867, she came home for her usual vacation, and with her she brought one of the "refined young ladies." Also as a guest at her house—to the astonishment of the villagers—was a "dark-eyed young blade with black sideburns and a fine luxurious mustache." Even when Miss Aiken stiffly let it be known that the young man was an instructor in French at her finishing school, there was headshaking, there were glances askance.

But there was something commanding about the man himself—he walked the streets as if he were pacing a quarterdeck—and though he was only 26, he carried off his fine clothes, his courtly manner and his oil-slicked whiskers, and the young sparks of South Yarmouth knew they had no chance with the beautiful off-Cape girl at Miss Catherine's.

Then the young furriner and the off-Cape girl suddenly disappeared. Miss Catherine received a letter a few days afterwards, saying they had gone to New York and had been married at City Hall. Miss Catherine shuddered at the thing she had brought about. She had known all along that Mary

Plummer was a silly little thing, "anchor-shy" and reckless as a coot. Miss Catherine could only pray they would be happy—Mary Plummer and Monsieur Georges Clemenceau, nine years later Tiger of France.

Where the Bass River Bridge takes you into South Yarmouth, a little more than a century ago Uncle Eleazar Kelley would have ferried you across at two cents a man, and for the price, you got a real piece of navigation. When the ferry failed to make it, you just went out to sea with Uncle Eleazar and hove to for the tide to turn. For you see, Bass River flows two ways—to the northeast on the flow tide, southwest on the ebb. To venture out cross-tide—come the ebb or come the flow—took the hand of a master, and sometimes—come the ebb—even Uncle Eleazar would find himself sliding broadside for Tuckernuck Island.

"A man that hath a covetous and deceitful rotten heart," a woman told her Quaker meeting, "lying lips, which abound among them, and a smooth, fauning, flattering tongue, and short hair . . . such a hypocrite is a fit man to be a member of any New-England Church."

To South Yarmouth, where the "cursed sect of haereticks" had spread from Sandwich, Marshal George Barlow came on his rounds to put down the "prodigious insolency" of these people—and to put into his pocket whatever lay along the path of righteousness. Upon the backs of Christopher Holder and John Copeland the Marshal brought down his "strapado" thirty-three times for each, while from the onlooking crowd a woman's voice cried out, "How long, Lord, shall it be ere thou avenge the blood of thine elect?" The year was 1658—not yet two-score years after the Pilgrims had come to the land, seeking "freedom to worship God."

In Yarmouth of old lived Thomas Hinckley, the "Antiquaker" whom Governor Prence chose for his assistant. There was in Hinckley's mind no inkling that three centuries later this part of Yarmouth was to be known as "Friends Village," and that guidebooks would be directing the traveler first of all to the little Quaker Meeting House; but certainly he was aware of their obstinacy, their maddening defiance, which invited the whip and then made martyrs for other men to follow. He had seen Humphrey Norton stand before Governor Prence himself and shout, "Thomas thou liest, thou art like a scolding woman, and thy clamorous tongue I regard no more than the dust under my feet!"

And the Quakers, taking capital punishment and dealing out verbal punishment in return, won out. A Yarmouth town meeting in 1717 voted to end the requirement that Quakers contribute to the support of the orthodox minister.

Turn right, off the highway, at the traffic signal across Bass River Bridge, and you may see the last meeting-house they built here, in 1809. The church is not used now, but the building and burial ground beside it are kept in trim. The little square stones on these graves carry only names and dates. Rather than have a minister pick me out my epitaph from a book of irrelevant rhymes, like a shoe clerk handing me down my Judgment-Day slippers without so much as a try-on to see if they fit, I believe I should like one of those plain white stones myself.

But the "Praying Indians" of Yarmouth have an even simpler burial ground, with no markers at all except a bronze tablet set up by the white men on a pile of rough stones. Like the Nobscussets of Dennis, this tribe has left the cemetery gardening to Mother Nature, and there, beside the pond, she has done a fine job of it indeed. To reach this cemetery, return to the highway, and make a right turn a short distance further, and right again on "Indian Memorial Drive."

What the white man left undone, in the wiping out of these Indians, the smallpox took care of; and before 1800 the last of the tribe was gone. There are no names on these graves, but "Deacon" Elisha Nauhaught, champion pray-er of the "Praying Indians," was a member of the tribe. Though the "Deacon" had not the wondrous volume of the Reverend Treat of Eastham, he could have surpassed him by several hours in any test of endurance.

In the beginning, the prayer of the Red Man to Kehtean, the Great Spirit of the Western Heavens, was a brief chant from some high place. When the white man came, the red man learned what marvelous exercise could be worked into a prayer —fine tricks of the throat, and words that could stretch on and on, till they made the simple old chant on the hill seem rude and uncertain of being heard.

Deacon Nauhaught set the pace for the tribe and then outprayed the white man too. He prayed so hard he was actually becoming a factor for the Devil to reckon with. And one day the Devil sent a hundred snakes after Nauhaught, to silence him. They wound around his legs and came higher on his body, and the boldest one reared up its head to dart down Nauhaught's throat. The Deacon looked him in the eye. Then he opened his mouth, and when the snake entered, with jaws grown mighty through his exercises, the Indian snapped his teeth together, severing the serpent's head.

For the best glimpses of South Yarmouth, cross the highway on your way back from this spot and continue on Crosby Street and then through the other shady byways bordering the "South Sea." Many of these houses were built for sea captains about the time of the Civil War. They hired ship's carpenters, who built as if they expected a hurricane to concentrate on every beam.

When a skipper chose a site a few hundred yards from the shore, he bought a three-foot right-of-way so that no one might have anything to say about how or when he was to unload his boat. Many of these narrow rights-of-way are still held.

Such a house was that of Captain Loring, on Main Street, a landmark recently reconstructed by its present owners. Captain George Wood, who spent his boyhood in the house now occupied by the library, had his own home built at the corner of Union and Pleasant Streets. Captain Wood commanded the clipper *Fleetwing* and circled the globe three times. His grandfather Zenas and his uncle Orlando had both been lost at sea, and when young George got his chance to go cook on a fishing boat, Par and Mar had to be talked into it.

He went, but the skipper said that as a cook George Wood wasn't worth galleyspace. Next he tried going cabin-boy. Then he shipped before the mast, and after three years, he was advanced to third mate.

A month before he was 21 he had come into his own command and was bringing his vessel into Boston Harbor. The harbor was not dredged then, and the ship was heavily loaded, so Captain Wood hired a fishing vessel to lighten his load. He invited the skipper to come aboard for dinner. The older fellow came into the cabin, stared at the young deepwater captain for a moment, and then said, "Sink me for a corpse! If it ain't George Wood! Well, *Cap'n* Wood, someone must have larned ye to put pork to the beans!"

# CHAPTER XVI

## HYANNIS & SOUTH SHORE TOWNS

*On State 28, between West Yarmouth and Mashpee. Ten miles
between Barnstable town lines.*

In a wind-raked corner of Happy Hollow which
shivering children named Cape Horn stood the
shanty of Barney Gould. Barney was "the duly
elected king" of that fey neighborhood up-back
from Lewis Bay—elected by the beggarfolk and
others who had taken pauper's oath at the time
that the rest of Hyannis went to the polls to choose
selectmen.

The Goulds were a proud family, farther down
the Cape—a "school of high-instepped marsh
herons with their bills in the air"—and of the lot,
only Barney had gone astray. After many wanderings, he settled down in Happy Hollow, and with
him settled Gentle Annie, a strapping specimen
of womankind whom Barney had recommended
"for the heavy work" to every blacksmith along
the South Sea. Zibe and Black Jane and Tamsey
Anne were their neighbors, and so was Three-
Fingered Ruth, who told fortunes to the "sea
captings' wives" whenever they could sneak off
to Happy Hollow while their husbands were
voyaging.

For his own living, Barney walked errands for
the townsfolk at ten cents each. He would go
miles—as far as Falmouth—for ten cents. But the
people he met along the way were asked to pay

what he called his "road tax." He was king of
Happy Hollow, and since the road passed through
his kingdom he viewed all wayfarers as subjects.
The "road tax" was two cents a man, and everybody knew Barney Gould, and most everyone paid,
so that the longer his errand, the better his "tax
revenues." Once a doctor gave him a dime, and
Barney congratulated him. "Now your road tax is
paid up for the next five years!"

One day early in November, 1849, while Barney
was pounding past Crocker Pond on an errand to
Falmouth Village, he fell in with Lemuel Davis,
and when Lemuel had paid his tax, he went along
with Barney and told him about "Californy," and
about the nuggets, big as sea clams, that were
lying loose on the ground out there. The bark
*Orion* was sailing round the Horn, and lots of Falmouth men were taking passage. Lemuel hadn't
the $150, but he was going anyway—in the crew.
Barney nodded gravely.

"It's the long way there," he said, "and Cap'n
Bunker's a driver. Ever been round the Horn,
lad?"

"No, but she's a long-legged ship, Barney,"
Lemuel answered happily. "And Cap'n Bunker—
well, you know what he can do with her!"

Barney knew. Bunker—a good sailor, but a big
blowhard, who wanted taking down a ratlin'.
When he reached Falmouth, Barney looked up the
Captain. In the presence of several Falmouth men,
he began to "bait" the old skipper about the speed
of the *Orion.*

"Cap'n Bunker," Barney said at last, "I'd like to
make you an offer, sir. I'll lay you my best shirt I
can beat you to San Francisco—Gould's Express,

going overland, agin the *Orion* going round the Horn!"

This put the skipper somewhat "on the spot." If they had been alone, he might have ignored Barney, or called him an impudent beggar, one remove from ijicy, and the whole affair would have been forgotten. But too many others were on hand, men who knew and liked the "old character." There was nothing for the skipper to do but lay his best shirt against Barney Gould's best and only.

The record of the *Orion's* voyage around the Horn with 123 passengers is preserved in a document now held by the Falmouth Historical Society. I can offer you no documentary evidence of Barney's journey overland, but the story as handed down is that when the *Orion* dropped anchor in San Francisco, and Captain Bunker stepped on the dock, Barney was there to meet him; and that Barney came back to Happy Hollow wearing the skipper's best shirt. From one prairie schooner to another, Barney Gould had raced his way 'cross-country—hitch-hiking in the gold rush of '49.

The Kingdom of Barney Gould is gone. South Barnstable, including the villages of Hyannis, Craigville, Centerville, Osterville and Wianno, has become ultra-smart. This is the same great tract of land that Sachem Yanno gave in 1666 to Nicholas Davis "for divers good reasons" (probably some shiny trinket, or even a pair of pants). Here a single lot—which fetched a bead or a pants button—sold for $500 in 1906; in 1926, the same lot was divided into three parts and sold, two parts fetching $25,000 each and the other $50,000.

On the South Shore, the transformation of Cape

Cod is complete. Summer people keep trade alive, summer residents pay the taxes; slim-waisted pleasure-craft have the harbor to themselves; and a captain's chart is a museum piece.

As for the hotels, restaurants, dance-floors, shops and tea-rooms, I am deliberately shirking my duty; I shall not go into the refinements as to which is best for this or for that—mainly because I distrust guidebooks on such matters myself, and secondly because these establishments change from season to season, sometimes from month to month.

I am also failing to identify Craigville Beach as "the fourth finest in the world." A journalist who happened to be visiting here some years ago gave this as his personal opinion. The statement was at once taken up and preserved for touring posterity. Craigville sand is fine and white, and the water is warm, the slope convenient; but I should not want the task of proving that no other beach on Cape shores is as well appointed. Possibly if the journalist himself could see the string of bath-houses that have been built since he first saw Craigville Beach, he might move it down a couple of notches.

It is true that the water of the Sound averages several degrees warmer than on the north shore, and considerably warmer than the rolling surf of the open Atlantic along the Back Side beach from Chatham to Provincetown. But what is one man's bath of bliss may be two fathoms of sheer boredom to another. I wholeheartedly recommend the bathing on South Shore beaches, but I would not care to miss the ocean for the bath-houses.

The lower temperatures on the Back Side have been attributed partly to the Labrador Current.

When a Canadian engineer hit upon an inspiration to change things, a few years ago, the Cape was quite upset about it. His idea was to plug up the Straits of Belle Isle, forcing back the Labrador Current so that Canada would have a warmer climate. The watchful press of Cape Cod was at once up in arms; the people were told that palm trees would spring up overnight on the windy hills of Truro, and one journal gravely warned that "if British and Canadian interests get to interfering with our weather, an international problem is bound to result."

From Main Street in Hyannis you can drive to a little harbor on Lewis Bay, by turning left on Pleasant Street. The Baxter artificial pearl factory is situated there, and the management of that unusual business has shown a tolerant spirit towards the poor inquiring tourist. Pearls of small price are made from fish scales, and the herring of Cape Cod provide the scales for the factory. It is a democratic fish; when it isn't circling fair white throats as an approximate symbol of worldly wealth, it is being spread as fertilizer on a hog-feed farm. And in either case, I suppose, it is all the same to the herring.

All alongshore here, a century ago, were the wharves, sail-lofts and other interests of the men who went "to the Island for cod, by the grace of God," and as late as 1904 there was one dealer in ship's stores and chandlery.

The sailmaker, with his rawhide palm and his three-sided needle, carried on a highly specialized business in his "loft." In machine-sewn sails, three rows of stitches are taken; in the day of the sail-maker, there were only two, yet the hand-sewn sails were the stronger. The sailmaker was as important to the Cape in those days as the motor mechanic is now, or the airplane technician will be in times to come, and the work was no less exact. Each suit of sails had to be drafted, either from blueprint or from the vessel herself; drawn upon the floor of the loft; and then cut, with precise allowance for stretching. Sometimes this was figured at a quarter-inch per foot, but much depended upon how the vessel was to be worked, how much strain was to come of hoisting and of pulling at the boom. Then the sails were sewn and roped, the stitching going through each lay of the rope, and the metal grom-mets worked into the corners. There are still a few sailmakers; and when a new suit of sails was wanted for the Eastham windmill a few years ago, it was necessary to go only as far as Province-town, where Sailmaker Maguire was "at his trade."

As soon as the rising young mariner of Barn-stable got his captain's berth, he began saving for a home; when the home was built, he sat down and pondered what type of weathervane was to go on the barn; and then, with that problem out of the way, married and had children.

The South Shore people, especially, were aware of the importance of a weathervane, and the sum-mer residents have kept the old feeling alive. You will see vanes of many kinds on your tour of the Cape—the full-rigged ship, the whale, the codfish, crow, swordfish, windmill, dart and "Sailor Jack." One of the finest is an old cast-iron racing sulky—

horse, vehicle, driver and all—riding the Barnstable winds atop a barn on Mill Way. Captain Thomas Hinckley owned the house and barn in the eighties, and the little sulky was there then, but who first set it up nobody knows. It follows a Currier and Ives design—very jaunty, the horse having all four feet in the air—and the present owner of the barn, Miss Ruth Snow, clerk of Superior Court in Barnstable, has had many an offer for it.

But the South Shore folks who keep up with the Joneses must now install *indoor* weathervanes, the latest stage in the evolution of the ancient golden rooster. A Boston newspaper made the faux pas in 1936 of referring to a "unique device" in a Dedham gymnasium, calling it "the only indoor weather-vane in the United States." Immediately there were outraged calls from Cape Cod. The new Coast Guard stations are all equipped with them, but more decorative ones are now in many Cape homes. The first to protest the Boston story was a resident of Colonial Acres, in West Yarmouth, who had just installed a handsome ship's compass, set in the ceiling of his home, with an arrow to show the wind's direction. The arrow was on a vertical shaft which went up through the roof, to a schooner that swung as an outdoor vane. Then other Cape homeowners began telling about their indoor vanes. One, in South Yarmouth, even had an elaborate electric arrangement, which flashed little ruby-glass lamps on the compass to show which way the wind blew!

In the library—the little gray-shingled house on Main Street—there are exhibits worth seeing if only to remind you that Hyannis was once a seafaring town, as unpretentious as any other on the Cape, and able to produce its deep-sea sailors. There was young Rodney Baxter, who rushed a cargo of corn and flour to the Irish in the famine of 1847. He drove his fore-and-aft schooner to Sligo in twenty-two days and came back in seventeen, beating Captain Allen Crowell, another Hyannis man, in the schooner *Cabot*.

The shops are farther along Main Street, and there are two departures from the highway to be given a note here—one to the southward, on Sea Street through the summer estates of Hyannisport, and the other northward to Shoot-flying Hill. For the latter, turn off Main Street on the Barnstable Road, and at the rotary traffic circle take Route 132 for about three miles, turning off left on a dirt road.

On the hill there is a fire tower, open to visitors. From the crow's nest the Cape and its waters are spread out for you like a vast map which sometimes blurs in a blue haze, sometimes stands out sharp and clear, but in either case is worth climbing to look at. If it is clear, you can see Provincetown to the northeast, Martha's Vineyard to the southwest, and the Canal up-Cape in Bourne; and in the foreground is Lake Wequaquet, like a nine-mile mirror for a vain and fickle sky.

Centerville is Cape Cod in its best go-ashore shirt. Osterville, Wianno and Oyster Harbors are the off-Cape world in a boiled shirt. Here the everyday tourist runs into closed gateways, and the landscape runs into money—mostly off-Cape money. There are a few houses with pasts of their

own, however. One is the large Safford home on
Long Beach, Centerville.

Although the architecture of this house is Cape
Cod throughout, it was, strangely enough, built in
Nottingham, N. H., more than two centuries ago.
Cape Cod would not come to this cottage, so Mrs.
John H. Safford, who inherited it, decided to bring
the cottage to Cape Cod. Over the 140 miles from
Nottingham to Centerville, the house moved in
sections. There were nine truckloads of it. Even
the flatrock doorsteps were fetched along. The
original chimney bricks were taken down and re-
set, with the three fireplaces in their former relation to the great flue. Sometimes I wonder what
this old "Cape Cod" cottage, this exile of two centuries, must think about—now that it has come to
the Cape at last, only to find itself a stranger still,
an alien amid the off-Cape mansions of the sum-
merfolk!

In Osterville the Crosby boatyard carries on a
century-old business, building "Crosby cats." And
at Oyster Harbors, where Goodman Hatch and his
many children pickled oysters for a living in 1660,
before they decided the broad acres of Falmouth
were a more respectable place to live, the Oyster
Harbors Club now shelters one of the most exclusive colonies on the Cape. It is, in fact, more exclusive and considerably more provincial than Falmouth Heights—that part of the neighboring
town's millionaire settlement where Goodman
Hatch betook himself.

The golf course at Oyster Harbors, one of nearly
a score of fine courses on the Cape, was still a
sandy wilderness in the early 1920's, until experts

were hired to see what could be done here about greens and fairways. Money was no consideration. The course was cleared and sodded, and grass was made to grow which all but curled its flourishing blades into dollar signs. With the grasses came Felix du Pont. Oyster Harbors was "made."

Throughout these South Sea villages, wealth seeks the waterfront. In Cotuit, for example, the "highground" and Cotuitport, south of the village, are considerably more dressed up in large estates, yacht club, golf course and other summer rig, than Cotuit Village. But Marston's Mills, to the north of the highway out of Centerville, is almost recognizable as Cape Cod, though little is left of this hamlet's ancient landmarks. One of these was the grist mill that gave the town its name and stood here 200 years.

Benjamin Marston came from Salem, built the mill on the stream and prospered. He sent his boy Nymphas to Yale. Nymphas became a judge, but when the trouble broke out with the mother country, he scandalized his Tory neighbors by his revolutionary leanings. He even put up the boys who were on their way to the defense of Falmouth, and when one of them, carried away by patriotic feeling or something, fired off a salute inside Nymphas's house and brought down the dining room plaster, the Judge assured the crowd it was all right, "if they would carry out their zeal in shattering the ranks of the enemy." The old mill came down in a gale in 1930. A. P. Gardner, a New York artist who had seen and loved it, made a painting of it, which was presented to the village library.

Marston's Mills lost another relic in 1937 when its century-old blacksmith shop was taken down, and an even finer one in the same year when the two Misses Baxter sold their ancient cottage on Osterville Road to a millionaire executive in the aluminum industry. This house, originally one room, had been moved at some time in the dim past from East Sandwich, and it is one of the reasons I have hesitated to call the Hoxie House in Sandwich "the oldest house on the Cape;" for nobody knows how old the house that came to Marston's Mills was. Captain Sidney Baxter, a coasting skipper, bought it in 1856 and added some rooms. The latest transfer removes it from its Osterville Road site, and—as far as the public is concerned—from Cape Cod.

The little blue bay of Cotuit, where some of the millions of "Cotuit oysters" sold in this country actually come from, can be reached by going through the village or by branching off on an oyster-shell byway marked Little River Road.

As in Wellfleet, South Shore oystering is not done now as it was in the Old Colony days—simply by raking up the native shellfish. The native oysters, like the native Cape Codders, are mostly gone from South Sea harbors. The "Cotuits" on your New York hotel menu, if they have seen Cotuit at all, have been there only long enough to get the flavor. In April the "seed" is brought from New Haven and Long Island and planted in the Bay to spawn. Propagation occurs during the summer. The harvest season begins September 1 and goes on until the next June.

The purity of the water and the chemical makeup account for the flavor of the Cotuit, which is known and demanded in many parts of the world. A number of orders come annually from England. But to produce a barrel of Cotuits costs about $3 more than any other kind of oyster, and the three firms that have oyster grants in the Bay have been up against a knotty problem created by hotels and clubs that promise "Cotuits on the half-shell" on their menus, and then dish out an inferior oyster that costs about 40 per cent. less to produce.

The industry was nearly wrecked, too, when a midwest newspaper, on its everlasting hunt for the sensational, started a nation-wide "oyster scare" in 1925 by printing a full-page story headed, "DEATH GERMS IN OYSTERS." There was no truth in the story, as a later investigation proved, but the damage had been done. The demand for Cotuits, along with all others, dropped temporarily to five per cent. of normal, and was some years recovering. The midwest newspaper, which has been one of the most clamorous defenders of "freedom of the press," was not penalized.

Gilbert Coleman, one of the holders of the oyster grants, has his "house" on the Bay, near those of the Cotuit Oyster Company. The firms plant and cultivate 100 acres along the waterfront. If you come to Cotuit in the months of harvest, you may watch the men take up the oysters with their long-handled tongs—which do not "bill" the edges of the shell—rate them for size, and then barrel them, ready for shipping; and if you come during the winter, you may see them sometimes cutting through ice a foot thick to rake the bottom of the Bay. Speed in opening oysters is as much a matter of pride in New England as hog-calling is out west. The official record for opening 200 oysters is 9 minutes, 27 seconds—and when they go that fast, the falling shells sound almost like a clog dance on the floor.

The road signs in this appealing little village of "Long Fields" will tell you that around 1835 every family had a sea captain—which is a good percentage indeed, though in some of the down-Cape towns they did even better than that, as in East Dennis with its twelve Captain Howeses for the postman to swear at.

When Mrs. Bethuel Handy died in 1820, Cotuit suddenly realized it had no burying ground—Handy or otherwise. In much haste a plot was laid out, fenced and landscaped with all modern improvements of the day; and when the job was done, they were very proud of it and called it Mosswood. Then they buried Mrs. Handy, and on her stone they put:

> *My bosom friend, come here to see*
> *Where lays the last remains of me,*
> *When I the debt to nature paid*
> *A burying ground for me was made.*

A road from Main Street leads off, just beyond the library, to the summer home of Dr. A. Lawrence Lowell, president emeritus of Harvard. Just outside Dr. Lowell's gates is a gray-shingled little cottage known as the Phinney House, built some time before 1797. It was once occupied—of course —by a sea captain; but no one has lived in it for forty-odd years. Now, beneath its silvered shingles the house is wistfully disintegrating.

Main Street leads out northeast to Santuit. As

you make a left turn onto Falmouth Avenue, you find four old houses bunched together, two on each side of the road. They still belong to the innumerable Crockers of Barnstable—those descendants of Deacon William who had so many children that poor Amos Otis, the genealogist, didn't know what to do. Zenas Crocker, who lived in the first house at the right, kept it open as a stage-stop for many years.

Long ago, before the Crockers or any other English folk lived here, a giant trout came into the South Sea. This was old Mish-que—in the language of the Indians, "great red fish." He was a thousand years off the coast of the Nausets, and another thousand years in the waters of the Monomoyicks, and how many thousands of years he had spent near the Mattakeesets, or the Nobscussets or the Payomets, nobody knew. But now, certainly, Mish-que was getting on, and no fish knew it better than he. He had peopled the ocean with his kind, his mission in life was done. In his old age he desired quiet water, and most of all, solitude; and there was a spot he remembered, a placid, lonely harbor on the Bay, across-Cape. But it was a bad thing, to be in the South Sea and suddenly to remember the waters of the Bay—and to be as old as Mish-que; it was disheartening to think of the long swim, all the way around, through the stormy waters to the far tip of the Cape and then across-Bay. Mish-que hesitated. And while he was swimming back and forth and pondering the situation, an Indian girl watched him from the beach at Popponesset.

"Old Mish-que!" she said. "Go find the quiet

water, where you belong now. You are as bad, my friend, as some of our braves in the tribe, who never know when they are *san-quoi!*" And because *san-quoi* meant old, and because the young girl was thinking of a thing that had happened, she laughed.

"I am not like your old men in the tribe," Mish-que answered stiffly. "If I could get to the quiet water, I would go there."

The girl thought of the short way to the calm waters—overland. "Come, old fish!" she cried suddenly, and beckoned inshore. When Mish-que obeyed, she jumped astride his back and headed him up the beach. Mish-que struggled hard over the sand, on through the fields and the woods, leaving a great gully behind him. The girl whispered and urged him on, but before he was half-way across-Cape, his strength failed him. He spied a pond, made for it, and dove in. The laughing girl of Popponesset was carried in with him, and neither girl nor fish was ever seen again. The pond is called Santuit—"place for the aged"—and from it now runs a river to the South Sea, the Santuit River.

# CHAPTER XVII

## MASHPEE

*State 130 to Mashpee Pond, one mile, rejoining State 28 in circuit of village, three miles.*

*May 17, 1648, an agreement was made between Paupmunnuck . . . and Capt. Miles Standish, of Plymouth, in behalf of the inhabitants of Barnstable.*

On through the legal rigmarole "Captaine Shrimpe" scrawled boldly and without pause. Waiting upon him at one side of the table stood Thomas Hinckley, deputy of Barnstable, and at the other Sachem Paupmunnuck of the South Sea Indians.

The Captain did not keep them waiting long. He knew precisely how to word the document; he had made many like it.

*. . . In witness of all and singular of the premises thereof, they have hereunto set their hands the day and year above written.*

He dipped his quill for a few more flourishes, signed the paper, "Miles Standish," and below wrote, "The mark    of Paupmunnuck." Then he handed the quill to the Sachem, who put a cross in the space left open.

That was all. Another great slice of Cape Cod —"all the land on the S. side, from the bounds of Marshpee, eastward, to Oyster River"—had been sold to the white men, "for and in consideration of 2 brass-kettles and one bu. of Indian corn."

Ten years later, Sachem Paupmunnuck came back to the white men, announcing that his tribes- men wanted the land. The South Sea Indians did not understand legal documents, he said. They were troubled, for the pleasant places to live were closed to them now, the good places to hunt and fish. They did not understand, and there were mut- terings among them.

The white men showed the Sachem his own mark on the deed. Josias Winslow read over the text to him. Patiently John Alden tried to make clear that such a paper was binding upon him who signed. But a third white man frowned and called the others to him, and they held counsel.

Clearly this third white man was powerful among them; for at his command a new paper was drawn up to take the place of Captain Standish's. In it, important concessions were made to the tribesmen, who in return would acknowledge themselves "fully paid, quietly satisfied and con- tented forever, without any further trouble."

Sachem Paupmunnuck nodded assent as he heard the new arrangement, "leaving the skirts of good land about Cotuite, alias Sautuite Pond, to the plantation of Indians dwelling there, accord- ing to the desire of Mr. Richard Bourne."

Richard Bourne, makeshift minister of Sand- wich, was himself a man of means and one of the town's biggest landowners. In the old country he had been an able lawyer; but here in the new, he was looking beyond white man's law, and he, too, was troubled. From Sandwich to Billingsgate, brass kettles were being traded for the homeland of an ancient people. Word had gone abroad, the

rush was on, the "settlers" jubilant. To Richard
Bourne alone among white men, the honey tasted
bitter.

He decided to make a haven for the Indians—
as large a tract of land as he could block off from
his English neighbors. On the other hand, those
who came there to live would be "Praying Indians"—Christians—and he himself would lead
them. He liked to preach. For twenty years, he
and Thomas Tupper had delivered the sermons in
the meeting-house at Sandwich. Neither he nor
Tupper had been ordained, but each had his followers; before the service, noses were counted, and
to him who could claim the bigger flock went the
right to preach the sermon for that day.

Now Richard Bourne laid out heavier work for
himself. In 1660 he obtained grants from the court
for a strip of land for his "Kingdome of Mashpee"—a tract of fifty square miles, reaching from
sea to sea across-Cape. There his converts were to
be forever safe from white men's bargainings.

The white men distrusted him and opposed his
scheme. The red men were slow to come into the
fold. But on a site in the Mashpee hills he put up
a rude meeting-house and labored mightily among
those who would join; and the "Kingdome" worried along.

Six years later, Governor Prence and a party of
clergymen came to Mashpee to see how things
were going. They quizzed the Indians, who "gave
such an account of their knowledge and belief, and
of the impression the gospel had made on their
hearts; and gave their relations with such affection, as was extremely grateful to the pious
auditory."

Probably it was a good deal simpler than all that, but respect for the Kingdome grew, and in 1670 John Eliot and John Cotton came to ordain Richard Bourne minister to the Mashpees. In a stirring scene amid the great pines, they "laid on hands" while praying braves—"such an multitude as would make a swaying sea"—encircled them. In the group were other leading men of the Colony —the governor, the magistrates, several ministers.

In 1674 the thing happened which Bourne had long feared. War broke out between the Colony and the tribesmen of King Philip of the Wampanoags, whose rule included Cape Cod. Elsewhere in New England, the war was a bloody affair; in the winter of 1675 a thousand Indians were killed, and nearly a hundred white men. But on the Cape, Treat of Eastham was taking good care of his flock of praying braves; Bourne of Mashpee was doing the same; and these tribesmen, who might have wiped out the white settlement, chose to keep the peace.

Bourne's Mashpee Kingdome had struggled in the wilderness, and had met destiny.

Where Richard Bourne is buried no one knows. There is no stone shaft for him. Even the town of Bourne is not named after him, but after Jonathan Bourne, a descendant. In 1684, however, a year before his death, a new meeting-house was built to replace the first Mashpee church, and it has been maintained to this day as his monument.

Richard's son, Shearjashub Bourne (take your time pronouncing it and put the accent on the "jash") completed legal details "so that no part or parcel of these lands might be bought by, or sold to, any white person or persons, without consent of all the said Indians, not even with the consent of the General Court."

But from the beginning the white men did not feel that the Indians were competent to rule themselves—a form of anxiety that seems to come over many a conquering people when they have taken over the land of others. The Indians of Mashpee were held in the legal status of paupers. They were governed by white overseers, and they had no voice in the selection of these men. And they complained against many practices which their spokesmen said were "insufferable." Their children, they said, "were taken by the authorities and put out to work, with an understanding that they need not be schooled, and they were badly fed, badly lodged, badly clad, and were constantly subject to the accusation of being degraded."

The Mashpees were stubborn about it. For nearly a century they kept demanding the right of self-government. Six years before the Declaration of Independence was signed, they sent one of their tribe, Reuben Cognehew, to London. Indian Cognehew went to King George III and told him the colonial government was oppressing his people. The King sent him home with orders to the colony to give Mashpee a better government. At last the Indians had won the right to elect their own officers.

In the Revolutionary War, "Mashpee District" gave more generously, in proportion to her population, than any town on Cape Cod. Twenty-two tribesmen enlisted in the first Continental Regiment, twenty-one died in action. When the war ended, there were seventy widows in the little community.

But now Massachusetts was no longer taking orders from King George. And promptly, in 1778, the colonial government again took from Mashpee her right of self-rule, putting her back under the overseer system. After helping America win her freedom, the tribe lost its own.

Meanwhile, within the district a strange fusion of races was taking place. A number of negroes had come there to settle, and there was much intermarriage with the Indians. Also *Bravas*—Cape Verde Islanders who had come over on whaling ships—began to make homes in Mashpee, and they, too, mingled in the already dusky concoction. Finally, in the Revolutionary War, a number of Hessian soldiers were captured, and this strain also was stirred into the melting pot.

The number of pure-bred Indians was fast declining; they were as rapidly being replaced by half-breeds; and this interbreeding has caused local historians to breathe many a sigh. (I find little in these same histories on the subject of inbreeding, for which the Yankee communities were notorious. But in his list of proud old family names, Otis, the genealogist, includes a surprisingly large number of strange items like the one about a poor lad who went about town flapping his wings in the belief that he was a duck.)

At any rate, the historians have held these motley newcomers to Mashpee responsible for what they call a "degenerate and degraded" condition of the town. Henry C. Kittredge refers to them as "scum drifting to Mashpee like weeds to the Sargasso Sea." *

Nevertheless, Mashpee went on fighting for freedom. Scum, weeds and all, her people struggled for fifty years after America had gained independence. In 1833 they assembled and drew up this set of resolutions:

> *Resolved, 1. That we, as a tribe, will rule ourselves, and have the right to do so; for all men are born free and equal, as says the Constitution of our country.*
> *Resolved, 2. That we will not permit any white man to come upon our Plantation, to cut, or to carry off, wood, or hay, or any other article, without our permission, after the 1st of July next."*

The resolution was signed, "Ebenezer Attaquin, President," and was taken to Boston by a delegation, and presented to the Governor.

On July 1, white men promptly put the resolutions to a test; and the Indians who tried to stop them from cutting wood on the plantation were arrested, convicted on a charge of rioting, and jailed.

Benjamin Hallett, Boston lawyer who was widely known for his orations and debates, had been born and brought up near Mashpee, and when the Indians went to him with their story, he agreed to help them. He told the legislature they were "grievously oppressed by the white people and borne down by laws which made them poor and enriched other men upon their property." He said the men who were jailed for rioting had been "as justifiable in what they have done as were our fathers in throwing British tea into Boston harbor."

By his efforts, the men were freed, and an act

*Cape Cod, Its People and Their History.

was passed in 1834 incorporating Mashpee, and authorizing the people to choose their own officers and manage their own affairs. And ever since, the "scum and weeds" seem to have done a rather good job of it. On the "Sargasso Sea" there have been few wrecks.

One morning a few years ago, Samuel G. Davis, wealthy citizen of Roxbury, was driving through Mashpee. The wind blew his hat off, and a dusky little Mashpee lad, who was on his way to school, raced after it. When he brought it back, Mr. Davis held out a dime. But the ragged little youngster shook his head and explained that his mother had taught him not to accept anything for doing favors.

Mr. Davis was touched by the incident, and upon his death shortly afterwards, it was revealed in his will that a part of his estate had been left to the town of Mashpee. The gift included real estate, stocks and bonds, and it was to be set up as "The Kind Good Manners Fund"—the income to be used for an annual award of medals and prizes for courtesy shown through the year by children of the Mashpee school.

The prizes were $5 and $10, and the whole outlay for one year was limited to $200. But when the estate was settled, the town found itself with about $50,000 in the "Kind Good Manners Fund," from which the income, even at a low yield, would amount to many times the figure allowed for the prizes.

Mashpee had long been in need of a new schoolhouse. The town was poor, most of its people making their living in the fields. The selectmen thought

a bright, clean schoolhouse, which the town could
not otherwise afford, would be an excellent invest-
ment of the surplus in the "Kind Good Manners
Fund." In 1936 they applied to Probate Court for
permission to use it in that way, pointing out that
they had several thousand dollars which could not
possibly go for "kind good manners." They explained, too, that the old school building was in
bad shape and in many ways inadequate.

The court denied their request.

Accounts vary as to when the last full-blooded
Indian died in Mashpee, but probably the pure
strain was gone more than a century ago. Yet as
you drive through this township, you will see people with high cheekbones, thin lips, straight hair, a
red tinge to the skin. Most of the faces, it is true,
are negroid, or partly so; but the exceptions are not
so rare that you are likely to miss them, even in a
brief drive through the scattered settlement.

Route 28, cutting southeastward through the
township, is the shortest way to Falmouth, the next
on your trip; but Route 130, which you can take
from Santuit, offers a better way to see Mashpee.
The "town" is more woods than village; and its
story is in its tall pines as well as its people. The
trees make of Mashpee a stately wilderness.

If you take Route 130, continue as far as the
Hotel Attaquin.

The Attaquins are an old family in this country.
The arrival of people from the *Mayflower* was a
passing incident well along in their family history.
Captain Solomon Attaquin built this little hotel in
1840 after he had given up seafaring. At the age of

12, Solomon had shipped as cook aboard a fishing vessel, and after two seasons on the Banks, he went into whaling, then into coastwise shipping, finally working up to a command of his own vessel in that branch. His body lies in an old Indian burying ground west of Mashpee Pond.

Later generations of Attaquins have kept the hotel. Its ancient register was stolen in 1910, presumably because of the long list of famous autographs that were in it. Among the signers had been Daniel Webster, Grover Cleveland, Joseph Jefferson, John Drew, Finley Peter Dunne, Richard Watson Gilder, Charles Dana Gibson and many other celebrities.

These people came to hunt in the woods and to fish in Mashpee Pond, which you can reach on a dirt road from the hotel. It is one of the largest ponds on the Cape, and its setting is one of the wildest and most beautiful. The little stream that serves as its outlet to the sea is an important herring run, and at a spot just beyond the hotel, sluiceways have been used for many years.

Retracing a short distance from the hotel on Route 130, you come to the crossroads again. Turn right and continue until you see a sign at the left, "Old Indian Church." A mile and a half through the woods—and the trees here are Mashpee's grandest—brings you to the place where Richard Bourne carried on his work among the Indians.

Here stands the meeting-house which was built in 1684 to replace his first church, and beside it is the burying ground where his flock sleeps. Unlike their heathen forbears, these Indians placed headstones over their dead. They figured out the Eng-

lish spelling of their names, and chiseled them on
the stones, but for some reason, they were very
sparing with epitaphs. Perhaps this was because
English came hard, but I prefer to think that, in
this matter of labeling eternal premises, the braves
would go only so far, and that at epitaphs, they
drew the line.

The Indian Church is never locked, and visitors
are welcome. Though it is the oldest church on
Cape Cod, much restoration of the original building was necessary in 1838, when the State provided
money for that purpose, and from time to time
since then.

In 1711 the Reverend Daniel Williams, of London, died, and his will entrusted a fund to Harvard
College, from which £60 a year was to be paid to
"a person of prudence and piety to preach to what
pagans and blacks be otherwise neglected."

Harvard chose Mashpee.

# CHAPTER XVIII

## FALMOUTH

*On State 28, eleven miles from Mashpee. To Woods Hole, from Falmouth Green, five miles.*

*Sunday, Janury 9—Sixtyfore days out of Falmouth Mass & not won single whale have we tuk yit. Our Capting has ordered the man on lookout to come down, says mebbe the Lord is taking his vengints upon us for looking for whales on the Sabbith. Hear after the lookout will not go aloft no more on the Sabbith xcept oncet every our. So ends, fine wether all day.*

*Monday, Janury 10—Vilents broke out in the galley today. The men says they would not eat the potatoe barging becaus there was too many cockroches & other incests ect. in it, and they maid Peter White, our neegrow cook, eat it insted. So ends this day, still no whales in site.*

*Tuesday, Janury 11—Peter White the cook compelaned of panes in the abdoming & died this day 3 oclock p m. The Capting has ordered the men queschinned trying to find out who is gillty of making him eat the potatoe barging, but all hands pleed innosents. So ends, not a whale in these onwholly waters.*

*Wensday, Janury 12—Fewnril sarvises was held at 11 a m for Peter White. All hands xept the lookout called on deck to witniss our last fairwell to our pore shipmate. He was laid in a box & the Capting begun to reed sourfully from the scripters after giveing worning that any man what udders a disrespective word is going to git seesed up in the riggin. Suddingly the lookout calls There she blows. The 1st whale we seen on the whole of this miserble viage. The Capting went on reeding over the departid & the lookout calls There she blows and breeches. Still the Skipper is reeding & the lookout calls There she blows & breeches & belches. Then the Capting drops his book and orders the men—*

356

*Heave that damed carkiss overboard and lower
away. But we was too late. So ends, our won
whale, the only whale we seen yit—gorn.
Thursday, Janury 13—The Capting give worning
this day to all hands not to die ontill we git our
first whale. No fewnril sarvises will be held. So
ends, not won miserble whale to be seen.*

For the story of Falmouth in her heyday, one
must seek among treasured logbooks that tell of
adventure thousands of miles from home. The village has been home-port of 148 sea captains, many
of them whalemen who did not find the waters
"onwholly." The stately old homes that still give
Falmouth much of her character are standing
evidence of their success.

Late in the Eighteenth Century, while his fel-
low-townsmen are going to sea, Shipwright
Hinckley is bolting together his stocky whaling
barks at West Falmouth. There he builds the
*Popmunnett* and the *William Penn,* while Quaker
neighbors stand around and shake their heads and
warn him of a dire fate for the latter vessel, because "too much Sunday work" has gone into her.
And their prophecy comes true; at the Navigator
Islands, the natives kill the mate outright and capture two boat-crews, who barely escape with their
lives.

A still bloodier voyage begins in 1833, with the
sailing of the *Awashonks* for the South Pacific. She
is a Falmouth ship, named after the queen who, the
Indians said, used to come to Great Hill (Falmouth Heights) and hold feasts there, on her summer rounds from Narragansett to the island of the
Gay Headers.

The *Awashonks,* Prince Coffin master, heaves to
half a mile off Baring's Island, to trade with the

natives for fruit. The islanders come aboard, and one of the first things to catch their eye is a box of "cutting-spades" over the quarterdeck. To satisfy their curiosity, Captain Coffin takes one down and shows them the thin, razor-edged triangle of polished steel at the end of a fifteen-foot pole. Swinging one over the side, he demonstrates how the men thrust the blades into a dead whale to strip it of the blubber.

Dark eyes watch the skipper put the spade back. The chief goes below with him to bargain, but the others can scarcely take their gaze from the box above the quarterdeck. Tension grows. At last a row breaks out. The natives rush for the cutting-spades. Eleven of them come at the crew with the deadly implements in hand. The deck of the *Awashonks* is washed with blood.

Through the ship the fight rages, until the natives are driven off at last with firearms. Of the ship's company, six have been slaughtered. Below, the skipper sits in his cabin—his head hanging by a small unsevered strip of his neck.

So much for the "blubber-boilers." There are other tales of Falmouth. The Indians who lived here long ago had stories that began even then with "long ago;" and though the people are gone now, a few of their legends and many of their names survive. They called the place "Suckanesset," which meant "black clam." Of the shells of that species they made "suchawhock" beads—black money, worth twice as much as the "wampum" or white money made of the shell of the periwinkle.

From the shadowy strip of Indian lore, the town's story passes like a spectrum of history through varied doings of men at sea and men ashore—of smugglers and pirates, of coast traders, of war heroes and of persecuted Quakers.

Isaac Robinson, "excellent and sensible man" of Barnstable, is chosen by the Plymouth Court to "frequent the Quaker meetings to endeavor to seduce them from the error of their ways." He goes to Sandwich and attends the meetings; but instead of carrying out orders, Isaac is himself "seduced." He accepts many of the Quaker doctrines, falls into the ill graces of the Court, and in virtual banishment, flees to the wilderness of Suckanesset.

Sandwich Quakers follow him. They hope to escape the impoverishing fines and the strapado of Marshal Barlow; but Suckanesset attracts other settlers too, and before many years have passed, Quaker Daniel Butler is "tied to a cart and whipped through the town." Thomas Bowerman is fined and jailed for refusing to support the Congregational Church. And fifty years after Sandwich has decreed an end to persecutions, the Constable of Falmouth strides into the home of Thomas Bowerman's son and seizes "one Linen wheel and one Bason, worth 20 shillings."

Tarpaulin Cove, the lonely harbor of Naushon Island, was a hiding-place for craft on mischief bound, both in time of war and in time of peace. In 1723—six years after Sam Bellamy had terrorized the Cape—"Pirot Admirall" Ned Low's sloop, the *Fortune,* drops anchor here.

Sam Bellamy was a young fool; but Ned Low is a madman. He fells a captive shipmaster, lays him out on the deck, cuts out his heart, and then has it roasted and seasoned and makes the dead man's mate eat it. A man-of-war is sent out to comb the South Sea for Low, but he escapes.

In the spring of 1779, a British fleet of ten sail anchors in Tarpaulin Cove, "with the avowed determination to burn the town." But Falmouth, forewarned of the plan, sends "expresses" to Sandwich and Barnstable for men and guns, and rushes to put up breastworks alongshore.

On the morning of April 3 the British fleet heaves in sight. They put over a landing party, but as the boats approach, they see themselves outnumbered by the four companies of Cape Cod militia —200 men—and so turn back. The warships then begin a "smart cannonade." A few buildings are hit, but most of the shots bury themselves in soft Cape sand. The fleet squares away. The "burning of Falmouth" is another of His Majesty's several disappointments on Cape Cod.

On the island of Pasque, which lies next to Naushon in the Elizabeth string, John Slocum stands in the doorway of his house, and gazes across the Hole. John is known to every man in Falmouth as a Tory, and it was here, at his house, that the officers of the British fleet had come "for a frolic" before they attempted their raid. At last Tory John sees a lone figure in a boat, rowing across the Hole. He goes down to the beach and paces it until the dory is pulled up.

"Well, lad?"

"All right, father. I told the men at Wood's Hole, and they sent the warning on. When the fleet came in, town was ready for them."

"Thank God!" says John Slocum, the Tory. " 'Twas more than a man could bear, to hear them talk so free of burning Falmouth!"

Today the ancient, well preserved villages of Falmouth are only so many little green crystals in a kaleidoscope. Acres of strawberry lands; miles of good beach and more miles of "improved" beach; everything in the play-world from curling to helmet-diving; in the world of culture, everything from summering college professors to editors of true confession magazines; sword-fishing fleets and yacht-racing fleets; old houses and new millionaires—they are all in the conglomeration that is Falmouth.

Once the town sank a fortune in the mushroom industry, and lost; another time it made several fortunes with a guano works at Woods Hole. In 1910, it was on the verge of launching a fleet of trolley cars through its streets. Cape Cod shuddered and Falmouth writhed. Civil war threatened. The cars were actually brought in, the rails piled on Main Street, and "dry-land skippers" taught how to man the helm. At the last minute the town rose up and scuttled the whole enemy fleet, in the fair name of Falmouth and for the honor of Cape Cod.

In Teaticket (a distortion of the Indian Tateket—"at the great river") the road to your right, marked Hatchville, leads through the strawberry country to Coonamessett. Here Cape Cod, in the hands of Chicago wealth, has been made over into a ranch. The Coonamessett Ranch Corporation, controlled by westerners, has bought up thousands of acres and has built Coonamessett Inn, one of the most exclusive hotels in this section. Here are golf, polo matches, an airport, and in 1937 plans were filed for a "dude ranch" plant to be known as

"Casa Del Rancho!" The plans included, in addition to pretentious hotel accommodations, "landscaping of the outside grounds on the lines of a Texas ranch." Whether a rodeo, a herd of longhorns, and a sprinkling of Texas Rangers are to be added to these properties, I am not prepared to say. At any rate, Casa Del Rancho of Cape Cod has not yet struck oil.

On a hill where the old Sandwich road meets the Hatchville road stands the East End meeting house of Falmouth, built in 1797. Those who lie in the burying ground here had hoped to make their neighborhood the center of trade and population. The East End was nearer the glory that was Sandwich, the grandeur that was Barnstable. For a time the rivalry between the East End and Falmouth Village was spirited, but the Village kept its supremacy. In 1830, when the poor East Enders, humbled and somewhat straitened, asked for stoves in their church, the Village Society agreed to put in the stoves if the East End paid $30 into the joint treasury. The church went unheated.

Coming back to the highway, you continue into the village, where a visit to the historical exhibit in the public library on Main Street may bring you relief if you are in need of orientation after inspecting the "rancho."

I shall let you do your own browsing among the relics here; but Elijah Swift, the gentleman with one eye, in the portrait on the wall, deserves an introduction. Starting as a carpenter, he went into the lumber trade and prospered mightily, becoming Falmouth's leading figure around the turn of the Nineteenth Century. His home stood on the spot where you meet him now.

When the War of 1812 was declared, Elijah had long been a loyal friend of the red-head captain of the "Falmouth Artillery Company," Weston Jenkins. "The Artillery" was Falmouth's pride and joy, consisting of two highly polished and much paraded brass cannons, which were kept in the "Gun House" next door, where the Lawrence High School is now.

In 1814 the British warship *Nimrod* had the audacity to make a formal demand that Jenkins surrender the Artillery. It was like asking him to tear out his heart and hand it to them on a platter. When Jenkins refused, the *Nimrod* sailed out of Tarpaulin Cove, trained her guns along Main Street and began a bombardment.

The townsfolk stood staunchly with Jenkins. Their houses might be razed—but the Artillery surrendered, never! Ann Freeman was visiting the Joneses. The house was in the line of fire, and the Joneses took their baby and ran. Ann stayed because she wanted to cook a dinner for the soldiers. A ball came through the wall, landed in a "piller-bear" and filled the house with downy white clouds. The alarm of fire was spread by people who saw the clouds curling out of the windows. But the story goes that Ann Freeman skimmed the feathers off a kettle of "yeller-eyed beans" and went on with her cooking.

Another shot came in through the front door of Ichabod Hatch's home, which Ichabod had refused to leave. He strode to the door, opened what was left of it and valiantly stood under the fanlight arch. "There, damn ye, John Bull, see if ye can do that again!" The next minute Ichabod heard a whine through the air, and ducked into the buttery. He ducked just in time, for John Bull had complied. Ichabod went out the back door, shaking his head and muttering that the ways of Providence in rewarding the valiant of heart were beyond all understanding.

A third victim was Elijah Swift. A shot crashed into his dining room and shattered his favorite wineset, along with other prized glassware on his sideboard. His first thought was that Weston Jenkins might have been a little more tactful in his handling of the British demand for those guns, but anyhow, he shook his fist at the *Nimrod* and swore revenge. And that same year, despite the alert blockade the British had laid around the Cape, he built a fifty-ton schooner in his yard, rolled her down to the beach, with "fifty yoke of oxen" to pull her through the streets, defiantly christened her the *Status Ante Bellum,* and sent her through the blockade to South Carolina. In 1821 Elijah founded an institution which became the goal of every whaling skipper through the decades following—the Falmouth National Bank.

While your car is parked you might look at the murals in the high school next door. They are the work of Karl Knaths, Provincetown artist, and they have attracted considerable notice, first from town authorities, who were cool to them because they were modern, and later from certain art circles, which praised them for the same reason. The center of controversy was the series depicting in symbolic form the phases of education.

A sign on your left, just beyond the library, directs you to Elm Arch Inn, once the house of the Joneses, where Ann Freeman cooked her yeller-eyed beans for the soldiers. It has been moved from its original location, but the Inn people can show you the place in the wall where the shot from the *Nimrod* came through and started the feathers flying.

The Village Green, ahead on Main Street, was the "training ground" for Falmouth's militiamen. Here Captain John Grannis engaged "thirty good, able-bodied, effective men," drilled them for the Revolution, showed them how to turn back the British if they should come to burn the town.

Captain Grannis's house still stands, the middle one of three at the "Head-of-the-Green," which is the short side of the triangle of these streets. The house to the left, as you face it, was built in 1804 by Braddock Dimmick. The Dimmicks were reckless fighting men. General Joseph Dimmick, father of Braddock, was in command over John Grannis and his men. In Joseph Dimmick's day, generals had not yet built up the tradition of dying in bed. "The most urgent entreaties could not induce him to protect himself in the trench," writes the local historian; "he continued to pace the breast-work whilst the balls were flying around him and with every report of a gun, would wave his sword in defiance."

On the other side of the Grannis house lived Captain Weston Jenkins, the man who would not part with the Artillery.

At the Head-of-the-Green once stood a fourth structure—John Jenkins' whaling supply shop, where the skipper came for his "codheads," pea-jacket and dittybag. Codheads were the stout knee-length boots of oiled leather, which the Grand Bankers introduced on the Cape, bringing them home from Nova Scotia. Fishermen nowadays wear rubber boots from the mail order houses, which are cold and give them rheumatism. The old codheads were as waterproof, and were warmer, but they had to be kept in condition. The seafaring man would bring them periodically to such a store as John Jenkins ran, and the storekeeper would fill them with "boot oil" and let them stand until the leather was saturated. Before he poured the oil into the boots he measured it, and before he poured it back into the barrel he measured it again. He charged the skipper for the difference.

One of the whaling skippers lived next to the church, in the house with the captain's walk upaloft. William Bodfish, young whaleman whose proposal to Mary Crocker between voyages was the talk of the town, built this place in 1814.

William had just made his proposal to Mary, in a house across the Green, and Mary had just nodded in assent, when a message came for the Captain from his owners. They ordered him at once to New Bedford, whence he was to take a cargo of oil across the Atlantic.

The skipper got off his knees and backed out the door, assuring Mary he'd "contrive" somehow to wed her before he sailed. When Mary turned to ask him whether he thought he ought to sail at all, William was already gone from the doorway. Before sailing across Buzzards Bay for New Bedford, he stopped on the shore at Quissett long enough to tell his troubles to his old friend, Captain Bill Davis; and together they "contrived."

Several days later Captain Davis stood on a hill in Quissett, looking over the passing vessels through his big spyglass. Suddenly he found the signal he was looking for—a blue shirt flying from the peak of a whaling bark—and off he galloped for the Green. He stopped at the Crockers' to shout up to Mary, telling her to "jump into your splicing-rig, girl, the Captain's on his way!" and raced back to Quissett to meet the skipper.

In brass-buttoned blue broadcloth and tall beaver hat, Captain Bodfish rode into the village beside his friend.

"Got to be off on the turn of tide tonight," he said anxiously. "Think she'll be ready for me, Bill?"

"Can't say," Captain Davis answered cautiously. "But if you can't be reliable-sure about her, you can about the tide."

When they dismounted at Mary Crocker's house, everything was ready except Parson Lincoln. He'd been called out on a sick-visit. Up and down the streets Captain Davis rode, through the afternoon, but Parson Lincoln was not to be found; it was not until ten o'clock that night that he was dragged into Mary Crocker's house. While he droned through the marriage service, Captain Bodfish stood on one foot and then the other— just like the vessel he was thinking of, beating "off and on" in the Sound. When it was over, the Captain hoisted his bride into the Bodfish buggy, whipped up the horse, accomplished his honeymoon—a gallop around the Green to the house next the church—kissed poor Mary good-bye, and was off for Bremen.

In the late eighteenth century, when "the pox" was ravaging the Cape, Falmouth voted that "inoculation shall not be set up in this town." The fever of debate ran almost as high as the fever of disease. Finally a pox hospital was established at Wood's Hole. The yellow house on the Green was the hospital, which was removed here for a residence by some courageous citizen in later years.

The Congregational Church was built in 1796, on the Green itself, and half a century later was rolled across the street to its present site. In the tower there is a fine old bell, for which the people paid $338.94, and in the Falmouth National Bank there is a receipt for this amount, signed by the maker of the bell:

> *One church bell*
> *Weight 807 pounds at 42, $338.94*
> *Received payment by a note.*
> *PAUL REVERE.*

There are more stories of the Village Green—for instance, the "melancholy crisis" of the fight between the "Herring Party" and the "Anti-Herring Party" over allowing the fish to run up Coonamessett River. The "Anti-Herrings" put a heavy charge of powder into a cannon on the Green, rammed it full of herrings and fired it as a demonstration—blowing to bits both the cannon and the man who touched it off. But I cannot tell all the tales, and there is Woods Hole yet to see. If you go from the church to the Head-of-the-Green, cross over and then turn right, you are on the way to Woods Hole, passing the birthplace of Katherine Lee Bates, a house on your right marked by a memorial boulder in the yard. Her best known poem is "America the Beautiful."

Falmouth's first summer residents were the Fays of Boston. They came down in 1852 and bought a house in Woods Hole, overlooking Little Harbor; and being summer residents, they thought of flower gardens. Roses bloomed fabulously at Woods Hole. The Fays brought in Michel Walsh to cultivate them, and here, in 1893, Walsh originated the rambler rose, cuttings of which have gone out to blossom the world over. You will see the Fay garden on your right as you pass the little cove in Woods Hole. This is a remarkable summer estate on Cape Cod, for the Fays are remarkable people. They will let you see their roses.

The buoy that bobs along the shipway, ringing its bell, flashing a light or giving out agonized groans, is like the brass rail at a bar; we take it for granted, we are lost without it; yet it has not grown there by itself and no provident spirit of nature keeps it polished. Buoys are of vital importance to mariners, but few sailors ever give a thought to the complex business of maintaining a buoy system. The U. S. Lighthouse Service gives you a backdoor glimpse of seafaring here, at its buoy-yard.

Every buoy must be "relieved"—float and sinker replaced—after one year of service. The buoys are lined up in the yard, to be cleaned, red-leaded and painted for another year at sea.

There is plenty of work for the relief ship at-

tached to the Woods Hole depot, hoisting eighteen-
ton buoys out of the water, with their 8,500-pound
sinkers, sometimes from as deep as sixty fathoms.
Occasionally a heavy buoy will break loose from
its mooring or slip from its position, sinker and all.
Then there is trouble-shooting for the relief ship.
In a full gale the great light-and-whistle buoy off
Peaked Hill Bars will sometimes drag anchor a
quarter-mile or more. The relief ship also services
the lighthouses, recharges the whistling and light
buoys and tests them regularly to see that enough
acetylene gas is in the tanks to keep them func-
tioning. There are other depots for this part of the
coastline at Bristol, Conn., and Boston.

The work of the United States Bureau of Fisheries at Woods Hole is one of the greatest unsung
achievements of our good government along lines
of conserving the nation's food resources. The
Bureau will have finished its main job of the year
long before the summer visitor arrives, but you
may go through the plant and see where it is accomplished, and because it is one of the most fascinating and certainly one of the most constructive
jobs of its kind yet undertaken on the Cape, it deserves some explanation here.

Winter flounders, or "black backs," as the fishermen call them, come into Waquoit Bay late in December to spawn. You will find that bay on your
map in the southeastern corner of Falmouth. Government men catch them in fyke-nets before they
have a chance to lay their eggs, and bring them
to the fisheries station, where they are placed in
special breeding tanks, 25 females and 10 males
to a tank. At night the female fish starts signalling

to the gentlemen by gently agitating the water. When she finds that she is not going unnoticed, she discharges the spawn, and the male fertilizes it. Each female black back lays from half a million to a million eggs before the Bureau considers her a "spent fish."

In the morning the eggs are collected and put in cleaning boxes, separated from the mass formation and washed. They are then placed in hatching tanks where salt water changes every seven minutes and is kept at the proper temperature, somewhat above 38 degrees. In from nine to twelve days, the fish emerge from their eggs. They are about an eighth of an inch long, shaped like a mackerel, with an eye on each side of the head and a large food sac on the upper side. This food globule rapidly disappears, and one eye moves around to the other side of the head, so that when the fish lies on the ocean floor, both are on the top side, where they belong on a flounder.

The Bureau ships the fry, half a million to a can, to the waters where they are needed, from Provincetown to Long Island, and dumps them over the side in places where the soundings show good firm bottoms where they can feed properly.

The hatching season reaches its peak in early February. The Bureau is then bringing out from ten to twenty million fry a day. The operations may go into March, depending on the weather. Flounder, like herring, come back to spawn in the waters where they were born. Those hatched at the plant cannot come back there, but a part of the hatch is taken back to Waquoit Bay and dumped, and three years later, being unable to come to their birth place, they do the next best thing, returning to the Bay, thus insuring a steady source of eggs for the Bureau.

The Bureau has also done this sort of work with haddock and cod, and it makes numerous experiments in "tagging"—marking the fish—and noting down observations, to compare with notes taken later when the same fish turns up again, and is identified by the tag. Flounders have been picked up after five-year absences. You may see the aquarium which the Bureau maintains, and there are sometimes seals and sharks in the outdoor pool.

The ketch *Atlantis,* of the Rockefeller-endowed Oceanographic Institute in Woods Hole, works in cooperation with the Bureau, but she is usually out at sea on some adventure of science. Her voyages reach from Maine to the Gulf of Mexico, and some of her work is spectacular. One of the few craft built solely for scientific research, she carries a fully equipped laboratory on deck, and another below deck.

Among the travels of the *Atlantis* have been trips to the Banks for valuable data on the food-fish resources; an investigation of the weird Sargasso Sea; a study of the commercial possibilities of shrimp-fishing in the Gulf of Maine, which may become an important industry of New England; and many tests of the ocean floor, both on the continental shelves and in the great deeps.

Sediment on the bottom of the ocean represents the undisturbed deposits of thousands of years, and is correspondingly valuable in the eye of science. But tests of more than a foot or so could not be made until the *Atlantis* sent down a new device in

1937 which could blast out cores of mud or rock
to a depth of eight feet.

Another problem the scientists have tackled is
the "Gulf Stream cycle." This is likely to be a
matter of many years' work, but they say if the
secret of the "cycle of currents" can be worked out
and proved, accurate weather forecasts can be
made over a six-months' span.

There is a third scientific establishment at
Woods Hole, the Marine Biological Laboratory.
Of the three institutions, this is the largest and best
known. It was incorporated in 1888, and in its early
years built up a reputation through many real accomplishments; but the original research work
now being undertaken by less widely publicized
groups on the Cape is coming in for a greater share
of the attention of specialists.

Down at the waterfront, where the Nantucket
steamer docks, you may find a few of the "Nomans-
land fleet" of swordfishermen tied up. These fling-
ers of the lily-iron follow a hazardous trade. While
modern whaling has gone into the use of bomb-
lancing, with a forty thousand-ton mother-ship at
hand, the swordfisherman still goes out in his small
craft, standing in the "pulpit" with iron in hand
while his mates keep watch from the masthead.
And if they are accomplished yarners, it is partly
because they do not have to draw heavily on their
imaginations.

Take Gasper Mano, for instance. A few years
ago, sailing off the territorial limit near Scatterie
Island, Gasper's skipper made fast to a huge fellow, tossed over the buoy attached to the harpoon
rope, and sent Gasper out in the dory to bring the

fish aboard. Gasper rowed out and made the buoyline fast to his dory. Suddenly the fish came to life
—to very lively life, in fact—and before Gasper
could get his oars into the rowlocks there came
a tug that nearly spilled him out astern. Then away
through the seas with the greatest of ease, the
young man went flying in his dory, on what is
known in whaling circles as a Nantucket sleigh-
ride. On such occasions there is nothing for a conscientious young fisherman to do but sit and watch
the vessel grow smaller and think of the long row
back.

Gasper sat and thought until his vessel disappeared. On went the swordfish, at a twenty-five-
mile clip. At last, just when they began to slow
down, the Canadian Coast Guard Cutter *Bay
Hound* hove in sight. Down she bore on Gasper
Mano, and he and his fish were taken into custody
on a charge of playing their little game in for-
bidden water, within territorial limits. Gasper,
after telling it to a judge, was finally released. The
story of his adventure—if you still don't believe
it—is on the records of the court in Sydney, Nova
Scotia.

From Nobska Light, reached by going back past
the rose garden and turning on Church Street, you
look across the narrowest part of Vineyard Sound,
to the island of Martha's Vineyard. The lighthouse
plant was equipped in 1937 with radio beacon and
two-way radio telephone, with the West Chop
light, on the island, likewise radioed to serve as
a "monitor station."

Offshore here lies sunken treasure, but perhaps

by the time you read this, it will be too late to do anything about it.

In 1918, a week before the Armistice was signed, the freighter *Port Hunter,* bound for France with supplies, was rammed and sunk in Vineyard Sound by the tug *Covington.* For more than eighteen years, to the time of this writing, she has lain on the bottom in seventy feet of water. She went down with a cargo of uniforms, narrow-gauge carwheels and car parts, 2,000 tons of steel billets, and a shipment of brandy valued at $75,000 then, and at $200,000 now. A diver looked her over early in 1937 and declared her well worth the trouble of bringing up. A Boston liquor dealer acquired the rights to the vessel, after a long legal fight, and prospective divers were warned that drinks were not "on the ship."

Continuing past the light on the Shore Road, you come back into Falmouth Village, on the way passing a tablet at your right which commemorates the founding of the town of "Sackonesset" in December, 1661, by Isaac Robinson and Jonathan Hatch, on the "Necke of Land lying by the Hering Broke."

As elsewhere, the early settlers here became involved in many land disputes. One such quarrel was settled by an Indian; and in the story was born a curious tradition that survives in the South Sea country to this day.

Indian John Horton had seen the first white men come to Suckanesset. He had watched them measure off the earth, and then dispute their own measurements. He had helped them build fences. He had come to understand many of their ways.

One day, when Indian John was a very old man, there came to him Jonathan Hatch, Isaac Robinson, Peter Blossom and eleven other white men. This time they were arguing over a boundary line between Five-Mile River and Coonamesset Pond. Years before, they said, the boundary had been set "from the edge of one high hill to another;" and some now contended that the "edge" of the hill was at the bottom, and others said it was at the top. Did Indian John remember exactly what was meant by the "edge of the hill?"

Indian John felt weary as the fourteen men gathered around him for his answer. Then he said:

"Yes, I remember. It went neither by the top of the hill nor the bottom, but halfway between."

But then they wanted to know what marker had been used, to show *exactly* where the line should run; and when Indian John said the marker was a great rock, they declared that he was lying, that there was no rock midway on the hill.

"Come with me," Indian John said.

Along the hill he searched, running now and then to a bush, a tree, a dead bough. And at last, under a pile of brush, he uncovered a great rock.

"Here," he told the white men, "is the rock where the people set their bound. Each time they passed it, to show their good faith they put on a bough. In time it became covered with boughs, and that is why you could not see it."

Because he was the only living witness, the white men believed him and were satisfied. Each of them put a bough on the heap. And Indian John was very thankful that he had found a large rock—for they are rare in the hills of Suckanesset.

Ever after that, the Indians sealed their own

agreements with piles of brush, to which each passerby added a stick, as a symbol of accord. As time went on, there were many brush-heaps in the South Sea country, and new generations carried on the custom without knowing why.

White men have misnamed the piles of sticks, calling them "Indian taverns" and giving strange explanations for them. But the story of Indian John Horton is on record, and near the Falmouth-Mashpee town line at Waquoit, there is a pile of sticks where, to this day, the people of Mashpee add their sticks when they pass by.

When you have taken the highway out of the village, watch in West Falmouth for a Kiwanis sign. Drive two-tenths of a mile beyond it, and turn off to the left on the road you find there. In the hollow you will see the house that Quaker Thomas Bowerman 2nd built about 1685.

It was this Bowerman who would not join the Congregational Church, nor would he help pay the minister. When he was in Barnstable Gaol in 1705, the Friends of Sandwich voted to send "a bed and bedding to Thomas Bourman 2nd he being in prison for the Priest's Rate."

The ancient dwelling now has the additions of generations of later Bowermans, and is widely known on the Cape as the "Rainbow Roof House." It is still owned by Bowermans.

There are several "rainbow roofs" on the Cape. The design is said to have originated with the sea captains—because of the resemblance of the roof to a heft-up ship's bottom—but I doubt this. The idea of a heft-up ship's bottom would not be a very pleasing one to a sea captain; and besides the resemblance really is a bit far-fetched.

The hand-hewn joists and rafters of the Bowerman house were fitted together around a great chimney of grey stones gathered from the hill. The bow-roof gives the attic interior an arch-ceiling effect in ancient umber-hued planks. Katherine Crosby, writing in the Cape Cod Magazine, describes it thus:

"A stone hearth holds a variety of clutter . . . left there from the days when this was the spinning room and the women did some of their cooking over this fire. . . . In the shadows under the eaves I counted six spinning wheels for wool or flax— no doubt each bride who came into the family brought her own wheel from home." There is an ancient high-chair there too, the writer adds, "its stout splint seat long ago worn out by a succession of restless infants and replaced by one of hard wood. This had lost two coats of paint and was worn smooth and thin."

In 1787 the Bowermans became the millers of the town. Their windmill remained until a few years ago, when it was sold and moved to Brockton.

On the shore of West Falmouth, before the Bowermans came, the Indians lived in large villages, and among these hills there is many an unmarked burying ground. Hundreds of arrowheads and other relics have been found here.

The meeting-house of the Friends is a small square structure on the left side of the highway, almost opposite the fire-house in West Falmouth. It is surrounded by the graves of Bowermans, Gif-

fords and others, and was built in 1841, on the site
of an earlier Quaker meeting-house.

Silver Beach runs parallel to the highway on
the Buzzards Bay shore. Promoters have tried to
put through some ambitious "amusement development" plans there, but the town fathers have denied permits, other than for a theater. They have
allowed no reproduction in whole or in part of
Coney Island. Restive souls who do not like the
simple Cape vista will have to be content with
ranchos and such.

And now, before you cross into the town of
Bourne, there is a historical detail that cannot go
untold—the tale of Captain Sam'l Dewey and how
the President of the United States was decapitated.

"For God's sake," cried the Whigs, "save this
ship from foul disgrace!"

Petitions, worded thus, floated down into Boston
streets from upper story windows on a July afternoon in the year 1834. Near Charlestown bridge,
anchored stem-to, lay the grand old frigate *Constitution*. Erect upon her prow, chin out, plug-hat in
hand, stood Andrew Jackson, big as life. The U. S.
Navy had had the audacity to choose him for the
new figurehead of Old Ironsides, and to turn him
so that all Boston town might—as Captain Elliott
put it—"admire."

Yankee Whigs, to whom Jackson's re-election
had merely meant another four years of cussing,
did not admire. But after all, the Navy was the
Navy, and Captain Elliott might have got away
with it if a Cape Codder hadn't chanced to be in
town at the time.

"You might have swung her stern-to, Captain,"

said Admiral Hull, Commandant of the Navy Yard. "The President does look a little defiant there where you've left him."

"It's what they need—damn Yankees!" retorted the Captain. "Blowhards! Not a man among 'em but would commit gross mopery on the high seas— and talk a lot of disloyalty at that!"

Commander Hull snapped him up, and the two men swung into a loud debate.

Captain Sam'l Dewey of Falmouth stood in the corridor and heard the whole thing. He went to his friend Henry Lincoln, a ship merchant on the Old Central Wharf, and told him the story.

"Got a good notion," Captain Sam'l wound up, "to go there myself and whittle me off a souvenir of that statue!"

"Dewey," Lincoln answered, "you do that and I'll give you a hundred dollars!"

On the night of July 22, a thundershower came down in sheets over the city. The downpour was so heavy that Captain Elliott's Marine Guards, stationed aboard the *Constitution* because of the tension in the city, took refuge below decks.

But the thunder of that night was gentle bird-song compared to the storm that broke over Boston and traveled like a hurricane down the coast to the nation's capital next morning—a storm of mingled profanity and rejoicing over the news that Andrew Jackson's head had been sawn from his body the night before by some scoundrel who had rowed to the *Constitution,* climbed up a rope hanging from her bow, and made away with the noblest part of her new figurehead!

Captain Elliott was wild. Though he had a new head made at once for the President, from his own pocket he offered a reward of a thousand dollars for the arrest of the guilty man.

Sam'l Dewey lay low, and Andrew Jackson's head lay lower. But along with his nerve, Sam'l had a New England conscience, which kept working at him until, many years later, he decided it would be "a good joke" if he went to Washington and told the authorities about Andrew Jackson's head—incidentally returning property of the United States Government.

If you go to New York from the Cape, at the Museum of the City of New York you can see today the figure of the seventh President of the United States. It is the same figurehead which Sam'l Dewey sawed off near the chin.

# CHAPTER XIX

## BOURNE

*On State 28, between Falmouth and Cape Cod Canal. Six miles from Falmouth line to Bridge.*

To the men who drew up plans for the Cape Cod Canal in 1909, Father Neptune and Mother Earth jointly posed a score of problems—problems that were even then nearly three centuries old. Many times, a canal across the Cape had been planned, and more than once it actually had been undertaken; but no permanently navigable channel had come of any of these schemes. In digging it through at last, and in widening and deepening it for the uses of commerce, modern engineering has scored a major triumph.

On the south bank of this waterway, in the town of Bourne, stands a curious little structure of ancient Dutch design. With its steep roof and leaded panes, it looks as if it had gone astray both in space and time. It is a replica of the Aptucxet Trading Post, established by the Pilgrim Fathers in 1627. And the story of the great artery of shipping that cuts across-Cape today is also the story of the little fur exchange that opened for business three hundred years ago. The need that actuated the building of both was the same. Thus, in the town of Bourne, one finds two exhibits of American commerce, the earliest and the latest, side by side.

Badly in need of earnings to apply against the
interest on their Old World debts—piling up at
rates as high as 60 per cent—the Pilgrims wasted
little time getting down to business, once the settlement at Plymouth had been accomplished.

Good opportunities were open, especially for a
profitable fur trade with Manhattan. In March,
1627, Isaac de Rassieres, secretary of the colony
there, wrote a letter to Plymouth. He flossed up
his salutation with many fine phrases, calling the
Pilgrims "noble, worshipful, wise and prudent
lords" (Bradford explains that it was a habit of
the Dutch "to be full of complementall titles")
but somewhere well down on the page he slipped
in the proposal that they swing a little deal or two.

Bradford made a civil acknowledgment of the
letter, agreeing that trade might be helpful all
'round, and only demurring modestly to "the over-
high titles more than belongs to us or is meet for
us to receive."

So far, so good. But between Plymouth and
points to the southward, Cape Cod stood out to sea
as a long and dangerous barrier. If the Dutch proposal were to be carried out, somewhere the route
of commerce would have to cut across.

Bradford remembered having seen the Indians
paddle up the Manomet River, which brought
them well inland from Buzzards Bay, then portage
their canoes over the few miles to Scusset Creek,
and paddle off again into Cape Cod Bay, thus
crossing the Cape. Therefore:

"That they [the Pilgrims] might ye better
take all convenient opportunitie to follow their
trade . . . they resoloved to build a smale pinass
at Manamet."

Bringing their goods down from Plymouth and into Scusset Creek, then carrying them overland to this vessel, they could "avoyd the compasing of Cap-Codd, and those deangerous shoulds, and so make any vioage to ye southward in much shorter time, and with farr less danger." And this, of course, is precisely what the Cape Cod Canal makes possible today, with the portaging eliminated.

Here at Manomet, the Governor's history adds, "they builte a house and kept some servants, who also planted corne, and reared some swine, and were allwayes ready to goe out with ye barke when ther was occasion. All which tooke good effecte, and turned to their profite."

Using "wampampeake" as a medium of exchange with the Indians, and selling the furs thus obtained, "beaver by ye pounde & otter by ye skine," they turned many a tidy profit indeed—enough to pay off all their debts.

Thirty years afterwards, the trading post was closed. Thomas Burge, who owned the land at that time, left it to his daughter, Elizabeth. She married Ezra Perry, and the property remained in the Perry family for more than two hundred years.

The post was reconstructed by the Bourne Historical Society in 1930, largely through the efforts of the late Percival Hall Lombard. It is as faithful a representation as months of research, in both this country and in Holland, could make it. On the site, only the foundations of the original building remained, and even those stones had to be dug out from the accumulation of the centuries.

Inside the building are many relics that were

recovered in the excavation. They tell of the past, and in some cases the past tells of them. There is the odd latten candlestick, for example, with two fine lines etched on the handle and a scroll design around the socket. Its age is unknown. But in the Berlin Gallery there is a painting, made about 1650 by the Dutch master, Pieter de Hoogh, and this picture, which is called "A Dutch Living Room," has in it an exact duplicate of the candlestick at Aptucxet.

Although the Pilgrims probably wished they had a canal, they made no immediate plans for digging one. But long before the trading post shut down, the idea was being talked; and with its closing, the colony had even more reason for speculating on the possibility of a waterway. Samuel Sewall, after a visit to Sandwich, which at that time included Bourne, writes in his diary for October, 1676:

> Mr. Smith rode with me and showed me the place which some had thought to cut for to make a passage from the south sea to the north. He said it was about a mile and a half between the utmost flowing of the two seas in Herring [Manomet] River and Scusset—the land very low and level.

In the years that followed, the subject was brought up again and again. During the Revolutionary War, it was a topic of speculation among Continental generals who saw in it a strategic aid, and a government engineer was sent to make a survey. George Washington, in a letter on the subject, wrote to James Bowdoin: "I am hopeful that you . . . have received all the assistance that Mr. Machin [the engineer] could give, in determining upon the practicability of cutting a canal between Barnstable and Buzzards Bay."

The engineer estimated the cost down to the last penny—£32,148, 1s., 8d.—but luckily for the estimate, its accuracy was never put to a test.

In 1791 James Winthrop was engaged by the colonists to make another survey for the canal. He looked things over briefly, and left a record dealing mainly with the ladies he met on his trip from Cambridge to the Cape. His findings were along the following lines:

> *Sabbath 15th. Attended meeting, drank tea at Mrs. Winslow's. Two agreeable daughters, both amiable. In the evening Major Thomas and Lady, the Misses Winslows, Miss Gorham and Miss Barr came to see Miss H. all the young ladies about her time of life. We had an agreeable evening. Monday 16th—etc.*

In fairness to Master Winthrop, however, it should be added that among his paragraphs approving of the Cape Cod girls, he did slip in a word here and there for the Cape Cod Canal; and those who had been agitating for it seized on his report and made what use of it they could. They brought the proposal before the Massachusetts Legislature, urging it chiefly on the ground that it would save life at sea. Scarcely a northeast gale swept in from the Atlantic in those years without leaving on Cape beaches the broken bones of some ship, the bodies of her crew.

The worthy members of the Legislature agreed with everything that was said about the treachery of the Back Shore run, and the number of sailors who had lost their lives there. And they promptly voted the project down by a large majority—for among these statesmen its defeat had been neatly

engineered by men who were acting for the stagecoach operators!

Through the Nineteenth Century, company
after company was formed to dig the channel.
Other routes were proposed; there was not a town
from Sandwich to Orleans where no hopeful lines
had been laid out for it. If all the paper "Cape Cod
Canals" produced in this period had been scooped
out, one alongside the other, they would have made
a corduroy of the upper Cape. As one official put
it, "every grain of sand was made the victim of
an algebraic equation."

Although the day of the sailing ship had passed,
and the terrors of the "Back Shore run" had been
further reduced by wireless and other aids to mariners, the project was still decidedly worthwhile
when August Belmont became interested in it early
in the present century. It would cut off seventy
miles, New York to Boston; and even for modern
power ships, the stretch to be eliminated was a
wicked run. In the years 1900-1920, there were 974
wrecks in Cape Cod waters, most of them on the
Back Shore.

Belmont tackled it in 1909. His company spent
five years and $13,000,000, and Cape Cod at last
had a canal, of a sort; not a very good one, not
even good enough for large freighters to go
through safely; but that it was a canal, and that
Belmont had been a jolly good fellow to dig it,
no one could deny.

The engineers had faced numerous problems,
but the greatest had been raised by the decision
of the company to put the channel through with-

out locks. The Panama Canal was first attempted that way, and the scheme had failed.

When you don't put locks in your canal, you have the tides to reckon with. Unless the tide-times and tide-levels of the two connected bodies of water coincide, the current set up in the narrow channel joining them will be spasmodically swift; and in that case, though the canal may make beautiful newspaper photographs and lend itself well to all sorts of publicity, it will not be safe for navigation.

Until the War Department took over the work, sinking many more millions of dollars into it, this was one of the troubles of the Cape Cod Canal. In Cape Cod Bay, the average rise and fall of the tide is five feet greater than in Buzzards Bay, on the other end of the channel. Also, between the two bays there is a tide-time difference of three hours. Thus Buzzards Bay is rising while Cape Cod Bay falls. Sometimes, in "spring tide" and high wind, there is a difference of nine feet between the two levels. To offset the dangerous currents thus created, the Canal had to be made almost half again as deep, three times as wide.

The government took it off Belmont's hands temporarily in 1918, as a "wartime measure," and a few years later bought him out for $11,500,000. I don't know whether the deal made the government as happy as it did Mr. Belmont, but by worrying through many a headache since, the War Department engineers have developed it into a really practical waterway for large seagoing craft; and by insisting that it is still "of definite strategic importance," the Army has managed to keep tolerably happy.

The engineers just can't leave it alone. They have dug it down and scooped it out; they have put two fine highway bridges over it, and one railroad bridge; they have primped it up, with improved highway approaches to the vehicular bridges; they have created a yacht basin on the Buzzards Bay side; in the Massachusetts Institute of Technology, in Boston, they have built a 115-foot working model of it, reproducing in miniature all the tidal currents and other conditions affecting it; and if inspiration for yet another finishing touch doesn't come to them on the scene at Bourne, they can go to Boston and contemplate the model.

The bill for the Cape Cod Canal and all that goes with it currently figures to more than $40,-000,000. With a thousandth part of that sum, the Pilgrim Fathers could have paid off "those deepe interests that kepte them low," and the principal as well. If we could turn back the calendar three hundred years and hand them the price of the bridge we cross in leaving Cape Cod today, their children and their children's children would be relieved of the "strain of making religion and profit jump together."

# BIBLIOGRAPHY

Bradford, William
*History of Plimouth Plantation*
Boston, 1912, 2 Vols.

Bangs, Mary Rogers
*Old Cape Cod*
Boston, 1920

Cape Cod Advancement Plan of the Chamber of Commerce
*Cape Cod Legends*
Hyannis, 1935

Cape Cod Advancement Plan of the Chamber of Commerce
*Ships' Figure Heads*
Hyannis, 1936

Cobb, Elijah
*Elijah Cobb, 1768-1848, a Cape Cod Skipper*
New Haven, 1925

Deyo, Simeon L.
*History of Barnstable County*
New York, 1890

Freeman, Frederick
*History of Cape Cod*
Boston, 1858

Irwin, Frederick T.
*Story of Sandwich Glass and Glassware*
Manchester, N. H., 1926

Jennings, Charles W.
*Provincetown; or, odds and ends from the tip end*
Yarmouthport, 1890

Jenkins, Charles W.
*History of Falmouth*
Falmouth, 1889

Kittredge, Henry C.
*Cape Cod: Its People and Their History*
Boston, 1930

Kittredge, Henry C.
*Shipmasters of Cape Cod*
Boston, 1935

Lincoln, Joseph C.
*Cape Cod Yesterdays*
Boston, 1935

Otis, Amos
*Genealogical Notes of Barnstable Families*
Barnstable, 1885

Pratt, Enoch
*History of Eastham*
Yarmouth, 1844

Pratt, Ambrose E.
*250th Anniversary Celebration of Sandwich and Bourne at Sandwich, Mass., 1899*
Falmouth, 1890

Reynard, Elizabeth
*The Narrow Land. Folk Chronicles of Old Cape Cod·*
Boston, 1934

Rich, Shebnah
*Truro—Cape Cod or Landmarks and Seamarks*
Boston, 1884

Sprague, Francis W.
*Barnstable Sea Captains*
Yarmouthport, 1913

Swift, Charles F.
*Cape Cod—The Right Arm of Massachusetts*
Yarmouth, 1897

Swift, Charles F.
*History of Old Yarmouth (Cape Cod)*
Yarmouthport, 1884

Tarbell, Arthur W.
*Cape Cod Ahoy!*
Boston, 1932

Thoreau, Henry D.
*Cape Cod*
Boston, 1896

Wayman, Dorothy Godfrey
*Suckanesset, a history of Falmouth, Mass. by Theodate Geoffrey*
Falmouth, 1930

Young, Alexander
*Chronicles of the First Planters of the Massachusetts Bay Colony, 1620-1636*
Boston, 1846

*A Modern Pilgrim's Guide to Provincetown*
Provincetown, 1934

## NEWSPAPERS AND MAGAZINES

*Cape Cod Colonial*—1937
*Cape Cod Standard Times*—1937
*New Bedford Standard Times*—1934-1937
*Provincetown Advocate*—1873-1937
*The Cape Cod Magazine*—1920-1937

# INDEX